William Thomas Stead

The splendid paupers

A tale of the coming plutocracy - being the Christmas number of the Review of reviews

William Thomas Stead

The splendid paupers
A tale of the coming plutocracy - being the Christmas number of the Review of reviews

ISBN/EAN: 9783741193859

Manufactured in Europe, USA, Canada, Australia, Japa

Cover: Foto ©Thomas Meinert / pixelio.de

Manufactured and distributed by brebook publishing software (www.brebook.com)

William Thomas Stead

The splendid paupers

BEING THE

Christmas Number of the Review of Reviews, 1894.

"We are not a rich aristocracy. We are many of us deadly poor, and all the poorer because tradition, society, and pride make us go on living beyond our means. It is not as if the aristocracy could set an example in this matter. They have been forced to go the pace which the *nouveaux riches* set. We have to live when corn is 30s. a quarter as when it is 50s.; but not only that, but to keep abreast, if not ahead, of the wealthy tradespeople who have come into land. The result is that we are, many of us, little better than splendid paupers."—LADY WARWICK, 1893.

REVIEW OF REVIEWS

EDITORIAL OFFICES: MOWBRAY HOUSE, NORFOLK STREET, LONDON, W.C.
PUBLISHING OFFICE: 125, FLEET STREET, LONDON, E.C.

PREFACE.

THE Christmas Numbers of the REVIEW OF REVIEWS endeavour to embody in the narrative form, which permits the chronicler to unite the license of fiction with the realism of fact, the most conspicuous events and ideas of the passing year.

In 1892, in "From the Old World to the New" I was able to describe in advance Chicago and the World's Fair. In 1893, the Liberator swindle suggested the subject for "Two and Two Make Four." This year, the fall in prices, the debates upon the death duties, the arrival of plutocrats from the United States, and the war between China and Japan, afford a not less obvious topic for "The Splendid Paupers."

It may seem to be audacious beyond measure to attempt to weave into a Christmas Number such forbidding and heterogeneous topics as death duties, bimetallism, agricultural depression, and the war in the Orient; but if fortune favours the brave, I may at least hope for good luck in my enterprise.

For the title I owe my acknowledgments to the Countess of Warwick; the characters, with few exceptions, are borrowed from real life, and most of them I fear are but thinly disguised.

MOWBRAY HOUSE, TEMPLE, W.C.
November, 1894.

W. T. STEAD.

CONTENTS

Part 1

WHEAT AT EIGHTEEN SHILLINGS A QUARTER

I.	Mr. Walledoff	5
II.	Lady Aenid	8
III.	The Duke of Eastland	12
IV.	The Radicals of Rigby	15
V.	The County of Blankshire	18
VI.	An Episode in Knickerbockers	21
VII.	The Modern Town of Garlam	25
VIII.	A Birthday Party at the "Radical Arms"	31
IX.	Exit Lord Bladud	35
X.	The Radical Campaign	38
XI.	An Unexpected Meeting	42
XII.	An Inquest at Sloane Hall	45
XIII.	The Plutocratic Microbe	49
XIV.	Defeated but Triumphant	53

Part II.

THE YELLOW MAN WITH THE WHITE MONEY

I.	A Shooting Party in the Highlands	57
II.	Messrs. Glogoul and Faulmann	61
III.	A Dinner Party at Westlands Castle	63

IV.	A Political Plot	67
V.	Bimetallism in Excelsis	70
VI.	The Wiles of Lady Dorothy	72
VII.	Chinafying Chatsworth	75
VIII.	A Gigantic Conspiracy	79
IX.	A Scene in Bouverie Street	81
X.	Roping them in	85
XI.	Jimjams and Cholera	88
XII.	The Yellow Man in Possession	90

THE SPLENDID PAUPERS:
A TALE OF THE COMING PLUTOCRACY.

PART I.—WHEAT AT EIGHTEEN SHILLINGS A QUARTER.

CHAPTER I.
MR. WALLEDOFF.

"SO the Duke says that he will have to sell Chatsworth?" said Sterling to his companion, a bright young girl who was looking down from a hill near Maidenhead upon the winding Thames.

"Sell Chatsworth? Nonsense! Will the Queen sell Windsor?" said she lightly. "Oh!" she exclaimed, pointing to the bend of the river, round which a crew of girls were swinging an eight-oared boat, "is it not splendid? Just look at that boat!"

"Yes," said Sterling; "they make a pretty picture. But they don't go the pace. Still, they keep time well, and the cox knows her business. Do you row?"

"Never have had the chance, save in an old tub at sea. But I mean to. I'm going in for everything—everything. Is it not perfectly lovely to think that no one will hinder me from doing whatever I've a mind to, any more than if I had been a boy?"

"Let us sit down here for a few minutes," said Sterling, "and enjoy the sunset. And you can tell me your plans just as well sitting down as standing up. Well, if you won't, I will. So there, Lady Ænid, by your leave."

Whereupon Sterling stretched himself lazily on the hillside. His companion looked down at him for a moment.

"Poor thing," she said, "he's tired, and is quite right to rest. But I have been doing nothing all day, and I prefer to move about. And do you know," she said eagerly, "I do believe I see Elma in that boat. No other girl has quite such a head of hair. What luck! Good-bye, I am off!" And before Sterling could rise, the girl was scampering down the hill towards the river.

"What a madcap!" he muttered; "she will break her neck some day. But that is just her way; helter-skelter, over field and through dyke. There's nothing like a woman for taking a bee line when the fit seizes her."

"ARE YOU HURT?" ASKED STERLING.

Meanwhile, the object of these reflections was rapidly nearing the bottom of the hill. The impetus of her own movements, accelerated by the steepness of the descent, was carrying her along so rapidly that she could not possibly stop herself before reaching a low hedge at the bottom of the hill. There was nothing for it but to fly at it as best she could. The girl was fleet of foot and agile. She had no time to think and no chance to stop. She leapt the hedge, cleared it like a stag, but, alas, she had what stags have not—the skirt of her dress caught on the stake in the hedge, and she fell heavily into the ditch.

"Hulloa!" shouted Sterling, "you've gone and done it now," and in a moment he was running down the hill, not knowing in what state of fracture he would find the girl on the other side of the hedge. When he reached her, she was sitting on the side of the ditch, with her face all glowing with nettle stings, and a long scratch across one cheek. She was still panting and out of breath.

"My dear girl," said Sterling, "are you hurt? I was scared to death when I saw you fall."

"It's nothing," she said, between her labouring breaths—"nothing at all. Only a few nettle stings and a nasty scratch. I fell soft, you see. It's all that confounded dress. I should have cleared the hedge splendidly but for it."

Sterling found it was as she had said. There were no bones broken. She had fallen soft, the force of her fall being checked by the skirt, which caught on the fence. The dress had held for a second, and then had parted, leaving a shred as a trophy to the stake. He busied himself getting dock leaves to apply to the blisters made by the nettles, listening silently the while to Lady Ænid's objurgations.

"It's all these hateful petticoats," she said, "dangling about one's heels. They don't give us half a chance. This is the second time they've served me this scurvy trick. The other time they caught on the pedal of my bicycle and flung me just as I was rushing down a splendid hill, and sprained my wrist. They'll be the death of me some day. Thanks, awfully," she added, as Sterling brought her some fresh cool leaves. "I'm almost better now. I wonder if Elma has passed."

"We had better go home," said Sterling. "If you lean on my arm, I think——"

Before he had finished his sentence the girl was up and off towards the river. She had spied her friend's boat, and was running towards the river, waving her handkerchief. Sterling followed slowly. "She's none the worse for her tumble," he said. "But if she only knew what a figure she cuts with that ragged skirt trailing behind her!"

But Lady Ænid did not care. Her friend had seen her signal and had sculled to the river side.

"Sakes alive," said Elma, with a strong American accent, "where have you been, Niddie? You look as if you'd tumbled off a haystack; and your face is bleeding. Dear, dear, Niddie, you've been to the wars indeed!"

"Only a scratch," said the girl. "Let me come into the boat and wash it off. Do introduce me to your friend."

"Lady Ænid, Mr. Glogoul—Mr. Glogoul, Lady Ænid. There now—no ceremonies—come on board."

"Mr. Sterling," said Ænid, turning to her companion, "you will come too, of course? This is Elma Dormer, my American friend. You'll like each other, I'm sure. Steady, now!" she added, as both stepped into the boat.

Sterling took his seat beside the young man, who was introduced to him as Mr. Glogoul.

"Have I not seen you before?" he said. "Both the name and the features seem familiar to me."

"Guess not, sir," said the young man. "Only arrived from New York day before yesterday."

"Glogoul, Glogoul—I'm sure I have heard that name before," persisted Sterling.

"Rather," said the young man, "who hasn't? But it was my uncle who made it famous. I have not had my turn yet."

"Oh, I remember," said Sterling. "And so you are the nephew of the famous professor? Is he still prosecuting his researches into the mysteries of human nature?"

"Guess so," said the young man. "Bit of an old fogey though, with antiquated notions. Why, I've actually heard him say that he had objections to vivisect any but incorrigible criminals. I've been rather ashamed of him since that."

There was for Sterling a strange attraction of repulsion about the young cynic.

"And you," he said, "would vivisect anybody?"

"Of course," he replied. "Why not? If you vivisect only criminals you only experiment upon the abnormal. You might as well vivisect only geniuses or lunatics. What we want in our physiological laboratories is the normal."

"You, then, are a pathologist, I suppose?" said Sterling.

"Oh, don't talk shop," saucily interrupted Elma, who was now rowing steadily up the stream. "Glogoul has been talking nothing but horrid stories of how they experiment in torture. I call it torture, but he says they don't feel—nobody feels anything. What looks like agony is only reflex action. We are all automata, and everybody does just what he must, and nobody's to blame. Niddie, how is the reflex action of the nettle rashes getting on?"

"Much better," said Lady Ænid. "What with the dock leaves and the river air I feel quite 'fit.' Is it not a lovely evening?"

As she spoke she pointed to the sun which was sinking slowly behind the Splendon Woods, as if unwilling to leave a scene of such perfect loveliness. The foliage on the trees was just beginning to change, here and there flecking the green wood with gold. The steady plash of Elma's oars in the water and the ripple of the stream against the boat alone broke the silence. Now and then a cow lowed in the meadows or a dog barked in the farmyard. The clouds in the eastern sky were beginning to glow with the reflected glory of the setting sun, whose long rays made the silver Thames glow like molten gold.

As they neared a turn in the river, they narrowly escaped bumping two eight-oared boats that were racing down stream. One was the boat whose girlish crew had first excited Lady Ænid's attention, the other was manned by men. The girls were leading.

"Look, look!" cried Lady Ænid exultantly; "who's going the pace now? We're leading a clear length. How splendid! Don't I wish I were one of them."

The boats swept by, the racing crews not vouchsafing even a glance as they passed.

"A spurt," said Sterling—"plucky spurt, but doesn't last."

"But they were leading," she objected.

"Had a start you may be sure," said Glogoul. "Women will always be whipped at that kind of thing—always."

"You're quite horrid," said Elma. "Give us a chance, a fair chance, and you'll see if you can hold your own."

"My dear cousin," said the young doctor, "you are totally wrong. Fillies have had as fair a field as colts since the world began, and even with an allowance for sex how seldom has a filly won any great race!"

"If only," said Sterling, "men would make women an allowance for sex the race might be more equal. But unfortunately women have not a filly's chance. Because they are handicapped by nature, they are further handicapped by man."

"No," said Lady Ænid, "by ourselves worst of all. Look at these hateful petticoats, for instance, to say nothing of corsets."

"Niddie," said Elma, blushing, "how can you? You are too awful for anything."

"Why?" said she, innocently. "I did not say anything, did I? Oh!" she added, laughing, "I forgot you are American, and Americans have no undergarments to speak of."

"Not before gentlemen, at least," said Elma, sotto voce, and there was again silence in the boat. Far away in the distance they heard faintly the refrain of a boating song. The boat was nearing the Splendon Woods. Already the high bank was rising on their left.

"Make haste," said Lady Ænid; "we must have a stroll in these lovely woods before dinner. There will just be time before sundown. I would not miss it for anything. Father has told us such jolly stories of the picnic parties he used to have under the fine old trees, that I always dreamed of coming here some day—and here we are," she said, as the boat slowed up and they prepared to land.

Hardly had the boat touched the bank, when a keeper stepped forward. "Out of that!" he shouted gruffly. "You've no business here."

"But," said Sterling, "I have landed here scores of times, and there never has been any objection. There must be some mistake."

"No mistake at all," replied the man. "I have my orders. Neither you nor nobody else must land here."

Sterling persisted. "My good man, I am sure you are wrong. I know the Duke very well, and he was always delighted that we should land here."

"The Duke be damned!" said the man. "What's he got to do with it? This isn't the Duke's any more. It's Mr. Walledoff's, and Mr. Walledoff 'll stand none of your blooming picnic parties and such flummery. So get out, will you, or I'll give you in charge as trespassers. S'help me, I will. Here, Baby!"

He whistled as he spoke, and an evil-looking cur came up showing his teeth.

"Off with you, do you hear, or I'll set the dog on you. Confound you; one would think the whole British public owned the property, and not Mr. Walledoff."

He gave the boat a push off with his foot as he spoke, and it began to drift down stream.

"Who is your master?" asked Glogoul.

"Why," said the man, "Mr. Walledoff—him as bought the *Latter Day Gazette*, you know."

Whereupon he turned on his heel and disappeared behind the trees.

"The devil!" said Glogoul. "To come across an American here!"

"I wish, cousin," said Elma, as she took up her oars, "that you would not use such dreadful language before ladies."

"I beg your pardon," said Glogoul. "But you see I don't believe there is a devil. So it is not profane, really. It is only mythological."

After a moment's pause, Sterling said, "I remember now hearing that the Duke had sold Splendon to an American millionaire. But I had no idea that even an American millionaire would deprive the public of privileges which they had enjoyed from time immemorial."

"Didn't you, though?" asked Glogoul. "Then you don't know the American millionaire. It was not he who said 'the public be damned,' but that summed it all up. And I guess the public will be pretty considerably damned, too, before our millionaires have done with them."

There was silence in the boat for a time. The mists were rising, and Lady Ænid began to feel chilly. "Put me ashore," she said, "and I will run along the river bank."

"Nonsense," said Elma; "what a guy you will look!"

"What do I care," she retorted, "if I can keep warm? There now; one moment," and then she sprang from the boat to the bank. She stopped for a moment to pin up her gown where it was torn, and then started off at a trot after the boat.

Glogoul watched her curiously through his glasses for a time as if she had been a new specimen in a museum. "And that," he said to himself, musing—"that, I suppose, is what they call a 'New Woman' in the adolescent state; a case of reversion—interesting but familiar."

"How?" said Sterling.

"Reversion," said Glogoul, "to barbarism. We are quite familiar with it in our country. Philanthropists occasionally catch a Red Indian papoose, bring it up a boarding-school girl. All goes well till one fine day boarding-school miss disappears. In her place squaw in a blanket, with hair hanging down back, and face daubed with red ochre. She reverts. And that new young woman reverts. The reversion to barbarism is a recoil from too straitlaced civilisation. I wonder how long it will last."

"What you call Barbarism I would call Nature," said Elma.

"But Nature is Barbarism. All civilisation is unnatural," said Glogoul.

"I take issue with you," said Sterling; "but here we are at the landing-stage; you go our way, I believe?"

"No," said Elma, "we go further down the river. But we may look you up after dinner."

Lady Ænid and Sterling turned away from the river. "I hate that man," she said; "he has the eye of a snake, and he dissects one as if you were dead—ugh!" and she shuddered.

Sterling said nothing. He shared her feeling to some extent. But there is a great attraction in excessive repulsion. If you throw a ball with great force against a wall it rebounds to your hand. Besides, the man was a type, and he liked types, especially when they were the logical ultimate outcome of ideas.

When they reached Flora Cottage they found dinner waiting. The Hon. Mrs. Truddlecombe, a neighbour who had been invited to meet Lady Ænid, was much scandalised at the girl's appearance.

"What would your mother think?" she observed, half under her breath, as the girl told the story of her adventures. She was too excited to notice the chilly censure implied by Mrs. Truddlecombe's manner. At last, she told with much mimetic power the scene with the keeper who warned them off the Splendon Woods. Then Mrs. Truddlecombe warmed up, "My dear, you ought to have known better than to try to put a foot on Mr. Walledoff's grounds. A lady should not needlessly expose herself to insult."

"Insult! Mrs. Truddlecombe; who was insulted? It was rude, no doubt, and I think this Walledoff is a churl, but we cannot be insulted by such creatures, surely."

"Well, well, Lady Ænid, you may think it no insult to be warned off as if you were trespassing, but I think otherwise."

"Tell me," said Sterling, "how long has this been going on?"

"OUT OF THAT!" HE SHOUTED GRUFFLY.

"Ever since the Duke sold Splendon. It seems in America they think a man can do what he likes with his own, if he pays for it. And this man no sooner got possession of the place than he shut the public out altogether."

"It must have made a great change," said Sterling. "When I used to come here, Splendon was one of the show places of the county, and every one had the use of the woods and grounds as much as the Duke himself."

"More," said Mrs. Truddlecombe—"much more. Why, we all rode and drove through the park just as we do through the Queen's park at Windsor. Boats always stopped on their way up and down at Splendon Woods. The Duke would often only come down once a year to see that all was in good order. Why, the whole place is now walled round, and every avenue of approach guarded as if it were the sally-port of a fortress."

"What a wretch!" cried Lady Ænid. "Do pass me some grapes, please. But what a selfish dog in the manger this Walledoff must be."

"Not exactly dog in the manger, Lady Ænid, for he at least enjoys his seclusion. But we who live in the neighbourhood feel very sore. Why, only the other day Sir Edward Rugby, who had ridden regularly through Splendon for the last dozen years, was stopped at the lodge by Mr. Walledoff's orders, and forbidden to enter. Mr. Walledoff's orders were positive, said the man, and there was nothing for it but to turn back."

"Then that," said Lady Ænid, "perhaps explains the meaning of that ugly wall we noticed the other day."

"Probably," said Mrs. Truddlecombe, "that was his wall. He has excited no end of dislike in the district, and this has even produced a pun from the stolid Berkshire rustic. His name, you know, is Walledoff, and they say he is Walledoff by name and Walledoff by nature. There is no one who lives here but wishes the Duke back."

"It must make a great difference to every one," said Mr. Sterling. "But why does he do it?"

"A case of reversion," said Sterling, quoting Glogoul. "Reversion to barbarism. Civilisation implies a certain measure of civility, and that seems to find scant favour in some quarters."

"They say," said Mrs. Truddlecombe, "that he lives in mortal dread of having his boy kidnapped, and so he builds this wall round Splendon to keep him safe."

"And then sends his boy to Eton, where he could be kidnapped any day! No, that story won't hold water," said Sterling. "I suppose it is simply and solely the desire to do what you like with your own. Our peers got that knocked out of them sixty years ago. But these parvenus of plutocracy have the lesson still to learn."

Lady Ænid laughed. "Don't look so miserable," she said; "come into the drawing-room and have some music."

But though Sterling followed her into the drawing-room, not even the merry music of Offenbach cleared the gloom from his brow.

"It is a bad look-out for England," he said, "this coming of the plutocrats. And if the Duke were to sell Chatsworth——!"

CHAPTER II.

LADY ÆNID.

WHEN Sterling came down to breakfast next morning, he found Lady Ænid's chair empty.

"Where has my lady gone?" said he to his wife.

"Oh," said Mrs. Sterling, "she left the kindest messages for you; but it was necessary for her to start early, in order to get to Eastland before sunset."

"What!" exclaimed Sterling. "You do not mean to say that she is going to try and make it in one day?"

"Yes," replied his wife. "The wind is from the west and the roads are good, and she thought she could manage the hundred miles without difficulty. So she packed her things at five o'clock this morning, and, after breakfasting alone, started at half-past six, leaving a note behind to say that she had gone. I just caught a glimpse of her gliding down the avenue as I was getting up."

It was as Mrs. Sterling had said. At the time this conversation was taking place, Lady Ænid was already twenty miles away, and had just struck the main turnpike which would take her within a few miles of her destination. Lady Ænid Belsover was the only child of Lord Belsover, one of the most eminent but impoverished of English nobles. He claimed his descent in direct line through Peveril of the Peak to the Conqueror himself. The centuries as they had passed, while they added to the antiquity of his house, had by no means replenished the resources of his exchequer. For the last two or three hundred years the Belsovers had contrived to keep up a tolerable appearance, living quietly on their estates at Six Elms, jealously maintaining their ancient traditions, preserving the family heirlooms, and from time to time ekeing out their inadequate rent-roll by discharging honourable and remunerative services to the State. The vicissitudes of the earlier generations of the Belsovers had struck the family less heavily than those of the last twenty years. They had survived civil wars, acts of attainder, Reform bills, and the Repeal of the Corn Law, always contriving to keep their heads above water; but the fall in the value of agricultural produce had brought them within hailing distance of bankruptcy.

Lord Belsover had seen it coming, and had done his best to trim his sails to the wind; but an ancient mansion and its fair domain can hardly be run on the cheap, and after all his efforts he found it impossible to make both ends meet. A colonial governorship which he held for five years gave him a respite, but on returning to Six Elms at the expiration of his term of office he found himself confronted by the problem of how to keep up a position in the county with practically no resources. With wheat at 50s., or even 40s. a quarter, the rent-roll of Six Elms enabled its owner to live in frugal ease; but when wheat sunk to 30s., and dipping still lower, touched 20s. a quarter, blank ruin stared him in the face. It was not merely that the margin of living income had disappeared, but the reduced rent-roll did not even suffice to cover the running expenses of the estate.

Lady Belsover, a silent woman, whose early ambitions had been somewhat cruelly oppressed by circumstances which rendered it impossible for her to find scope for the natural instincts of her somewhat lavish disposition, was the first to realise the perils of the situation. She made up her mind to face the worst. Belsover could not be carried on for long unless a change came, and of a change there was no hope. Rents were all dragging downwards, every year added to the number of farms which were left upon their hands to be cultivated at a loss. Her husband's party was out of office, and even if they did return to power, she had little hope that another Commissionership or Governorship would enable them to stave off impending ruin.

To keep up Belsover even on short commons entailed an expenditure of a couple of thousand a year, and expenses could only be kept down to this figure by postponing all repairs and reducing to the irreducible minimum the usual outlay on hospitality. The Belsover estates, with a nominal rent-roll of £12,000 a year, showed a net receipt of £1,500 after all charges had been defrayed, and last year's drought had wiped out even that. Lady Belsover's dowry, which was securely invested in Consols, brought in £500 a year, and by this means they were able to scrape along with difficulty. But prices were still tending downwards. The sanitary authorities were insisting upon the rebuilding of some of the cottages upon the estate; another large farm was about to be thrown upon their hands. What was to be done?

The assets of the Belsover estates were comparatively few. They consisted first of the land, which no one would buy; secondly, Six Elms Hall, with its heirlooms and pictures; thirdly, Lady Belsover's jewels; and fourthly, her daughter, Lady Ænid, who was to be presented at Court next season, and who, notwithstanding her lack of dower, had every chance of carrying off the first prize in the marriage market. The brief survey of realisable assets convinced Lady Belsover that there was only one course to pursue. If they could raise a mortgage on their estate that would enable them to carry on for a short time. If that failed them she could at least pawn or sell her diamonds for sufficient to carry them over another year. As a last resort there were the pictures, especially the great Raphael, which for two centuries had been the glory of their house, and for which they had repeatedly refused offers which would have kept Belsover going for five or six years. By these means they would be able to keep their heads above water until Lady Ænid had made the match which they hoped would enable them to contemplate the future with composure.

Lord Belsover acquiesced in his wife's proposals. What else was there to be done? The great thing was to keep their heads above water. Something might turn up; prices might rally, and meanwhile he would postpone the evil day as long as possible, and hope for the best. Lord Belsover's consent his wife had taken for granted, as her custom was. It was with more misgivings that she approached the daughter, upon whose success in the marriage market hung the future of Belsover. Lady Belsover was too shrewd to broach the subject directly to Lady Ænid, who was in the first exuberance of youth, and had ripened in the freer atmosphere of the colonies. Although the heiress of the Belsovers could boast some of the bluest blood of England in her veins, Lady Ænid had taken with a passionate eagerness to the free, democratic ways of the Australians, who had surrounded her when she entered her teens, and whose ways of looking at things she had imperceptibly adopted as her own. When she returned to the Old Country she found great difficulty in reducing her free and easy manners to the more conventional standard of Eng'ish society. She chafed against its restraints, and was never so happy as when, in the comparative seclusion of Belsover Park, she could give free scope to her natural energy.

"Oh, Ænid, Ænid," her mother would often exclaim in despair, when her daughter came in with streaming hair and sunburnt face from a wild ride across country, "you ought to have been born a boy!"

"Don't say that," Ænid once answered petulantly. "I wish to heaven I had been! I should have had some chance then! It was not my fault that I was born a girl. I never should have been if the choice had been left to me."

Her mother sighed, but deemed it wiser not to argue with the headstrong girl, feeling confident that the atmosphere of society and the pressure of circumstances would reduce her to docility. Nor was there absent a certain amount of calculation in Lady Belsover's acquiescence in her daughter's escapades. The one thing necessary was that Lady Ænid should marry, and marry well, which of course meant marry wealth.

"Times are changing," thought Lady Belsover. "A girl such as Ænid would have had no chance thirty years ago. But who knows, what with the talk of the 'New Woman' on the one hand, and the chance which mere originality and notoriety give to a girl, Ænid may perhaps be instinctively following the shortest cut to the indispensable goal. Certainly she will have a better chance by following her own bent than if I were to attempt to reduce her to the regulation pattern."

So it came to pass, partly from necessity, partly from calculation, that Lady Ænid was allowed to go her own sweet way. With this result, that at the age of nineteen she was cycling her solitary way across country from Berkshire to Blankshire, unattended by groom or chaperon, on her way to her uncle's.

She lunched at the "Royal George." There was only one other guest at the hotel, a man of about five-and-twenty, a cyclist like herself. He seemed indisposed to conversation, and beyond a few commonplaces about the roads and the wind the meal passed in silence. When it was over he went out into the yard, leaving behind him the paper which he had been reading when she entered. She took it up and glanced at it. It was the *Radical Bugleblast*. Lady Ænid looked at it with some curiosity, and her eye wandering over the columns was attracted by a double-leaded article in which the name of her uncle appeared somewhat conspicuously. Hitherto, partly owing to her absence from the country, and also to the disinclination of a girl to concern herself with affairs in which she is not permitted to take any responsible part, Lady Ænid had bestowed so little attention upon politics as hardly to know the issues on which they were split. The article in the *Bugleblast* proclaimed the opening of a campaign against the Duke of Eastland, whom she vaguely saw was regarded as a kind of tyrant-incubus upon the district in which he lived. The Radical candidate, one Edmund Wilkes, was on his way to carry the fiery cross through the country-side where the Duke's influence had hitherto been supreme. She had read so far when she was interrupted by the return of her companion at lunch.

"I beg your pardon," he said. "I am afraid my tyre is punctured. Have you a repairing outfit?"

"Certainly," said Lady Ænid.

As Lady Ænid was getting the repairing materials from her saddle-bag he was removing the tyre and proceeding to immerse the tube in a tub of water which was standing in the inn yard. There was no difficulty in locating the puncture, for a stream of bubbles rose to the surface of the water, indicating plainly enough the source of the mischief. A thorn piercing the outside tyre had punctured the air-tube. But for his meeting with Lady Ænid he would have been practically crippled. As it was, a small patch was soon placed over the hole, the tube replaced and inflated, the wheel refixed, and the cycle was ready to start.

"By-the-bye," he said, "could you tell me how far it is to Rigby?"

"About sixty miles, I think."

"Good roads?"

"Very, but rather hilly; at least, there is one stiff hill, but you will have no difficulty in finding the road."

"Good-bye," he said, "and thank you!"

Before she had time to reply he was rapidly cycling down the road. "I am going the same way," she thought to herself, "but I am glad he has got the start, as there will be no temptation to racing now."

Thereupon she looked to her tyres, and leisurely pedalled along the northern road.

The day was warm and the sun high. For a long time she pedalled along steadily, and after toiling up a long hill she could not resist a sigh of delight as she saw a steep incline stretching before her. It was easy at first, but seemed to become steeper as it curved to the right. She could only infer that the descent was rapid, for the road seemed to reach the valley by large curves. Lady Ænid was, however, too hot and dusty to dream of losing the chance of a splendid run down hill, in spite of all the curves in Christendom. She put up her feet and glided down the hill. As every cyclist knows, there is nothing so exhilarating as a splendid run down hill on a first-class machine. The speed, continually increasing without effort, comes nearest to the sensation of flying, while a sense of danger is sufficiently present to give a fascination to the descent. Lady Ænid rode the first strip of road with perfect ease, but on taking the curve she became aware that it was rougher riding than she had bargained for. Disdaining, however, to use the brake, she swept on, and, with continually increasing speed, rounded another curve, when to her horror she saw, standing in front of her, waving both arms and shouting vigorously, her late companion at lunch. Immediately behind him the road turned sharply to the left, and it was evident that there was some obstruction which led him to stand where he did.

This flashed through her mind in a moment. She at once put on her brake, but the impetus with which she was going was too great to be checked in a few yards. She had a bewildering sense of coming smash, and then she was upon the man. She swerved slightly to one side in order to clear him; she was suddenly stopped, and her machine went flying into the hedge on the side of the road, while she was grasped round the waist by the strong right arm of her companion, and fell heavily into the middle of the road.

SHE WAS GRASPED ROUND THE WAIST BY A STRONG ARM.

Fortunately beyond a severe shaking she was not hurt, and speedily scrambled to her feet. Her first impulse was one of blazing indignation. She was on the point of crying, "What mischief did you do that for?" when she saw that he had not risen, but was still lying on the road apparently unconscious. Her wrath vanished in a moment, and she knelt down to see what was the matter. The young man was lying on his side, breathing heavily. She turned him over, and going to the side of the road dipped her handkerchief into a pool of water at the bottom of a ditch, and returning washed the dust off his face. The coolness of the water revived him, and he opened his eyes.

"Are you hurt?" she asked.

He moved uneasily and put his hand upon his chest. Then she saw that in stopping her the handle-bar had struck him on the chest with such force as to knock the breath out of his body, and as he fell the shock had deprived him of the little sense he had left. However, he was soon sufficiently recovered to sit up.

"Now," said she, her wrath suddenly returning as she saw he had recovered, "will you tell me why you spilled me like that?"

"Look," he said; "if I had not stopped you, you would have charged right into a flock of sheep which are coming up the hill. I was coming down the hill with my brake on, and saw them a sufficient distance in advance to get off in time. I had caught a glimpse of you flying behind, and perceived in a moment that it was a case of stopping you or of letting you run headlong into the flock of sheep, to the ruin of your machine, and possibly to the loss of your life. So I did my best to stop you in time."

Just at this moment the leading sheep of the flock could be seen coming round the turning which passed through a pretty steep cutting, on either side of which the more adventurous animals were nibbling the herbage, while the main body were completely blocking the roadway. Up to this time neither of them had looked at the machine, which was lying in a more or less doubled-up condition on the side of the roadway. Supporting her companion on her arm, Lady Ænid led him to the roadside, and then began to examine the damage that had been done to her machine. It was much less than appeared at first. It required a good deal of trouble, however, to straighten the brake, the lamp was smashed beyond repair, and the handle-bar was soon put back to its proper position. As for her companion, he seemed to have recovered with the exception of a slight stiffness in one leg. After a while they mounted and rode slowly down the hill. After riding thus for about half-an-hour he began to fall behind.

"What is the matter?" she said.

"I am afraid my right leg is hurt. I have been working only with my left leg for some time."

She stopped until he came up to her, and was pained to see the wearied expression on his face. It was the first time she had really looked at him. He was not more than five-and-twenty, with yellow-brown hair slightly curled; his features indicated an almost rude strength; the whole figure was full of the vigour of the athlete accustomed to the ups and downs and the rough and tumble of life.

THE WATER REVIVED HIM, AND HE OPENED HIS EYES.

"I am so sorry," she said. "Can I help you?"

"I don't see very well how, ——; but I do not know your name," he said.

"My name is Belsover—Ænid Belsover," she said simply.

"Well, Miss Belsover, I do not see very well what you can do for me, excepting to leave me to jog along as best I can, until I come to a cart or something else that will give me a lift."

"Nonsense," said Ænid. "I am not going to leave you in distress, especially as the injury was received in endeavouring to save me."

"But," said he, "what can you do?"

Lady Ænid hesitated. The man was a stranger, but after all he was crippled, and it was she who had done it, and the least she could do was to lend him a hand, so she said, "Do?—why I will give you a tow. You don't mind taking my hand, do you?"

He blushed, the blush showing red against the pallor of his skin. "I cannot think of it. You have enough to do without thinking of me."

"Oh," said Lady Ænid, laughing. "There is no one so proud as a man. If I had been lamed you would have given me a hand, and seeing that it is you who are lamed, why should I not do the same? Believe me," she added mockingly, "this is no disparagement to the superiority of your sex. 'All rights reserved,' and take it 'without prejudice,' as the lawyers say."

Thereupon, seeing that the sun was setting and that he had not much chance of getting on, he accepted her offer, and grasped her extended hand. They started off again with fresh heart. He was sad, and she was rather tired, and there was not much conversation as the two pedalled along side by side, till at last, at a turn of the road, she gave a sigh of relief as she saw the towers of Eastland Castle in the distance.

"Oh, there is Eastland. I am almost at home now."

"Eastland," said her companion—"are you going to Eastland?"

"Certainly," she replied. "I forgot you were going to Rigby, which is nearly five miles further on; but when we get to Eastland it will be all right; we will get you a carriage and send you to your destination."

"Excuse me," said he rather coldly, "I cannot go to Eastland, neither can I accept a carriage from the Duke."

Lady Ænid looked at him in blank amazement; then suddenly what she had read in the *Radical Bugleblast* came to her memory, and she said, "Excuse me, but is not your name Mr. Wilkes?"

"That is my name," said he shortly—"Edmund Wilkes, at your service."

Whereupon Lady Ænid burst into a merry laugh. "What a joke," she said—"what a screaming joke!" and she laughed more heartily than ever.

"Excuse me," said he, rather tartly, "I do not see where the amusement comes in."

Lady Ænid stopped laughing and said, "I beg your pardon, and I quite understand why you object to go to Eastland. But for all that common humanity compels me to insist that you shall at least permit me to provide for your conveyance to Rigby. Come now," she said imperiously, "it is the least I can do. If you have saved my life, why should I not show my gratitude by what is the country equivalent to paying your cab fare? No, not a word; that is settled."

Quickening her pace slightly, she rode up to the lodge gates.

"I suppose, Mr. Wilkes," she said, "you will prefer to remain here until I come with the carriage. But don't be afraid; no one will know who you are or anything about you, and I will drive you over myself." Thereupon she rode down the carriage-drive to the castle at a rate which would lead no one to suspect that she was completing her hundredth mile.

Instead of going to the hall, she rode straight to the stableyard.

"John," she said to the groom who took her bicycle, "get out the pony carriage at once."

The groom, who evidently was familiar with the impetuous girl, answered, "Certainly, my lady."

"I cannot wait a moment," Ænid said. "Let me have the carriage at once, and don't tell any one I have arrived, until I come back."

In a few minutes the carriage was ready, and jumping in she rattled down the avenue as fast as she had come up. But when she reached the lodge gates Mr. Wilkes had disappeared.

"Dear me—how tiresome! What idiots men are, to be sure!" and whipping the pony she drove off in the direction of Rigby, after the departed cyclist. She had not far to go. About half a mile down the road she came upon Wilkes seated upon a stone-heap ruefully contemplating his machine.

"Come, sir," she said, "you ought to have had more sense."

Wilkes was evidently suffering; he raised himself with difficulty and needed to be helped, half lifted, into the carriage. Lady Ænid then placed the bicycle on the front seat and started off for Rigby. Wilkes was chagrined and mortified. He loathed to accept this favour from any one at the castle; while Lady Ænid, piqued at his refusal even to allow her to acknowledge her indebtedness for his kindness, was too human not to feel a little exultation over his discomfiture. They drove on in silence in the gloaming until they reached the outskirts of Rigby. Rigby was a manufacturing town which stood on the borders of the Duke's estates.

"I will spare your feelings, Mr. Wilkes," Ænid said, "by not taking you any further. We will stop at the nearest cab-stand. It would never do for you to drive up to the 'Radical Arms' in the Duke of Eastland's carriage."

Wilkes' eyes flashed fire. He bit his lips, but said nothing.

"I beg your pardon," said Lady Ænid; "I should not have said that. Forgive me, Mr. Wilkes, and thank you for all you have done for me to-day."

Angry though he was, there was something about the girl's face and demeanour which softened his ire. "Goodbye, Miss Belsover," said he; "you have been very kind." Another moment and he was alone, and Lady Ænid was driving rapidly back to the castle.

CHAPTER III.

THE DUKE OF EASTLAND.

THE dressing-bell was just ringing when Lady Ænid threw the reins to the servant and ran up the steps into the hall.

"Aunty! where is aunty?" she shouted, and in another moment she rushed up to the Duchess of Eastland, who, hearing her voice, came forward to meet her.

"Oh, aunty, aunty, dear!" cried the girl, throwing her arms round her neck and kissing her, "I am so glad to see you."

"Where has my harum-scarum, flibberty-gibbet come from now?" said the Duchess, looking down upon her tenderly. "We were afraid that you had had an accident. You know this habit of young girls riding across country all alone is one which I am too old to appreciate. But come my dear, we have not too much time, and you can tell me all your adventures at the dinner-table."

But when Lady Ænid got into her room she began to consider. The Duchess's words had roused a train of reflection. If she were to tell the story of her accident, she would never be allowed to ride alone while she was at Eastland; and as she intended to remain for a good while, she did not relish such a restriction of her liberty. And, besides, the more she thought of it the more clearly she came to the conclusion that it would never do to confess her adventure with Mr. Wilkes; it might embarrass the Duke as much as it had embarrassed Mr. Wilkes. Besides, she had promised that no one should know the service she had rendered him. So on the whole Lady Ænid decided, before she had put the last touches to her simple toilet, that she had much better draw a discreet veil over the incidents connected with her adventure.

Fortune favoured this resolve, for when she descended to the drawing-room she found the whole place one hubbub of conversation concerning the approaching election. The Conservative candidate, with his chief supporters, was dining at the castle that night. In the hubbub of electoral discussion, in which the ladies freely joined, Lady Ænid found no difficulty in keeping her adventures to herself.

In the eyes of the Duke of Eastland Lady Ænid was a mere child whom he had never taken seriously, and who to tell the truth had hardly taken herself seriously even now. She was the favourite of the Duke's eldest daughter, Lady Muriel, a slight fair girl of seventeen, whose features showed a budding beauty which in a few years would develop into the glory of perfected womanhood. The Duke, an honest painstaking peer, had the overlordship of a great stretch of the Eastern Counties, alike by tradition and inheritance. Before the Reform Bill the Dukes of Eastland had sent their nominees to Parliament for all the boroughs within fifty miles of Eastland Castle. Since the Reform Act the Eastland interest had remained supreme in three counties. After the emancipation of the county householder the Eastlands had lost two of the county divisions in which hitherto their interest had been in the ascendant. But the county division in which Eastland Castle itself stood was regarded as impregnable both by friend and foe.

Although by a fiction of the constitution it was supposed that the Duke took no part in elections, it was perfectly well known in the division that he was in deed and all but in name the Great Elector. The Conservative Association, which had its headquarters in the neighbouring town of Rigby, and which was conventionally understood to manage elections in the Conservative interest, was merely the veil behind which the Duke exercised his power. Everything was managed in strict accordance with the requirements of the constitution, but the moment you pierced the veil it was his Grace here, his Grace there, and his Grace at every corner. The cost of registration, for instance, was met by the Conservative Constitutional Association, but no one knew better than the treasurer of that association that but for the funds supplied by the Castle the association would be in "Queer Street." The choice of the candidate was ostentatiously left to the decision of the executive of the Constitutional Association, but the boldest member of that executive would never have dreamed of starting any candidate who had not previously secured the imprimatur of the Duke. Yet no one could truthfully allege that the Duke used his power in any illegal or unconstitutional fashion.

His was the oldest family in the division. If the county had to select by *plébiscite* one man who best knew the needs of the country-side, and who was personally most trusted by the rich and poor, the Duke's name would have issued from the ballot-box without a rival. Nearly one-half of the electors in the division were either living on his property or earning their daily bread by the tillage of his lands. In every good work the Duke was foremost in his county, nor did he consider good works in too narrow or skimpy a spirit. His pack of foxhounds was one of the best in the Eastern Counties. He subscribed alike to church and chapel. The Duchess's balls were conspicuous as the meeting-place of all sorts and conditions of residents in the county of Blankshire, and Eastland Castle was the centre from which every kind of philanthropic or social reformer found it easiest to reach the uttermost corners of the county. It was therefore only natural that a magnate with a traditional position confirmed and established by his personal merits, entrenched behind enormous wealth, and served by a multitude of willing and devoted vassals, should be able to hold very cheap all attempts to assail his influence in his own county.

The Dukes of Eastland down to the repeal of the Corn Laws had been Whigs, but they had never been able to see the possibility of maintaining the landed interest unless it were buttressed by a Corn Law; and when England veered round to free trade, the Dukes of Eastland went over bag and baggage to the opposite camp. That they carried their county with them goes without saying, and from that time downwards the county of Blankshire had been one of the strongholds of Conservative reaction upon which Lord Derby and Lord Beaconsfield, no less than Lord Salisbury, had confidently relied to stem the rising tide of Radicalism.

The present Duke succeeded his father shortly before 1880. He had been suspected of Whig proclivities, but they were speedily checked by the development of the Irish question, and among the 400 peers who threw out the Home Rule Bill, there was none who gave his vote with a heartier conviction than the Duke of Eastland. All the same his Grace was by no means easy in his mind.

"We are too strong," he kept saying, "we are too strong —400 to 40 is unnatural. Had we a majority of two to one it would have been another matter, but ten to one is too much."

The Duke, however, was too reserved and reticent to talk about his own misgivings. He had travelled much and had seen the evolution of democracy in many lands. He was painfully conscious of the rancorous spirit of social hatred that prevailed in certain quarters of the French nation against the *noblesse*, and he recognised the full significance of the fact, that in no English-speaking country among all those which have been peopled from our shores has a single attempt been made to establish an hereditary aristocracy, to say nothing of an hereditary Chamber. Proud and sensitive as he was, he disdained to reply to the accusations which formed the stock-in-trade of the agitators in the press and on the platform who habitually assailed his family and his administration. Sometimes, when too flagrant a lie was published, his agent would appeal to him to refute it. He always refused. "These fellows must say something," he would reply. "If you refute one lie they will invent another. You had better let them stick to their old stock-in-trade. It makes no difference in the long run what they say."

In all county matters he was an ideal public servant. No one was more constant in his attendance at Quarter Sessions than he, and when they were superseded by the County Council he was at once elected chairman, and took his place with its titular and semi-feudal authority consecrated by the votes of the householder-democracy. But although he did his duty faithfully and well to the best of his power and ability, he was penetrated with the conviction that the end of the existing order was drawing near. How it would come he did not know, but he was convinced that the old landed interest of England was going under. He was one of the last of his race, standing guard over a fortress which was on the point of capitulating.

"We might have lasted," he would say to the Duchess, who exhorted him to take a brighter view of things—"we might have lasted for another century yet if we had had to do with democracy alone. We could have weathered the storms of the Reform Bills, but we cannot stand up against the consequences of Free Trade, and largely," he would sometimes add, "we are falling by our own fault. An absentee aristocracy is as a tree girdled for the axe of the revolutionist. How many of us refused to lead when our people were clamouring to be led, and now how few of us have the means, even if we had the opportunity, to take our rightful place at the head of our counties! When wheat was quoted at 20s. a quarter, it registered our doom. No power on earth can stand up against that. We are undone; our order has no longer an economic foundation; we are like men in charge of a sinking ship—we can at least stand to our posts, but the hole yawns in our timbers, and the vessel is steadily sinking before our eyes."

It may be imagined therefore that the Duke was not in very good spirits when he welcomed the candidate and the officials of the Conservative Association on the eve of what promised to be the first serious attempt to deprive Eastland of the prerogative which it had exercised for centuries.

Lady Ænid understood little of the buzz of talk that went on around her at the table, but she vaguely understood that these horrid Radicals were going to bring out a candidate in opposition to the Duke, and that all present were determined they would give him such a lesson, that he would not show his face in Blankshire in a hurry again. Lady Ænid was consequently very glad when the ladies rose and retired to the drawing-room, leaving the gentlemen to talk over their wine undisturbed by the presence of the more frivolous sex. In the drawing-room, however, Lady Ænid found the conversation as political as it had been at the dinner-table. One elderly lady, who was a Primrose Dame of high degree, waxed very eloquent in denunciation of the "outrage," as she called it, of "that low-bred Radical foisting himself upon the county to oppose the Marquis of Bulstrode, who was not only the son of a duke, but was the chosen and approved candidate of Eastland Castle. "What is the world coming to?" she exclaimed indignantly. "Why, only the other day I heard that a greengrocer in Rigby, whose wife had been laundry-maid in the castle, actually declared that he would vote for that low-bred Radical. There is no such thing as gratitude nowadays."

"Who is this Radical?" said Ænid to Muriel.

"I really don't know," replied Muriel. "He is a total stranger; no one has ever met him before, but the Radical Club in Rigby is bringing him out, and I believe he had to make his first speech to-night. Probably the meeting is being held at this moment."

The Duchess made a sign to her daughter, who at once crossed the room. Returning, Lady Muriel said that her mother had asked her to go down to the office where they had arranged to have the progress of the Radical meeting reported by telephone. There was a strong feeling in the Constitutional Party, she said, in favour of breaking up the meeting by sending a large contingent of Loyalists to the meeting. They had issued such urgent appeals against anything of the sort, that they hoped the meeting would be held in peace. Still they were uneasy, as any violence on the part of the Unionists might irreparably damage the Castle cause. It was therefore necessary to have reports, and their agent in Rigby would telephone any news that there might be, so that they might be relieved of all anxiety before separating. The two girls eagerly accepted the commission, and went downstairs to the office, where the attendant was in charge of the telephone. He said that no message had been received, but that he would ring up and ask. In response to his inquiries they learned that the Radical meeting had been postponed; no one knew why, but they were making inquiries, and would telephone later. Great was the jubilation in the drawing-room, and afterwards in the dining-room, when this message was repeated. But curiosity was on tiptoe as to the cause of the sudden abandonment of the Radical attack. The girls, nothing loath, went back to wait for the next message. Hardly had they entered the room than the message was received. "Radical meeting postponed, owing to accident to Radical candidate. Leg broken or some other accident, rendering it impossible for him to appear."

Lady Ænid slightly quivered when she heard the message.

"I did not think it was as bad as that," she said, half to herself.

"What did you say?" asked Muriel, sharply.

"Nothing," said Ænid. "I only said I did not think it was anything so bad as an accident which had led to the postponement of the meeting."

When they returned to the drawing-room and delivered the message, a feeling of complacent satisfaction went through those present.

"Quite providential," said the old Primrose Dame to Lady Ænid, who was standing near, who could not resist the temptation of remarking—

"What an odd thing for Providence to do, is it not?"

"True," said the old lady, not noticing the girl's face, "it would have been so much better if Providence had broken his neck."

Lady Ænid felt so savage at the brutality of the old lady's remark that she would have said something very rude had there not been a general stir through the room as the gentlemen entered.

"Well, what have you settled?" asked her Grace of the Chairman of the Constitutional Association.

"Lord Bulstrode will take the field at once, and there is no doubt that we shall be able to give a very good account of ourselves."

"Who is the Radical candidate, may I ask?"

"Oh, the poor fellow who has broken his leg!" said the chairman. "I really do not know. But let me present to your Grace the editor of the *Rigby Fugleman*; he knows all about him." The editor of the *Fugleman* bowed and coloured up to the roots of his sandy-coloured hair. He had been a foreman printer a year or two ago, and this was his first introduction to high life.

"Do tell us who is our opponent, Mr. Spitz."

"His name," said the editor somewhat pompously—"his name, it is Edmund Wilkes. He is believed to have been descended from John Wilkes, of whom you have, of course, heard."

"Yes," she replied smiling; "but how comes he into this county?"

"A case of natural selection, your Grace. He naturally ought to be one of us. His father is a country gentleman in Gloucestershire. He is, indeed, quite well to do, has a great deal of money invested somewhere, I don't know how, but said to be very wealthy. Well-educated, too, so that he cannot have the excuse of ignorance for his misconduct. Took honours at Cambridge they say. But quite bitten with Socialism, he is a Land Nationaliser and a member of the Fabian Society, and I do not know how many other horrid things. We could not have had a better candidate to rally round the castle all the Conservative forces of the county; and your Grace," said he, seeing an opportunity of blowing his own trumpet, "may rely upon it that the *Rigby Fugleman* will do its duty."

"I have no doubt of it," said her Grace, smiling pleasantly, while the treasurer of the Constitutional Association, who was standing near, with difficulty repressed a broader smile, for the *Rigby Fugleman* was a "kept" organ, and the cheque which met its quarterly deficit came from the castle treasury. ' Of course Mr. Spitz was not expected to know this, for it is best to allow editors to imagine that they are doing themselves to death for the pure love of a sacred cause, when in reality they are simply engaged in the prosaic task of earning their daily bread.

the cab. In getting him out of the vehicle they twisted his knee, and the shock of the pain recalled him sufficiently to consciousness to enable him to explain what had happened. They summoned a doctor, who said that the muscles of the knee had been badly strained, and that he must on no account put his foot to the ground for a week. Great was the chagrin of the committee, but the pallor of Mr. Wilkes' face, and the obvious impossibility of his being able to endure any physical fatigue, convinced even the most turbulent that there was nothing for it but to postpone the meeting.

"LET ME PRESENT TO YOUR GRACE THE EDITOR OF THE 'RIGBY FUGLEMAN.'"

CHAPTER IV.

THE RADICALS OF RIGBY.

WHEN Mr. Edmund Wilkes found himself deposited at the cab-stand at the entrance of the town of Rigby he was painfully conscious of the fact that the injury to his knee was much more serious than he anticipated. He hobbled with difficulty to the nearest cab and desired to be driven to the "Radical Arms," where a committee would, he knew, be waiting to receive him. Such indeed was the case, and when the cab drove up to the door of the hotel, great was the dismay of the committeemen to find their candidate in a dead faint inside the vehicle. The cabman explained that the gentleman had been driven up by a lady, that he was quite lame, and must have fainted in

Immense was their disgust at having to abandon their first attack, but there was nothing for it but to yield with as good a grace as possible. The committee broke up in ill-humour, which, however, was somewhat alleviated when on passing the Town Hall they found it surrounded by a dense crowd of their political opponents, who had taken up positions at all the doorways with the view of entering the building and preventing a word of Radical oratory being heard. When some half hour afterwards the crowd were informed that the meeting had been abandoned owing to an accident which had befallen the Radical candidate, there arose a contemptuous storm of cheers, for they were convinced that the accident was a put up job in order to save the Radicals from what, it was evident, would have been a complete fiasco.

The town of Rigby, with which Mr. Wilkes was making his first acquaintance under such unfavourable circumstances, was the one Radical stronghold in the county. Its Radicalism dated from the time of the rivalry between town and country which came to a head in the great Free Trade struggle. Rigby, crowded with artisans, went for the cheap loaf, while the country round about it, which was a wheat-producing district, went solid for Protection. Rigby as a borough, however, had its own member, and the contagion of its Radicalism was not sufficient to leaven the agricultural district of which it was the natural capital. The greater part of the ground on which Rigby stood belonged to the Duke of Eastland, and it was the ground-rents of Rigby which enabled the Duke to stand the racket of the ruinous fall of rents. If Rigby, however, had done much for the Duke, the Duke, in his turn, had done much for Rigby. A statue to his predecessor stood conspicuously in the market-place, and an inscription recorded the fact that the new market had been laid out and presented to the town by the Duke of Eastland, who also had rebuilt the town-hall and laid out the public park for the benefit of the citizens. The living of the parish church was in the gift of his Grace, and the *Fugleman* was practically his kept paper. Against influence so pervading, so subtle, and so powerful it was inevitable that there should be a strong revolt. Human nature, especially British human nature in a provincial town, dislikes to be perpetually told that the patronage of the castle goes to your neighbour and not to yourself. Those who from one cause or another were, or believed themselves to be, in the black books of the castle, succeeded in forming themselves into a tolerably strong party of Anti-Eastlanders. It was the old story of Aristides over again. They had no fault to find with the Duke, but he was a duke, and they met him at every turn and were heartily sick of him, and wished to be done with him once for all. In the latter days this party, which had always existed in the town, had been re-inforced by the Socialist agitation, which had spread from London on the one hand and from Norwich on the other, and had as its objective the taxation—or as the more candid Socialists expressed it—the confiscation of the Duke's ground-rents.

The Duke's property included the best sites in the town, and was in the best condition. It had from of old been a tradition of the Eastland estate never to grant a lease excepting on conditions which enabled the agent practically to dispossess a leaseholder who brought the property into disrepute, and it was the exercise of this reserve power in the case of a publican and jerry-builder that gave the Duke of Eastland his most virulent opponent in the town of Rigby. This man, Joseph Brassy by name, had succeeded to the lease of a fully-licensed house on the Duke's property. The license was transferred without any objection being made to the character of the new lessee, but after a time the conduct of the house began to attract the attention of the police. From being one of the best conducted of the old hostelries of the town, it became under Joe Brassy's management the rendezvous of all the poachers of the countryside. Whenever the police wanted a doubtful character they could find him or traces of him in the parlour of the "Red Dragon." Raids were arranged there, and were carried out by gangs working into each other's hands in remote districts, so as to distract the attention of the police and throw the keepers off the scent. The Eastland estates were not strictly preserved, and the tenants had more of such game as there was than the Duke himself. But along with the poachers, many of whom were professionals from London, there came professionals of another sort, and of the other sex, who established a centre of disorder and demoralisation in the town, so as to compel public reference in the Press, and subsequently n the town council. The local Radical organ was very sarcastic concerning his Grace the Duke's disorderly house, and at last, after many warnings, the Duke's agent availed himself of the reserved right in the lease and turned Brassy out. This started him with a grievance. Being unable to obtain a license, owing to his bad character, he opened a temperance hotel in some of his own jerry-built property in one of the lowest parts of the town, where he was shrewdly believed by the police to do a good deal of shebeening, especially on Sundays. If this was the case, it was carried on so secretly that they were unable to secure evidence sufficient for conviction.

Brassy at once threw himself viciously into the campaign against the Duke. He was a powerful speaker, and now that he had opened a temperance hotel he became the sworn ally of the temperance people, who at first looked at him rather askance, remembering how lately he had been holding the license of a public-house, but finally passed an act of oblivion on his behalf, and welcomed him to the fold as a useful ally against the other publicans.

Brassy was present at the "Radical Arms" when Wilkes arrived, and had succeeded in inspiring the Radical candidate with an unconquerable disgust. The keen sensitiveness of the young man detected in a moment the false ring of Brassy's protestations, and when he called subsequently to inquire after the candidate's health the candidate absolutely refused to see him. The man was surprised and offended, for he knew that Wilkes, so far from being too unwell to see any one, had had a long conversation on the previous day with the Congregational minister, who had called upon him on a similar errand.

The Rev. Ebenezer Brown was, however, an altogether different sort of man from Brassy, with whom he reluctantly consented to act "for the sake of the cause"—that formula which has covered so many strange alliances. Ebenezer Brown was a comparatively young man, delicate and intense, wearing his life out with the strenuousness of the exertions he was making to pitchfork Rigby into the Kingdom of Heaven with one stroke, as a rustic pitches a sheaf of corn to the top of the stack. Rigby, however, as the young minister said, "was swollen hard with wickedness and sin," and was saturated with the conservatism of some centuries of history of which it affected to be not a little proud. Brown was unmarried, an exception among Nonconformist ministers, one of those exceptions which not only prove the rule, but which illustrate its general utility. For if Brown had been moored to this world by the soft loving arms of a wife and child he would never have wandered away into the fantastic idealism which was the chief characteristic of his ministry. The young minister, full of fervour, nourished himself on the denunciations of the Hebrew prophets, and Sunday after Sunday preached against those who added field to field and house to house, so that his more impressionable hearers shuddered, and the older pewholders whispered to each other approvingly, "Ain't he givin' it 'em hot!" Brown kept it up weekday and Sunday, faithfully following his duty as he conceived it. Brown was a Fabian and a diligent reader of the *London Daily Tribune*, from which, as from an inexhaustible cruse, the fires of social Radicalism were every day replenished. Everything that went wrong in town or country was debited to the existing social order, and the Duke as the local head of the social system came in for no small share of the objurgations of this dissenting Boanerges. With his diatribes against the powers that be, were mingled eloquent descriptions of the glories of the time that was coming, when everything that is would be turned upside down, and when everything that now belonged to the individual would belong to the collective whole. "Whatever is, is wrong," might be taken to be the starting-point of his gospel; and while he admitted that there might be doubts as to whether the salvation of mankind was to be brought about by the adoption of collectivism, he was quite willing to chance it.

But no one could meet him without being convinced of his transparent sincerity and of the enthusiasm that consumed him. Of this he had given an example not many months before. One of the leading members of his congregation, a trustee of the church, and a deacon whose contributions were believed to be the largest of any individual in the fold, carried on a flourishing business under the sign of the Three Balls. He was, in fact, the leading pawnbroker in Rigby. No one among all Mr. Brown's congregation had drunk in so eagerly all that was said as to the iniquities of landlordism and the duty of nationalising the land, but he could hardly believe his ears one Sunday when he heard from the pulpit an energetic appeal for the municipalisation of the pawnshop. There was no mistaking Mr. Brown's earnestness. He took his text from Leviticus, and illustrated it with facts and figures quoted from Mr. Donald's articles in the weekly paper *London*, proving beyond all doubt that our pawn system was less Christian, nay, less human even, than was the Jewish system, and that we had lagged far behind the more civilised nations of the Continent.

Mr. Tantrum's face during the delivery of this sermon was a study to behold. So at least the congregation seemed to think, for they looked at him all the time they were not gazing at Mr. Brown; in fact, the minister seemed to be the only person in the building unaware of the effect which his discourse was producing upon Mr. Tantrum. When he had dismissed the congregation and descended from the pulpit, he found the deacons in vain endeavouring to control the fury of the indignant Tantrum. The moment the pale face of the minister appeared at the doorway of the vestry, Mr. Tantrum flew at him as if he would have

MR. TANTRUM FLEW AT HIM AS IF TO KNOCK HIM DOWN.

knocked him down. "How dare you, sir," said he—"how dare you try to take away a man's living in the very house of God—a house, too, which me and mine have done more than any other people in Rigby to build and maintain!"

"But, Mr. Tantrum——"

"Don't Tantrum me," said that worthy, "not another word from your lips! To think of all these years that I have supported this cause! I call it downright robbery, sir—robbery! I helped to build this chapel as a house of prayer, and behold! you are making it a den of thieves!" Whereupon Mr. Tantrum shook off the dust from his feet upon the tabernacle, the doors of which he never again deigned to darken. The following Sunday he attended the parish church with his family, and the next number of the *Rigby Fugleman* announced that Mr. Tantrum, "that eminent and distinguished citizen," had formally severed his connection with the Radical Association, and had applied for enrolment in the Conservative Club. Mr. Brown mourned over his defection, but so innocent was he of the world's ways, that he could not for the life of him understand the suggestion of his deacons, that in future, when he ventured to deal with any subject which was somewhat out of the usual course, he should take counsel with the officers of the church.

With this fervent apostle of collectivism Mr. Wilkes found many points of agreement, and together they discussed the best way of conducting the campaign against the Duke. The two men, very dissimilar in their theological standpoint, were nevertheless at one in a fierce impatience of the evils of the present social system. Both were young, and both were so consumed with compassion for the sufferings of those whose hardships they realised, that for the mere chance of relieving them they were ready to sacrifice the interests of all other sections of the community.

But what was much more serious from the political point of view was their utter inability to measure the forces of resistance or to adequately estimate the quality of the

C

troops upon whom they depended for support. Because the individualistic system had worked and was working cruel injustice to multitudes, therefore they considered it was a case of "Sound alarums and advance all along the line" to make a clean sweep of the accursed thing. But they had no idea of how strongly entrenched was the enemy, or how few and straggling and ill-disciplined were the hosts which could follow their lead.

The Rev. Ebenezer Brown saw the battle afar off, as a kind of preliminary skirmish of the battle of Armageddon, and prayed and preached and canvassed in the sincere and honest belief that he was contributing his mite to fulfilling the prophecies of Micah and Isaiah, upon whose inspired words he nourished his soul. Mr. Wilkes studied Karl Marx more than the Old Testament, and candidly avowed that he regarded the Bible chiefly as a useful arsenal from which he could extract texts with which to barb the shafts he launched at the enemy. In this he was no inapt pupil of Mr. Labouchere, the English politician who has most of the letter and least of the spirit of Scripture in his discourses. But notwithstanding their different standpoints, he felt the true handgrip of mutual faith and mutual confidence, and Ebenezer Brown, in the secrecy of his closet, poured out long and passionate supplications that the Lord of all mercy, who had led His servant so far along the true path, would vouchsafe the further blessing of illuminating his soul with Divine grace, and enable him to see the true bearing of the present social struggle amid the eternal plans of the Providence of God.

Another member of the Radical committee who was hardly less interesting to Wilkes, and who was always welcome to the room in which he lay nursing his knee, was John Hopton, the secretary of the Trades Council of Rigby. Hopton was a man of thirty, and much more practical than either Wilkes or Brown. He had begun life as a crow-boy at the age of ten, and had picked up such book learning as he possessed in the intervals of a life of continuous labour. Hopton had from his youth formed an almost superstitious reverence for the principle of association. Nothing was more constantly on his lips than Mazzini's declaration that the era of individualism was at an end, and the epoch of association had begun. In his eyes the mere principle of association was the sum and substance of all religion—the key of all progress and the one hope for men on earth. He promoted unionism as a Jesuit preaches Catholicism. It was to him the one hope of the world. It was owing to his initiative that the various straggling Trades Unions of Rigby were joined together in a Trades Council, and it was to his powerful influence and persuasive eloquence that the council, after being constituted, continued to live and thrive. Hopton was a mechanic employed in an agricultural implement factory, and he had steadily refused all proposals to quit his forge for the Town Council or even for a higher position. Sincere and enthusiastic, he had neither time nor opportunity to study very deeply questions social, political, or economic. What he saw with his rough instinct was that, as every Church had found it necessary to have a devil, so in his own Church, founded on the principle of association, it was necessary to have some incarnation of evil which would act as a constant incentive to action, and would serve as a bond of union. This incarnation of the Evil One he found in the Duke and the system which he represented. Of the Duke personally he had nothing to say but what was pleasant; but the system which he represented —that of hereditary power and the principle of class and caste distinction—he regarded as emanating from the bottomless pit, and he went for it with a whole-hearted enthusiasm which, together with the religious enthusiasm of Brown, made up three-quarters of the working capital of the Radicals of Rigby.

CHAPTER V.

THE COUNTY OF BLANKSHIRE.

THE county of Blankshire, which had Eastland Castle as its governing centre in old times, was one of the worst hit by the agricultural depression. The heavy clays which enable it to produce wheat were once the despair of agriculturists elsewhere, but since Indian wheat had driven the price down to eighteen shillings a quarter, the land was practically unsaleable. Rents had fallen year after year, until the margin of landlord's profit had ceased to exist. Land, in fact, in Blankshire had touched prairie value, and in many cases had gone below it. The Duke of Eastland, for instance, with a rent-roll of £25,000, was receiving half the amount drawn by his father only twenty years before. In 1875 the rent-roll of Eastland was about £50,000 per annum. Of this sum about £25,000 was spent in maintaining the estate and the various charges with which it was encumbered. These charges had not been diminished, neither had the cost of keeping up the estate decreased one iota; and the result was that while the spending charges had remained the same, the actual income had fallen fifty per cent. The Duke was left practically without an income, every farthing being hypothecated before it came to his hands. His father had sunk, in the improvement of the estate, in erecting labourers' cottages, in rebuilding farmhouses, and in bringing the land up to the high standard demanded by scientific agriculture, nearly a million sterling. The Duke had added to this a further outlay of a quarter of a million. What is called the net rent-roll, therefore, was hardly two per cent. upon the actual capital spent in the last fifty years in the improvement of the estate. Actual rent, as an Irish landlord understands it, that is to say, payment made by the tenant for land without improvements, had ceased to exist. The Duke of Eastland would have been practically penniless had he not had two other sources of revenue. First, there were the ground-rents of Rigby, and secondly, the dower of his wife. He had married a banker's daughter, and her dowry, together with the ground-rents, enabled him to keep up the ancient style of the Dukes of Eastland without confessing to the outer world the decay of the ducal resources.

The day after the Constitutional Association had dined at the castle the Duke was closeted with the secretary of the association and the Conservative agent, whom he had summoned to the meeting. The agent was a new man from London, Wirham by name, sent down by Captain Middleton to undertake the organisation of the campaign on behalf of the Marquis of Bulstrode. Wirham was quick, keen, and energetic. He was clean-shaven, plainly dressed, but in excellent taste. He spoke little, but seized points with the rapidity of a thrush picking up the early worm from the castle lawn. He knew nothing of Blankshire excepting, as he remarked, that it existed. Would they kindly consider that he knew absolutely nothing of their local affairs and instruct him accordingly. "It is always the best way," he said apologetically, "to regard the agent in such circumstances as the present as a sheet of blank paper on which you must write the latest information as you know it. Not until that is done can he even so much as outline the plan of campaign."

"I think we understand," said the Duke. "The situation, unfortunately, is very simple. The key of the situation is to be found in the fact that wheat was quoted at Coleford Market yesterday at 18s. a quarter. In Blankshire," continued the Duke, "the situation is about as bad as bad can be. This is equally the case whether it is regarded from the political or the social point of view."

"Would you explain," said Mr. Wirham, "exactly how it affects Blankshire."

The secretary replied, "It affects it at every point and in every portion. The distress is already attaining lamentable proportions. The great failure of crops, which last year resulted from the drought, led to reductions of wages in all directions, and what is much worse, to the throwing out of employment many labourers. Wages in Blankshire are always very low; but they have gone down during the last few weeks to starvation point. In one district the agricultural labourers are not receiving more than 8s. a week, and they are glad to get that. In the Rigby Union workhouse there are at the present moment sixty more inmates than ever before at this time of the year. Usually the labourer succeeds in tiding over the October and November months by means of the earnings he has made during the harvest. But last year there was hardly any harvest to gather. The outlook is very serious."

"That is bad for the labourer, no doubt, and for the little tradesmen, yet our strength does not lie with the labourers, but with the landlords. Are they holding their own?"

The Duke smiled grimly.

"In Blankshire nearly every large place is either let or shut up, owners being unable to pay more than the taxes and rates on their properties. They are powerless to sell, the estates being entailed. The labouring class does not profit by this. They work for strangers who may or may not take an interest in them, but who more often, having no old associations in the place, refuse the sympathy and ready help that the old landlord's family took in every man, woman and child on his estate. The inhabitants of the villages round depend on work from the great house and estate—forty years' service being common to the men. These have to be pensioned or starve. A man prefers to let his place to the rich *parvenu* rather than turn off his dependents and live in the midst of them in their distress."

A map of Blankshire was spread out before them. It was a picture in itself. It was coloured all over with black patches as if they had been sprinkled over it from a pepper-caster, and each black patch represented a farm which had gone out of cultivation from the impossibility of finding any one who would work it even rent free. Quite as conspicuous upon the map were the round discs of white which were pasted at irregular intervals over the county. On closer examination these were found to mark the seats of country gentlemen which were now untenanted or left in the charge of caretakers owing to the hard times. It seemed as if more than half the country places in Blankshire were empty.

"It is a bad showing," said the secretary as he handed a list of the polling districts to Mr. Wirham. "In three quarters of these divisions we have not a country gentleman left."

"Is it so bad as that?" queried Mr. Wirham.

"It is indeed," said the Duke. "I have carefully gone through the county list, and you can see at a glance how the depression has thinned our ranks. Property," he continued, "has a very reduced garrison in Blankshire. We are very much in the position of a general after a Pyrrhic victory. All our strongholds have been depleted by the hard times, and there is hardly any one left to hold the fort."

"What about Sloane Hall," asked Mr. Wirham; "are things better there?"

"No," said the secretary. "I am sorry to say that things are very bad. The young earl is almost the only landowner in the county left who has any amount of money to spare. He is squandering his fortune. I was over there the other day, and the place is a regular hotbed of Radicalism. If we should lose the seat——"

The Duke visibly winced, but the secretary went on stolidly, "If we lose the seat it will be more owing to the blackguardism of Lord Bladud than to anything else."

"I should hardly have thought that Lord Bladud's extravagance would have had precisely that effect," remarked Mr. Wirham. "It is not the spending of money, but the withholding of it, which loses elections."

"That is no doubt true," replied the secretary. "But circumstances have changed. The Countess, whom Lord Bladud has treated so shamefully that she had to appeal to the Divorce Court, was well known and liked in the neighbourhood. There is a great deal of sympathy with her. This might not have mattered had it not been that the Methodists have a terrible tub-thumper in the neighbourhood, who seems to imagine that the mantle of John the Baptist has fallen upon him, and he denounces Bladud and his mistresses in every conventicle in the countryside. The Socialists have taken it up, and quote Lord Bladud as a typical example of the whole of the aristocracy. There, they say, you have an accurate object-lesson of what the Peers do with the tribute they wring from the People."

"They are working it hard," added the Duke. "I hear they are circulating a report of the Countess's proceedings in the Divorce Court, at the bottom of which is printed the single line, 'These be your rulers, O Israel.'"

"How does the shutting up of these country places affect the electorate?" asked Mr. Wirham.

"Almost always for the worse," said the Duke. "The shutting up of the country houses means less work and more starvation. Radicalism is only hunger in dilution."

"Do you mean to say that Radicals have much chance of defeating the Marquis of Bulstrode?" asked Mr. Wirham.

"No, things are not so bad as that. But there is no doubt that for the first time in our lives the Radicals have some chance of success."

"Everything depends upon their candidate and their organisation," said Mr. Wirham confidently. "What are they like?"

"They have next to no organisation, and so far as I can hear no money at all. We are badly off, and they are worse, but they will work night and day to carry their man. They are hungry and lean. Your fat, good Conservative will vote, but will do nothing else—sometimes is too lazy even to do that."

"Have none of these country houses been let to new people?" said Mr. Wirham.

"Yes," replied the Duke, "but it would be better for us if they had not been."

"How is that? If the house is tenanted even by a new-comer, money is going, men are employed, and a new element of stability is introduced into the county."

"I am not so sure of that," interrupted the secretary. "The new-comer is usually a vulgar, purse-proud creature, whose first idea is to get the utmost value for his money. He is a merciless game preserver, and will hear nothing of the little usages and privileges which make rural life go easy, and he treats the rustic, when he has to deal with him, with a supercilious hauteur which is bitterly resented. I would rather a country house were vacant, than that it should belong to a City man who attempts to run his establishment on the principles of the counting-house."

"Well, that may be so; but are any of them likely to help on one side or the other?" asked Mr. Wirham.

"One or two of them," said the secretary, "may help us, but as a rule they are too selfish and too little interested in the affairs of the county and of their country to bestir themselves in politics. Stay, there is one exception, and that is a very important one; it is Mr. Faulmann, who last year bought Netherton Priory, on the other side of Rigby."

"Well, what of him?"

"He is immensely rich, and for some reason or other pretends to be a fanatical partisan of the Radicals; in fact, I believe I am correct in saying that but for his support we should not have had a Radical candidate in Blankshire. He is a German Jew, a banker of the City, and chemical manufacturer of Garlam. I think you will find that he will be the Chairman of the Radical Committee."

"Then how could you tell me that the Radicals had no funds?" asked Mr. Wirham sharply.

"I referred to the organisation," replied the secretary. "Mr. Faulmann has plenty, but if he is to finance this election you may depend upon it it will be run on the cheap. Some of the contractors who have been refitting Netherton Priory according to his ideas declare that it is easier to get blood out of a stone than to get Mr. Faulmann to meet his bills."

"The situation," said Mr. Wirham, "reduces itself then to this. Every one is hard up; the other side, at least, as much as we. They have one ally which we have not—hunger; for the depression which depopulates our ranks fills theirs. The situation is serious, but by no means desperate. Here at Eastland we are on firm ground. This is the key of the position; but we must make overtures to Lord Bladud to secure his support at the other end of the county."

The Duke's face fell. "Do you think that that is indispensable? Lord Bladud is in such evil odour in the county that I think we should be stronger without him and his support."

"There is no room for sentiment in politics," said Mr. Wirham, sententiously. "Bladud may be somewhat lacking in the Christian graces, but he owns thirty thousand acres of land, he has plenty of money, and we cannot afford to make a gift of his influence to the Radicals. Between Eastland Castle and Sloane Hall we shall be able to rope them in, never fear."

The Duke glanced at the secretary. "I think, Mr. Wirham," said that gentleman, "you had better leave the question of Lord Bladud over for the present, until you have had more opportunity of learning the feeling in the county concerning him."

THE DUKE AND THE ELECTION AGENT.

"Certainly, certainly," said that gentleman. "It will never do to be too squeamish. Elections are not won with rosewater, and if you refuse to co-operate with any one except saints you will infallibly land at the bottom of the poll. Remember the Radicals have no such scruples, otherwise they would hardly have Mr. Faulmann as chairman of their committee. But adjourning that question; what about the Primrose League?"

"Her Grace," said the local secretary, "is at the head of the Order in Blankshire; but it has been run more from the point of view of sociability and charity than from partisanship."

Mr. Wirham shook his head. "Magnificent, no doubt," said he, "but not war. These fine sentiments, which do her Grace much honour, will hardly contribute to the success of Lord Bulstrode."

The Duke was nettled by this reflection upon his wife, but looked out of the window and said nothing.

"You see," said the Conservative secretary, "Blankshire has never been considered to be a contested county, nor was there the need for subordinating everything to political considerations which there is in less happily-placed constituencies."

"Of course," said Mr. Wirham, "I understand. The explanation is obvious, but the remedy is much more difficult. I suppose we can depend upon the clergy?"

"Yes," said the local secretary, "we can get them into line by working the Welsh Church cracle, otherwise they are not very keen partisans. But I am afraid that the Radicals, as far as I can make out, intend to say very little about the Welsh Church, and nothing about Home Rule."

"Oh, Home Rule does not count," said Mr. Wirham airily; "of course they will say nothing about Home Rule—that is our card, not theirs. But our first duty is to rally the Church to the defence of the Constitution. The first step in the campaign is to issue a special appeal to the clergy, urging them to form committees in their parishes to assist in resisting the attempt to destroy the Welsh Church. Each of these committees will serve as a local electoral centre for Lord Bulstrode's return. By-the-bye," said Mr. Wirham, carelessly, "if they are not going to fight on Home Rule, and are going to say nothing about the Welsh Church, what do they mean to fight on?"

"The land for the people, I think," said the Duke with a somewhat sardonic smile. "At least, that is the idea of the London man whom they have brought down. I don't think he will find much response in Blankshire, where land can be had for the asking by any one who will undertake to pay rates and taxes."

"What about allotments?"

"On my estates," said the Duke, "every one has had an allotment who cared to ask for one, but as you know, Blankshire clay is not very suitable for allotment purposes."

"Oh, the allotment cry," said Mr. Wirham, "counts for very little in the county where people know what land is. Its great pull is in towns. You will find more electors keen about allotments in Rigby and Coleford than in the rural districts."

"Now," said the Duke, "I think we have given you all the information at our disposal."

"What about the register?" asked Mr. Wirham.

"It is in excellent condition," said the secretary. "His Grace has seen to that. If you will come with me to Rigby, we will go to the office and begin operations at once."

Thereupon the London agent and the local secretary bowed themselves out and drove off to Rigby. As soon as they reached the office, Mr. Wirham said—

"Now the first thing to be done is——"

"Hold meetings," suggested Mr. Holdem.

"Sir," said Mr. Wirham, "that is the last thing to be done. The first thing to be done is to prepare the ground. Get envelopes addressed to every clergyman and curate in the county. We can do nothing without the Church. Remember it is worth more to tune the pulpit than to rouse the platform. The first thing to be done on our side is to rope in the parson. We must prepare a circular and enclose with it the ammunition issued by them in defence of the Welsh Church. I think you will find that is a stinger," said he, throwing a double-leaded, black-lettered leaflet, which Mr. Holdem took up and scrutinised with some interest.

"Pretty stiff," said he. "'Blasphemy,' 'sacrilege,' 'plunder.' Don't you think it is pitching it rather high, for after all it only affects a beggarly quarter of a million a year?"

"Sir," said Mr. Wirham, "you amaze me. Read what his Grace the Archbishop of Canterbury has said. You will find it quoted at the end of the leaflet. You see in the Archbishop's opinion this is the greatest crisis which has ever confronted the Church since its founding in these islands."

Mr. Holdem gave an incredulous whistle.

"It is all very well for you to whistle," said Mr. Wirham testily, "but I defy any clergyman to whistle in that fashion. Why, it would be flat mutiny, in face of the Archbishop's opinion, for any mere parish priest to hold aloof from the sacred cause. But I must be going."

"Where are you going?" said Mr. Holdem.

"Ha—hum," said Mr. Wirham, hesitating, "I have just time to catch the train; I am going to dine with Lord Bladud at Sloane Hall."

"What!" cried Mr. Holdem, "was it not understood——?"

"I don't know what his Grace understood," said Mr. Wirham airily. "What I have to do is to win this election. That is my business; his Grace can do as he pleases." Whereupon Mr. Wirham departed.

"Hum," thought Mr. Holdem, "these London men are pretty smart, but they will overreach themselves, I reckon, if they consider that they will run this election without considering his Grace's opinions."

CHAPTER VI.

AN EPISODE IN KNICKERBOCKERS.

LADY ÆNID'S fears that some inquiry might be made about the accident on the road to Eastland were unfounded. The commotion occasioned by the coming contest caused her arrival to be overlooked. As she had always come and gone in a very independent manner, it occasioned no remark when, early on the following day, she announced casually at breakfast that she was going to ride into Rigby to get a new riding-skirt. On arriving at Rigby, Lady Ænid left her bicycle to be repaired, and went off to a ladies' tailor to be measured for a cycling suit. "I have risked my life often enough," she said to herself, "with these horrid petticoats. On a cycle, at least, they are not compulsory." By the time she had been measured and had strolled round the town her machine had been repaired. As she cycled down the High Street she passed the "Radical Arms," and, gazing up, caught the eye of Mr. Wilkes who was looking down into the street from one of the windows. He started, but she preserved her composure, and was soon lost to sight.

For the next few days Ænid found abundant occupation in teaching Lady Muriel to ride the bicycle. The castle was full of guests. The great time was coming on when the pheasants were to be massacred, and the talk at meals and afterwards almost exclusively turned upon sport. To Lady Ænid, who had never killed anything in her life, the monotony of the ceaseless talk of shooting and hunting was rather wearying, and she was delighted when one day the post brought her a letter from an old Australian acquaintance who had come over to this country for the purpose of devoting herself to the profession of nursing. The letter, which had been forwarded from Six Elms Castle, ran as follows:—

Dear Lady Ænid,—I haven't the ghost of an idea where you are at present, but if you are within a hundred miles of Liverpool Street I beseech you of your charity to come and cheer the eyes of your devoted but desolate friend. I am here, like Robinson Crusoe, on a desolate island in the most out-of-the-way place you can imagine. If ever there was a God-forsaken place in this world it is Garlam, where I am in sole charge of an improvised hospital. There is plenty to do, for typhoid fever is epidemic, and I have been sent down to relieve a nurse who is invalided. It is a manufacturing village, which has been created by the lead works—and such a village! If ever you are inclined to be discontented with your lot, come and see how these people live. I have a spare room in the hospital, and could put you up in the matron's quarters. So, do come, if you can find time. I am simply languishing for some one to talk to. Do come—Yours affectionately, ETHEL.

P.S.—I forgot to tell you that the only civilised person to whom I can talk is the doctor, and he is away just now and has sent the oddest *locum tenens* in the world, a Dr. Glogoul, or some such name. He is an American, and the most tiresome person you ever saw. I believe he is not a Christian a bit, and his sentiments are those of a cannibal.

The moment Lady Ænid read the letter she determined to go, and was the more disposed to do so for her new cycling suit had just arrived from the Rigby tailor, and she was burning to wear it. At the same time she was rather in awe of the Duke, and feared to make her first appearance in the sacred precincts of Eastland Castle.

"Has any one any idea," she asked at lunch, "where Garlam is? Is it far from here?"

"Garlam!" said Lady Muriel. "I have heard the name, but I do not exactly know where it is. After lunch we will ask the agent."

"Wherever it is," said Lady Ænid, coolly, "I am going to cycle there if it takes me a week. I am going to start to-morrow morning first thing, before any of you are up, and then you see, Muriel," she added almost timidly, "I shall be able to air my knickerbockers, and get accustomed to them before any one in the castle sees them."

After lunch they found the agent, who told them that Garlam lay at a distance of about sixty miles from the castle. It was just on the other side of Lord Bladud's place at Sloane Hall.

"Could you pick out the road for me on my cyclists' map?" said Lady Ænid, producing her well-thumbed copy of the road-map of Blankshire.

"Certainly," said the agent; "but you are surely not thinking of going?"

"I am going there to-morrow," said Lady Ænid.

"Perhaps you have some friend in the neighbourhood?"

"Why," said the girl, "surely it is not such an out-of-the-way place as your remark would imply?"

"Well," said the agent, "it is not a place a young lady can go to very well by herself. It is a miserably dirty place, with a couple of gin-shops, half-a-dozen beerhouses, and not a decent hotel in the place. There is certainly no house in which you could find accommodation. The distance is too far for you to come back in the same day. It measures almost seventy miles on the map."

"Well," said Lady Muriel, as they left the office, "you will not go, then?"

"Won't I, though. There is nothing so nice as a spice of adventure. Besides, I am going to stay with my dear Ethel."

"You did not tell me that," said Muriel.

"Read her letter then," said Ænid, handing it to her.

After Muriel had read it she asked, "But are you not afraid of Dr. Glogoul?"

"Not in the least," was the airy reply. "I have seen him before. I met him when I was staying at the Sterlings. He is not a favourite of mine; but afraid of him—no! Muriel, did you ever know what it was to be afraid of a man? I never did, and I don't intend to!" said the young girl, in all the conscious might of a gymnast of nineteen.

"Well," said Muriel, "if you mean to go, I suppose you will go. All the same, I do not like it. There was something in the tone of the agent which seemed to imply more than he expressed."

"So much the better!" said Ænid recklessly: "You do not know what a charm there is in cycling by yourself through an unknown country. You feel like one of the knights of the Round Table pricking forth in quest of adventures. In these prosaic times, when you never ride unless you are followed by a groom, and for the most part drive in broughams or ride in railway carriages, we have lost the whole charm of romance of the olden days. But it's all coming back with the cycle."

Muriel put her arm round Ænid's neck, and kissed her. "For you, perhaps, Niddie, but for me life has no such fascinations of adventurous romance."

"You poor thing!" said Ænid sympathetically.

Lady Ænid spent an hour that afternoon overhauling her cycle. After seeing that all was in order and ready for the morning, she left orders that it was to be brought to the hall door at six o'clock. She consulted the barometer, and then tripped over to the gamekeeper's lodge to hear from the chief authority how he thought the wind was likely to blow on the morrow. She was a great friend of the gamekeeper, not so much for what he killed as for what he kept alive. The cottage was a perfect menagerie of pets, among whom Lady Ænid was very much at home, and with the gamekeeper she had struck up an intimate acquaintance.

"And so you are going to Garlam?" said the keeper. "It is a queer place for a young lady like you to be going to all alone. They do say that the devil is not so black as he is painted. The Garlam people be rough, but maybe they would not do you any harm."

"Why, what harm could they do me?"

"Heave half a brick at you, put a stick between the spokes, or cut your tyre, or anything else that might come into their savage minds. It is an outlandish place, is Garlam, with never a soul to look after any one."

"Oh, yes there is!" said Lady Ænid. "I am going to see the nurse at the hospital. She looks after the sick folk, anyhow."

"Hospital!" said the keeper; "that's new. Not so long ago—not two years ago—when our Dick was helping in Lord Bladud's preserves, they had no more a hospital than they had a church, or schoolhouse, or anything. Bad as they are, they are better than the folk at Sloane Hall. There is the civilised savage, and there is the rough savage, and the civilised savage is the savager of the two. There be many hell-holes in this Christian land, but saving your pardon, m' Lady, the helliest hole of the lot is Sloane Hall."

He was an old man, the keeper, and privileged withal.

Lady Ænid had the vaguest idea of what the keeper meant by his warning about Lord Bladud. Life had gone easily with her. Although she had had the run of all the newspapers, and had been brought up in the free and easy atmosphere of Australian life, all she had read or heard of the dark and lurid fringe of human life had left no definite impression upon her mind. Therein she differed very little from the majority of girls at her age. That there is evil, and plenty of it, misery and crime, they know, but it is a thing apart, nor do they ever dream that the sharp and rugged edge of circumstance can ever tear its way into their lives. The passions, and all the havoc they work with human lives, are to them a kind of stage-play which they witness from their cushioned stalls, causing them a passing thrill, but they regard them as apart from their own existence. It was, therefore, without alarm or anything beyond a certain heightened sense of enjoyment, that Lady Ænid, on being called at five o'clock the next morning, arrayed herself in her new costume and surveyed herself in the glass. It was a new sensation for her. At first she hardly realised that the saucy, piquant young woman in the coat and knickerbockers looking at her from the glass was Lady Ænid Belsover, her very self. She felt a little strange, and took a turn or two in the room just to try what her clothes felt like. Then she looked again in the glass, and a sense of the delightful but innocent impropriety of it all caused her to flush just a little. "After all," she thought, "I do look well in it, and it will be twice as easy to cycle in, and not nearly as dangerous."

But in order not to scandalise the servants at the castle, and to prevent any gossip after her departure, she carefully robed her knickerbockered limbs in a convenient skirt and went down to breakfast. Her travelling kit did not weigh more than fifteen pounds. It was speedily fastened to the handle-bar, and shortly after six she was dashing down the avenue to the park gates.

The sun had not yet risen, and there was a slight frost in the air, which made active exercise all the more delightful. She could see the deer already browsing in the glades, and now and then a rabbit popped out of the bracken and ran across the road in front of her. Nature was profoundly silent. The solemn silence which the air holds at sunset differs from the silence of early morning, not in its intensity, but in its solemnity. There is a briskness about the early morning air and a sense of the vigour of life to come which is lacking at eventide. Lady Ænid never slowed up until she reached the lodge gates. A moment more and she was out on the turnpike road.

She bicycled on for a mile or two, and then, looking carefully behind and before, she dismounted, unbuttoned her skirt, strapped it on the handle-bar, and remounted, not without a sense of guilty shame, which was transmuted into a sense of devout thankfulness that there was no one near to see her. It was a delightful sensation, feeling that she need not trouble herself about her skirts. The first hill which she glided down, with her feet up and no fear of her petticoats catching in the rapidly revolving pedals, was a delightful experience which she never forgot. As she neared Rigby, she began to wonder whether or not she should put on her skirt in passing through the town, and whether she might be recognise l. Reflecting, however, that it was barely seven o'clock, and that there would not be many people about, she rode on without stopping. Soon she found herself in the middle of the High Street.

There were more people about than she bargained for. Workmen were going to breakfast, and carts laden with agricultural produce were coming into the town, and there were all the usual signs of awakening life. It was too late to stop now, so Lady Ænid, looking as unconcerned as possible, passed the carts and the groups of workmen down the eastern road. The men stopped and looked at her, interchanging remarks among themselves, but that was all. It was not until she was beginning to congratulate herself upon having got through the town, that a hobbledehoy, coming out of a cottage, set eyes upon her.

For a moment he stared with open eyes and mouth, then he cried, "Oh my, look! Come here, Jim!" Thereupon Jim, apparently his brother, emerged from the cottage with his mouth full of bread. "Look there—look there, there's a girl with breeches on! Hi!" and thereupon the young lout, anxious to have a nearer view of this unwonted phenomenon, started clattering down the street after her. Lady Ænid flushed hot to the tips of her ears, and bending forward, rode her cycle speedily out of earshot of the objectionable young ruffian. He had done her no harm, but his rude exclamation of startled wonder and the clattering of his hobnailed boots on the road behind her made her somewhat nervous. When she reached Coleford, the next town through which she passed, she dismounted before reaching the suburbs and donned her skirt. She felt it was a weak compromise, but the memory of the lout scampering after her was too vividly impressed upon her mind for her to risk a similar experience.

By degrees the influence of the morning air, the exhilaration of rapid movement, and the intoxication of physical health, obliterated the painful reminiscence, and she delighted in the new sense of liberty and of power. Cycling, which is a convenience for a man, is a necessity of life for a woman —of life, that is to say, real life, for off their cycles many girls are never conscious of a moment's independent existence. They are the bond-slaves of Mrs. Grundy, and generally held in by some other will than their own, whether it is that of an individual parent or guardian, or the impalpable, undefinable opinion of the general community. The cycle is fatal to the chaperone, and the girl-cyclist who launches out on her wheel is as free as any wandering knight of olden time, to go where she pleases and meet what adventures seem good in her own eyes. For the most part the adventures are of the mildest, but there is sufficient possibility of the disagreeable to give a charm to even the most commonplace excursion.

Of this Lady Ænid was soon to have a rather unpleasant experience. She lunched at a roadside village which could boast of an inn, a relic of the coaching days, and therefore not lacking in accommodation for cyclists. After lunch, when she came to pay her bill, she wanted a £5 note changed. The waiter said that it would be necessary for him to go to the bank, which was some little distance off, in order to get change. She said she would wait at the corner of the street. She had lunched in her knickerbockers, and thinking nothing of the village public, she had not resumed her skirt after her meal. As she stood at the street corner waiting for the return of the waiter, her costume attracted the attention first of one and then another of the rustics. They had just finished dinner, and were about to return to work. Presently, almost before she knew how it happened, she was surrounded by a crowd of from twenty to thirty men and women, who interchanged remarks at the top of their voices which were the reverse of complimentary. The bucolic mind is essentially conservative, especially in the matter of dress, and the viragoes of the village were quite savage with the "girl in breeches."

"It's a scandal, it is," said one. "A houtrage, I calls it," said another; "it oughtn't to be allowed."

"That it oughtn't," chimed in another. "Where's the police? I would give her in charge if he was only here; but he never is where he is wanted."

All the while Lady Ænid stood as composedly as possible, waiting for that waiter. Would he never come? Attracted by the clatter of women's tongues, and seeing a crowd which always seems to indicate that there is something worth looking at, people came running up from all parts of the village. The women were meanwhile beginning to work themselves up to a state capable of physical violence.

"What are we comin' to?" asked one, "when young hussies can go about in breeches like this?"

"What right has she got to breeches?" said another matron, wiping her hands upon her apron.

"Tak' 'em off her," shouted a mischievous urchin on the other side of the crowd.

"So I will," shouted the woman, who began to approach Lady Ænid with the intention of carrying out her threat. There was no knowing to what length the virago might have gone. Lady Ænid was in despair. Just at this moment the waiter came hurrying up with the change. The little crowd shrank back in silence, and before it closed again Lady Ænid had mounted her bicycle and was riding down the street with an outward dignity which sadly belied her real feelings.

"What savages!" she thought; "what would have happened if that waiter had not come just when he did? How horrible!" For the first time in her life a sense of the grimmer realities of existence dawned upon her mind. For a moment she was cowed and miserable. Then there came to her a thought which always comes to those who suffer in breaking, by however short a road, through the palæocristic sea of use and wont. She felt that, however horrid it might be, still it was worth while to suffer that others who came after might enjoy a larger liberty and be free from insult and threatened outrage. So with a pardonable feeling of the pride of the martyr, she continued her journey through the pleasant wooded country of Blankshire.

The birds were singing gaily in the sunshine. The early frosts had coloured the copses. The cattle looked lazily up from their pasture as she went by. Every now and then she came upon fields overgrown with thistles, hedges untrimmed, and ditches uncleaned, and all the outward and visible signs of a derelict farm. Twice on her journey she passed country houses shut up, with the grass growing in the carriage drives, no smoke issuing from the chimneys, the windows closely shuttered, and everywhere a look of blank desolation.

Girl though she was, she had still some knowledge of the

"TAK' 'EM OFF HER!" SHOUTED A MISCHIEVOUS URCHIN.

carping cares which accompany the decadence of the property of the household. Six Elms Castle had always kept a brave show to the outside, but at what a cost of heart-breaking economy and starving of the household within Lady Ænid knew only too well. "How much pleasanter," she thought, "to cycle through the country than to own it. I have all the fun of it and none of the nuisance. Now at Six Elms we have pretty nearly all the nuisance and none of the fun. I wonder which is the road to Garlam?—there is the sign-post in the distance."

With that she quickened her speed. The sign-post, that indispensable finger-post of civilisation, pointed in two directions—one was to Sloane Hall, and the other to Garlam. She took the Garlam road. It was still early in the afternoon, and as far as she could make out she was about ten miles from her destination. From the summit of a hill, over which the road ran, she could look down upon the sea, which stretched away as far as the eye could see to the eastern horizon. The road led directly towards a hazy, smoky blot in the landscape, through which one tall chimney towered aloft. "So that is Garlam," she thought; "I shall be there before sunset." But remembering what she had heard of the inhabitants, she carefully arrayed herself in her skirt before venturing to ride through the long, narrow, dirty, muddy streets which she was rapidly approaching.

"How odd it is," said Ænid, as she was buttoning on her skirt; "I really have found a new test of civilisation. Places through which you can ride without being insulted are civilised, and those where I have to wear my skirt are barbarous. At least, I think so, if civility has anything to do with civilisation."

CHAPTER VII.

THE MODERN TOWN OF GARLAM.

THE town of Garlam was one of those products of the nineteenth century of which civilisation has reason to be ashamed. Not that civilisation had anything to do with Garlam. It was an excrescence rather than an outgrowth of civilisation. When the Patent White Lead Company, Limited, of which Mr. Faulmann was the chief shareholder and managing director, cast about for a locality in which it could manufacture the commodity which gave the title to the firm, Mr. Faulmann selected the little fishing village of Garlam. There was a small inlet which, with a little dredging, could be converted into a dock-basin, where ships could load and discharge at all times of the tide. There was no local authority in the place, a fact which the observant Mr. Faulmann duly noted. There were no sands or rocks upon the sea coast, only a long stretch of mud, over which the tide lazily spread itself twice a day, and then subsided.

The nearest town was ten miles distant. All the surrounding property belonged to the Earl of Bladud, who was perfectly willing to part with as much ground as the company wanted in return for cash down. The capital of the company was about £100,000, but its business was extremely profitable. Mr. Faulmann, during his continental travels, had succeeded by some means or other, into which it is better not to look too minutely, in inducing the Turkish Government to entrust him with a monopoly for the supply of white lead throughout the Ottoman Empire. Of this monopoly or concession Mr. Faulmann and the men of straw who were associated with him on the Board made the most. They only did business with Turkey, and exported the whole of the output of Garlam to various ports in the East.

The company was one of the most flourishing in the business. For the last five years—that is to say, since the monopoly was granted—the Patent White Lead Company had paid a dividend of twenty per cent. over and above the handsome allowance which they made to the managing director. The works were conveniently situated for the export trade. That was the only thing for which Mr. Faulmann cared. When he built his works it never occurred to him to inquire about the nature of the subsoil, which was marshy clay, or as to the water supply, which was confined to a brackish and sluggish stream that emptied itself into the inlet by the side of which the works stood. The works were built by contract, and the contractor who put them up brought his men down from London, bivouacked them in huts in the neighbourhood until the job was finished, and then carted them away again.

When Mr. Faulmann opened the works he was confronted with the difficulty of finding accommodation for the men—labourers for the most part, who were sent down by the labour registries to whom he had duly reported his want of labour. There were only half a dozen cottages in the original hamlet, and these, although they took in lodgers to the utmost of their capacity, were unable to provide adequate shelter for Mr. Faulmann's hands. Some rumour of this state of things having reached Rigby, Brassy, the jerry-builder, had an interview with Mr. Faulmann, and before the week was out foundations were being put in for a row of jerry-built houses in the immediate vicinity of the works. The foundations were little more than a few courses of brick below the level of the ground. There was no pretence at draining the houses which were reared in this marshy clay. They stood back to back, without yards or any necessary accommodation. The ashes and refuse were thrown into middens on the opposite side of the road. Mr. Brassy built at the corner of the first street a public-house, for which he secured a full license. He did not, however, stop there, but placed it in charge of his nephew, who had served his time as barman and tapster at the "Red Dragon," at Rigby.

Such was the beginning of the town of Garlam. By-and-by, as the business flourished and more and more workmen came to the town, other streets were built in a similar fashion. The Rural Sanitary Authority, however, had its attention directed to several cases of enteric fever. They sent down their inspector, and insisted that some elementary precautions should be taken to provide the people of Garlam with the first essentials of sanitary existence. Mr. Faulmann never entered the village which had grown up round his works. It was none of his business, he said; private enterprise must supply houses. It was enough for him to manufacture white lead. He paid good wages, none better; and if the working man was worth his salt, he would see that he was properly lodged and had all necessary conveniences. When the inspector pointed out to him the need for an improved water supply, Mr. Faulmann said he entirely agreed, but it was none of his business. He had not a house in the place, and all his attention was devoted to the management of the works. He was not going to convert free and independent workmen into servants and vassals by troubling himself with what they did with their wages when they left his works. He had no more to do with them than they with him after work hours.

Now most of the property belonged to Mr. Brassy, who had put it up, and was charging his wretched tenants more than would have been a fair rent for good sanitary property with all the necessary appliances for health. Mr. Brassy expressed his willingness to do anything, and in earnest thereof sank cesspools at intervals throughout his property in which the sewage of the neighbouring houses could accumulate. He also sank a well in the immediate neighbourhood of the stream from which they had hitherto drawn their supply of water. For this he charged a halfpenny a pail, for water was too precious a commodity to be had without payment. Besides, the less water there was, and the more one had to pay for it, the greater was the probability that the inhabitants would find their way to the bar of the "Green Man."

The workmen were as a rule Welsh and Irish, and were divided into cliques mutually antipathetic, neither of whom would dream of cordially co-operating with one another for the attainment of the greatest possible good for the town. There was no resident vicar or any place of worship. Occasionally a Catholic priest came to the village to see that the children were baptised; but for his ministrations there was little call. In this way there had gradually grown up a township of 5,000 or 6,000 inhabitants, utterly destitute of all means of grace, excepting an iron mission-room, which had been opened by the benevolent exertions of the Countess of Bladud, who on one occasion after her separation from her husband had been called to Garlam to see an old lady's-maid who was dying there, and had been so penetrated with a sense of the squalid misery of the place, that she had opened a mission-hall, which three Sundays out of four had no service. On the fourth Sunday an occasional local preacher or a curate from a neighbouring parish would read the lessons and deliver a discourse, which was listened to by a congregation small but by no means select. The adult male population spent its time in dog-fighting, poaching, and pigeon-flying, and made the "Green Man" their headquarters for the transaction of such business as was of a general and public character. There was one old midwife in the town who presided over the arrival of such infants as were so unfortunate as to be born into Garlam. A doctor came once a week to a dispensary, where those who were ailing had their wants attended to.

The cesspools were occasionally emptied, but for the most part remained reeking with their poisonous filth in the midst of the community. The death-rate was high, there was no bath or washhouse in the whole village, neither was there a library, reading-room, or hospital. Meanwhile the Patent White Lead Company divided its twenty per cent., and Mr. Faulmann prided himself on possessing that commercial enterprise which is the glory of this free country. Conscience, Mr. Faulmann had none; but a rudiment of a conscience might possibly be discerned in the uneasiness with which he contemplated the arrival of Her Majesty's factory inspector. The appliances for making white lead were of the best; of that he had no fear. He paid to have good machinery, and good machinery he had. The fact that haunted him was the way in which the inspector would speak of his negligence in not supplying the requisites of health to his employés. This, however, was not a statutory offence. He took care to keep himself strictly within the letter of the law, and if a large proportion of the hands suffered from lead-poisoning, that was their look-out, not his. If they chose to accept the work which he offered, they ought not to complain. The consequence was that if the Patent White Lead Company paid higher dividends than any other white lead company, it also had the worst array of miserable and wretched workpeople.

All this, however, was incidental to the manufacture of white lead. If the world needed white lead, a certain number of workmen must be poisoned in its production.

One day, Mr. Faulmann's attention was called very sharply by the inspector to his failure to supply what he had frequently pointed out was necessary to prevent a wholesale excess of mortality.

"Why," said Mr. Faulmann, somewhat impatiently, "you forget that these things cost money."

"Of course they cost money," said the inspector; "but if you do not supply them they will cost men."

Faulmann shrugged his shoulders. "If the people do not like their work, that is their look out, not mine." Beyond that the inspector could get nothing out of him. He reported adversely upon the works, roundly condemned the lack of sanitary appliances, and went as near accusing Faulmann of manslaughter as an inspector could in a report. But the reports of factory inspectors are seldom read by the public, and if they were there was no means of compelling Faulmann to comply with the inspector's recommendations.

So things went on, until one fine day an epidemic of typhoid fever broke out in the wretched place. Death followed death with alarming rapidity. The sanitary inspector reported the existence of an epidemic which demanded immediate attention. The Rural Sanitary Authority sent down a temporary hospital, with a trained nurse and an emergency doctor for the purpose of attending to the worst cases. The hospital was soon overcrowded, and still the epidemic showed no signs of abatement. A special committee from the Sanitary Authority with the doctor made a special survey of the place and condemned it root and branch. The houses were badly built; there was no system of main drainage; the whole surface of the subsoil was saturated with sewage; the water supply was tainted; there was no provision made for cleanliness, and, in short, it would be difficult to conceive a set of human beings more hopelessly doomed to disease and misery than the inhabitants of the town of Garlam. Mr. Brassy, as the owner of most of the house property, was duly served with notices which he calmly disregarded.

It was to this town when affairs were in this condition that Lady Ænid made her way in search of her friend Ethel Merribel, who was doing duty at the hospital as nurse. After the first excitement of welcome was over, Lady Ænid was startled to see the change which had come over her Australian acquaintance. In place of the buoyant, buxom, healthy girl from whom she had parted but two years before, there was a haggard woman, with a weary look in the eyes, and an expression about the mouth which told more plainly than words could do that she was suffering from a terrible overstrain tending to nervous collapse. It was evident that Lady Ænid's visit was a profound relief to her friend.

"You don't know," she said, "what a pleasure it is to see a friendly face again."

"How long have you been here?" asked Lady Ænid.

"I have been here six weeks. It is horrible. It is very different in the big hospital in London where I have been. There the work is hard, no doubt, but it is shared with many, and you feel at any rate that there is some one caring for you. Here it is not so; nobody cares—it is a God-forsaken place."

"Does the Company not do anything?" asked Ænid.

"Company!" said the nurse, with a bitter smile, "Company! Much the Company would care if every one in this hospital were to die before midnight. Nor would many other people care, and some would be very glad."

"How do you mean?" said Lady Ænid. "But don't talk now. Take your tea, and you can tell me afterwards if you like."

"No," said Ethel, "it is a relief to tell you. The constant pressure of want, disease and misery, and—I was going to say, sin," she added wearily. "But you don't feel that it is sin any more, and that is the worst of it. Vice and crime seem to come as naturally to these wretched people as breathing, and who can blame them? It is poisonous—the atmosphere is poisoned. They are poisoned with lead when they work, and when they come out they are poisoned with the beer they drink, and poisoned by the fœtid miasma which rises from the marsh on which they live. Poison and dirt,—

they never escape from them from the hour they are born till they die. How can you expect such people to be other than they are?"

Lady Ænid was seriously alarmed at the vehemence with which her friend spoke. It was evident that the tension was proving too much for her, and that if she remained there much longer she would collapse, and stand in need of nursing as much as any of the patients in the hospital.

By every means in her power she tried to turn their conversation from the vice and misery of these poor people to the pleasanter memories of the days in Australia when they were girls together. Fitful gleams of pleasure would glow upon the nurse's pale cheek, but only for a moment. With the regularity of a pendulum her mind would swing back to the ever-present weight of misery, and the squalid horror of the place was never absent from her mind. When tea was over, Lady Ænid insisted that they should go out for a short walk. The moon had risen, and the view from the hillside on which the hospital stood was not unpleasing, for the sea stretched right before them in the silver moonbeams. However hideous a man may make the land, the sea at least is beyond his power.

"Are there no county families," Ænid asked, "to whom you could appeal for help?"

"County families!" said the nurse indignantly. "There is only one county family, and it is worse than none. You have heard, of course, of the Earl of Bladud? I sometimes wonder, when I am sitting up at night watching by my patients, which is the greater curse to the countryside—the Earl at Sloane Hall, or Mr. Faulmann at his factory. The Earl is young, reckless, drinking himself to death, gambling, spending his substance in riotous living, and thinking only of his own brutal pleasures. On the other hand, there is Mr. Faulmann, bent on making money, as keen in grasping it as the other is in spending it, with a result that you can see."

"But how does Lord Bladud affect you?" said Ænid.

"Come and see," was the reply. "It is not merely Lord Bladud himself, but the servants and keepers at Sloane Hall take him as an example, and live as he does to the best of their ability. It is all drinking, and rioting, and worse," said Ethel. "Come here."

Lady Ænid followed her into the hospital. They stood beside a bed on which lay a fair young girl, on whose features death had placed his unearthly seal. Clasped to her breast was a miserable, puny child, whose face was marked with scars and ghastly running sores. Lady Ænid shuddered. She had never seen anything like it before.

"Tell me, what does it mean?" she asked.

"That is one of the Earl's babies, marked with his sign-manual, they say. It is the third of the kind. All ricketty,

"WHAT A PLEASURE IT IS TO SEE A FRIENDLY FACE!"

all rotten from their birth, they cannot, fortunately, live long. This one will follow its mother to the grave."

"But," said Ænid, horrified, "how did he come to have anything to do with her?"

"They tell me," said the nurse, "it is impossible to keep a pretty girl in the village. They are born here, I suppose, as elsewhere, but there is nothing to keep them. There is always a demand for pretty housemaids at Sloane Hall, and they all go the same way. This one, thank God, is dying. She caught the fever and will go even before her baby. The other two are now walking the streets of London. Oh, it is maddening," said the nurse, "maddening to think of it all —what that house might have been to such a place as this, and what it is!"

The door opened. "Oh!" said the nurse, with a sigh of relief, "here is Dr. Glogoul! Dr. Glogoul—Lady Ænid."

"Delighted to see Lady Ænid. We have met before, nurse. But, Lady Ænid, this is no place for you."

"I am the best judge of that," she replied airily. "But how did you come here?"

"Come to my room," said the doctor, "and we will have a talk." The two girls followed him to his room. "There is no mystery about me," continued the doctor. "Mysteries do not belong to my profession. After I left you I went to London to see a friend. I no sooner found him than he asked me if I were disengaged. 'For,' said he, 'my brother, who is medico at Garlam, is breaking down with the strain of a fever epidemic. It would give you an experience which you cannot get elsewhere. You can conduct what experiments you please, and make what observations you like. There are some five thousand persons among whom the epidemic is raging, and there is no one to look after them excepting my brother, who is breaking down, and a nurse who has broken down. You need not be afraid of newspaper fellows, because they do not go near the place; nor of the authorities, for they are ten miles off. Here is your chance.' So," said Dr. Glogoul pleasantly, "I came, and I have had a pretty lively time."

There was something uncanny about the doctor, and Ænid understood better than before how it was that Ethel had described him as worse than a cannibal.

"But what experiments are you making, doctor?"

"Invaluable experiments," said he. "I am cultivating the bacillus of typhoid fever. I have converted this hospital into a physiological laboratory. Have you ever been at Pasteur's establishment in Paris?"

"No," said Ænid, "never. Is that the horrid place where they vivisect animals?"

Glogoul glanced at her with infinite scorn. "Yes, they are reduced to animals at Pasteur's; here we have humans."

"You don't mean to say that you are vivisecting men and women!" cried Ænid, indignantly.

"Well, you need not call it vivisection if you do not like. I am cultivating the virus of typhoid fever. By starting fresh cultures from weakened ones I hope to have it sufficiently attenuated so as to be able to inoculate every one against typhoid fever; I am almost on the point of success. Indeed, in another day or two I shall have arrived at results which will justify me in writing a monograph on the subject for the Academy of Medicine."

Ethel here remarked, " Of course, doctor, you only experiment when you are quite sure it is sufficiently attenuated?"

"My dear nurse," said Dr. Glogoul, "I am surprised that any one in your profession should be so ignorant of the first condition of experiments, when you know positively there is no need for experiment. The other day I inoculated five perfectly healthy subjects. It is true that they were healthy—that is, healthy at the moment I pricked them—but they were not healthy five minutes afterwards; and after all it is only a question of time. They took typhoid fever in due course, and are going through all its stages."

Ethel's eyes were dilated with horror. "You don't mean to say that you give healthy people typhoid fever merely in order to experiment?"

"Of course," replied he, "we all do it. What are your great London hospitals for but to collect the poor in order that they may be used as experiments for the benefit of the rich? Surely you don't need me to tell you that."

"But suppose," said Lady Ænid, "any of the patients you inoculate should die?"

"One of them did," said the doctor calmly. "What of that? There is only so much more organic matter reduced to its elements. The death of a thousand such cattle as these," said he airily, "cannot be compared with the gain to science which my discovery will be."

Ethel Merribel remained quiet, but her fingers worked convulsively in her apron.

"It seems to me," said Lady Ænil angrily, "you stand a good chance of being hanged as a murderer, Dr. Glogoul."

"Not nowadays," said he carelessly; "we are too civilised for that. There is a certain risk, of course, but the pioneer must often take his life in his hands and be ready to die if need be that others may live."

"Now, Dr. Glogoul," said Lady Ænid, "don't talk like that. It is odious to hear you talk science; but when you come to cant, it is really more than I can stand."

"Well, well," said he, "I am now going to inoculate a baby with the matter from the infant whose mother is dying."

Ethel rose without speaking a word, and left the room. They could see her through the door go down to the bedside of the dying woman.

"Dr. Glogoul," said Lady Ænid, "you are not going to inoculate a healthy child with the poison from that infant?"

"Such is my intention, madam," said he, indifferently.

"But you are not going to do any such thing," Ænid replied.

Somewhat amazed at the tone of quiet decision, he looked up. "Why not?" he asked.

"Because if you do I shall have you arrested within twenty-four hours for attempted murder."

"Bah, what folly is this? There is no one here to arrest me, and supposing you do bring a constable from Sloane, there is no evidence against me. But," said he, changing his tone, "if it annoys you, I will not make the experiment until you depart."

"Your word of honour?" said Ænid, looking at him intently.

"I will not pursue my experimental researches until you have left Garlam."

"Thanks," she said. "It is a bargain. I must rejoin nurse."

At her approach Ethel looked up furtively, as if expecting to see the doctor. "Don't be alarmed, Ethel dear," Ænid said in a whisper. "He has promised he will not do anything as long as I am here."

"Then," said Ethel, "you will stay here until he leaves."

Lady Ænid pressed her hand, and they remained silent by the bedside of the dying woman. Dr. Glogoul made his round, left his written instructions and departed. Presently the woman began to moan feebly.

Lady Ænid knew instinctively that for the first time she was in the presence of death. She was awed and silent. Ethel, with the trained habit of a nurse, busied her self with little ministrations of tenderness and mercy.

"Where is he?" whispered the dying woman under her breath. "Why does he not come? I have waited for him so long—oh, so very, very long!"

She spoke brokenly, with pauses between the words. Ethel took the wasted hand in hers and caressed it softly.

The patient slowly opened her hollow eyes and fixed them on the two girls with a half vacant, half puzzled air.

"Who are you?" she said at last, slowly. "Why are you here?"

"Taking care of you, dear," said the nurse. "Now, don't talk, or you will tire yourself. Come, take a spoonful of this; it will do you good."

"Tire myself!" said the girl-mother, as she swallowed the medicine, with a slightly reproachful accent. "If only he would come!"

The child lying by her side gave a piteous little moaning cry—miserable in its weakness. Its mother slowly turned her mournful eyes to the puny little bundle of disease and pain. "He told me nothing would come of it," she moaned; "and now he has never come to look after his child."

She was silent; her eyelids sank heavily upon the long underlashes. Lady Ænid's eyes filled with tears. The little hand of the baby was clutching its mother's ear. Then a change came. The girl shuddered and moaned. Then she opened her eyes almost with a jerk, and tried to speak.

"You have not come!" she said, "not yet. And it is too late—now. But—but not here! Yonder! Do you hear?" she gasped. "You must meet me there, and ——" her strength flickered, her voice failed, and ceased.

Lady Ænid thought all was over, and was rising. Ethel restrained her with a look. The dying woman heaved a long, slow breath; the closed eyes opened heavily, the thin lips quivered. And the watchers by the death-bed heard her mutter:

"And soon!"

A slight tremor passed over the body, the breathing censed. Her great hollow eyes stared impassively into vacancy. The woman was dead.

The two girls slowly made their way to the matron's room. Hardly had they shut the door than Ethel dropped into a chair and buried her head in her hands. She swayed her body to and fro, saying nothing.

"Ethel dear," said Ænid, "bear up. It is better so."

Ethel looked up. "I am not thinking about her, I am not thinking about her. Yes, it is better so. But the others. There seems to be such an endless succession. How long will that bed be empty? It will be filled almost before we have had time to lay out the corpse of its last occupant. I cannot stand it. It is not as if it were unavoidable. Three-fourths of the misery which I have seen since I came here has been distinctly due to two men—Lord Bladud on the one hand, and Mr. Faulmann on the other. When I sit up at night listening to the moaning of these people, or when I go out to the village and try to do something for the miserable victims of lead poisoning, I know that it is due to the determination of the company to have twenty per cent. rather than to be content with fifteen. I feel as if I were going mad. I know how Charlotte Corday felt when she killed Marat."

Lady Ænid put her hand upon her friend's lips. "Hush!" she said. "Do not speak lightly of murder."

"Murder!" said Ethel. "Murder! What do you mean by talking of murder? Who is murdering—who has murdered that girl whose death-bed we have just left? Who has murdered all those who are dying in the village at the present moment? Murder! Do you call it murder, that swift death by shining steel, or swifter bullet that kills painlessly and at once? And do you not call it murder when death is delayed by long drawn-out torture? No, Ænid, no. Let us call things by their right names."

"My dear Ethel," said Ænid firmly, "you will never be able to get through your work if you give way like this."

"My work has got through me," said Ethel grimly. "It is no use working any more. What is the use of my patching up the wrecks of bodies, when those two men are allowed to shatter them wholesale? You say my nerves are giving way—it is no wonder. Do you know what I see night after night in the darkness when I lie in my bed trying to sleep, and being unable to get these dreadful thoughts from my mind? People talk of haunted houses and of ghosts of the dead, but what are they to the ghosts of the living? Yes, there are two ghosts, horrible as demons, which never leave this place. Oh!" said she, and her fingers began to work convulsively, "can you not see them? Look! by the side of that dead woman whom we have just left there is the phantom form of Lord Bladud! He stands there and he laughs, and then buries . . . . oh, horror!" cried the almost frenzied girl, pointing in the direction of the death-bed. "Do you see what he is doing?"

"No," said Ænid, "I see nothing."

"You are blind," said Ethel savagely. "He is burying his teeth in her bosom. He is eating, eating his way to her heart! Oh, the foul vampire that he is! Now he stands up—his mouth is all frothing with blood. Oh, Lady Ænid! Lady Ænid!" she cried, "help me, help me, I am going mad!"

"My dear Ethel," said Ænid firmly, "you certainly will go mad if you do not allow me to put you to bed and give you a sedative."

"Sedatives are no good. I have tried them all. It is no use, no use. That loathly vampire stands there with his bloody jaws, but even he is not so bad as the other one. The other one never leaves the place. Lord Bladud only comes sometimes, but the other one is always here. Do you not hear him?" asked the girl. She raised herself upon the bed where Lady Ænid had laid her. "Do you not hear him? Hark how he goes from bed to bed."

"No," said Ænid, "the place is perfectly still. There is only the ticking of the clock on the mantelpiece."

"You say that," Ethel cried. "You say that to deceive me, but you cannot. You must see what he is doing."

"No," said Lady Ænid; "what is it?"

"He is going from bed to bed, and at each he stops and listens; and when the patient moans he smiles, and when they writhe in pain he laughs and rubs his hands. For why?—oh, for why?" she said. "Do you know for why? Because every pang they suffer means gold—yellow gold—in his purse! It is full of the souls of miserable men, who have died that he might be rich. Oh, the little children! Do you hear them crying, Lady Ænid? I do—crying through the night for their father who will never come back to them any more, and for their mother who is in the cold, cold grave because of that man's greed! It would have cost so little," she said piteously—"so little! Only to sink the well a little higher up the hill. It would not have cost him one per cent., but he would not do it. And now he is coming here—he is coming to me to take away my reason, and make me as the others! Oh, help, Lady Ænid! help!" she cried, and then, shuddering convulsively, fell back in a dead faint.

Lady Ænid hastily summoned the servant in attendance, and together they succeeded in putting Ethel Merribel to bed, and prepared a sedative which they administered to her as soon as she came to herself again.

"What will you do?" asked the servant.

"I will remain with her through the night."

And Lady Ænid remained not only for that night, but for many days and many nights, nursing the nurse back into life, and helping as best she could in the administration of the hospital. The Duchess, without wishing to appear to sanction such unorthodox procedure, thought it wisdom not to challenge opposition from her self-willed niece, and confined herself to acquainting Lady Belsover with Ænid's latest whim, and to sending her such necessities and small comforts as the occasion demanded.

"YOU ARE NOT GOING TO INOCULATE A HEALTHY CHILD WITH POISON!"

"OH, HORROR! DO YOU SEE WHAT HE IS DOING?"

A Birthday Party at the "Radical Arms." 31

CHAPTER VIII.

A BIRTHDAY PARTY AT THE "RADICAL ARMS."

EDMUND WILKES' knee recovered slowly. He chafed bitterly against the enforced inaction. It was impossible for the Radical campaign to begin until he had at least two legs to stand upon. At present he had only one, and the doctor warned him that if he attempted to address a meeting he would be lamed for the rest of his natural life. His irritation was increased when he heard from correspondents in all parts of Blankshire that Lord Bulstrode's party was preparing for the campaign. Not that any meeting had been held, but Primrose Dames had been seen flitting about mysteriously. In many parishes there had been heard sermons against spoliation and sacrilege, which to the rustics who heard them seemed to have no practical meaning beyond an exhortation to vote for Lord Bulstrode, although, of course, his lordship's name was never mentioned.

Sociable by nature, and accustomed to meet men and women of his own age, and to be in the midst of the life and movement of the day, he found it terribly dull being cooped up in the best room of the "Radical Arms," with no one to speak to with the exception of an occasional Radical committee man who would look in to tell him how things were going; and as they were not usually going his way, these visitors tended rather to aggravate than to alleviate his irritation. His acquaintance with the minister, Ebenezer Brown, ripened into something like friendship, and Hopton looked in every evening; but still Wilkes felt very lonely. As his birthday was approaching he, in sheer despair, wrote to two or three of his friends in town to ask them to come down and cheer him in his loneliness at the "Radical Arms." "Come down," he wrote, "I beseech you, and have compassion upon my solitude, and let the light of your countenance shine once more upon the afflicted prisoner, Edmund Wilkes."

In response to that appeal, three or four of his old college friends came down from London and spent his birthday with him in Rigby. There was Sir Artegal Haddon, a Conservative of the Conservatives, but absolutely free from prejudice or bigotry. As to the old order, he saw they were changing, and giving place to a new and not by any means a better order. But, even if the change were advantageous, it would be all the better if it were not rushed, he thought. He defended all the superstitions and prejudices of his class, not because he believed in them, but because it seemed to him they were temporarily useful in retarding what he regarded as the hothouse growth of Radical nostrums. With him came Dick Milman, one of the bright and shining lights of Balliol, whose friends were quite sure that he would be Prime Minister some day, or if not Prime Minister, then Viceroy of India, or Archbishop of Canterbury, or anything else he chose to desire. For Dick had been born under a lucky star, and whether he devoted himself to journalism, finance, or to administration, it was all the same. An unseen power seemed to thrust him forward from behind, landing him at the top of the tree before his rivals had reached the first branch. He was a man of detached mind. Secluded by his position from active partizanship, yet he was closely linked both by personal and social ties with leaders on both sides. He saw as much of the game of politics as most men, and judged them with the impartiality of one who is without and the knowledge of one who is within.

Another old crony of Wilkes' was a man of a very different stamp. It would be somewhat difficult to locate precisely the political position of Mr. Rawton Silvertongue. He was the most cosmopolitan of the group. Born heir to an Irish estate, he speedily discovered that it would yield him but a miserable subsistence; so, without abandoning his ancestral acres, he applied himself with the courage and resource of an Elizabethan adventurer to build up a fortune for himself. In this quest he had travelled much and far. He had owned cattle by the hundred thousand in the great Western ranches, and then when they were smitten by the drought he transferred himself with equal facility to the Court of Seringapatam, where he occupied for a time the position of confidential adviser to the Maharajah. Wearying of the limitations of the feudatory prince, he returned to the Western world, and spent his time between Washington and London. No Englishman was so versed in all the intrigues of the lobby at Washington, or more familiar with all the ins and outs of the political and financial world in London. After trying many modes of diversion he finally came to the conclusion that you got more sport for your money in hunting the currency hare than by any other pursuit known to mankind. Mr. Silvertongue therefore became the impassioned advocate and apostle of bimetallism, in which he saw the only hope of unregenerate man. He delighted to haunt the *salons* of the great in order to whisper in the ears of his hosts warnings of the revolution and disaster which awaited them if they refused to remonetise silver.

One day he would indite an article in one of the monthly reviews, proving irrefutably, from a survey of the history of the world, that civilisation had only one hinge, and that hinge was the ratio of silver to gold. Another night he would be dining with a Rothschild, describing to the financial magnate how his house in Piccadilly would some day be surrounded by a howling mob, while he, Mr. Silvertongue, would endeavour to pacify the crowd by handing out all the plate. At third time he would be addressing a Chamber of Commerce, and setting forth the fact that the insatiate devotion of the white man to the yellow money would lead to the transfer of the industrial supremacy of the world to the yellow man with the white money.

With these three came a young peer, who had just succeeded to a heavily mortgaged and encumbered estate—a man full of generous illusions, resourceful, open-minded, well-informed, and resolute to carry out whatever seemed to him to be the duties of his position.

Such were the four companions whom Edmund Wilkes gathered round him at the "Radical Arms," in order to celebrate his birthday. Very pleasant was their talk, and many the reminiscences of college and other days which they indulged during dinner; but it was not until the cigarettes were produced and they fell to smoking, that they began to talk seriously of politics. Of course, they began with a speculation as to the result of the coming General Election.

"Oh, we shall lose of course," said Wilkes, "outside Blankshire I mean," he added, smiling. "You fellows have the game all in your own hands."

"I am not so sure of that," said Sir Artegal. "Never prophesy unless you know is a good rule at all times, and an especially good rule when you are dealing with that very dark horse, the British public. No one knows what an hour may bring forth. That is one of the charms of politics. You are always face to face with the inscrutable."

"I don't know," said Milman, "the one thing certain is that the outs always win a General Election. Parties have their turn in office, just as two elevens have alternate innings in the cricket field."

"But sometimes," said Sir Artegal, "you have to 'follow on' in cricket."

"Sometimes," said Milman. "But in politics it happens so seldom that it does not count. I should say the betting was five to one for a Conservative majority at the coming election."

"Ten to one, I should say," said Silvertongue, "since the glamour of Lord Rosebery has been dissipated and Ladas has lost the St. Leger."

"Well," said Sir Artegal, "I have known Lord Rosebery since he was a schoolboy. He is shrewd, resourceful, reserved. He is by no means a heaven-sent statesman; but neither is he the idiot which our side is attempting to make him out to be. He has a very difficult game to play, and is playing it much more adroitly than any of his censors could do if they were in his place. But they are overdoing it, and the next thing will be that, before we know where we are, he will once more be a heaven-sent statesman as he was when he first became Prime Minister."

"I have been very much disappointed in him," said Lord Eastwell. "We had hoped he would have come out strongly on the Imperial line."

"And," interrupted Wilkes sarcastically, "wrecked his Government before it had been a week old. What would you have thought of him then? Surely Mr. Gladstone's experience in 1886 should have cured Liberal leaders of the desire to execute curves with too great a rapidity. The situation does not call for heroics of that kind; indeed, it very seldom does, excepting when the Forum gapes for your Quintus Curtius, and it might gape until the day of judgment before Lord Rosebery would leap into it."

"There you are wrong," said Sir Artegal. "He is quite capable of doing that, if only because he has gained everything which he can expect to obtain. Remember—

Worse than adversity that befell,
He felt the fulness of satiety.

"Do you think he has achieved everything?" said Dick Milman. "I should say that he had only found the tools with which he could do anything. Here is the British Empire practically waiting reconstruction. Never had a statesman a greater chance. To speak of him having achieved everything merely because he has in his possession that which will enable him to achieve everything, seems to me to be absurd. But a truce to this endless discussion about Lord Rosebery, which always ends in the discovery that he is a darker horse than we imagined. What are you going to do in Blankshire?"

"Get my knee better first," said Wilkes, "and then make it as lively as I can for the Duke."

"What particular strip of Liberalism do you affect?" said Lord Eastwell.

"Oh," said Wilkes, "I would be an Independent Labour candidate if I had ever done a stroke of work in my life, which I haven't, and I am not quite capable of masquerading as a working-man."

"The scruple does you honour," said Milman, laughing. "It does not seem to trouble some gentlemen with whom you are in the habit of colleaguing."

"You see," said Wilkes, "I am a Socialist and a Democrat. I do not care a straw for the present Government of monopolists and of landowners and large employers of labour. It is a Government composed of the natural enemies of the working-man. If we can only threaten them enough, we shall succeed in making them give us some unwilling concessions which we shall accept as instalments. But nothing will content us except the nationalisation of all means of production, commencing with the land."

Lord Eastwell pricked up his ears. "Really, why beginning with the land?"

"The land," said Wilkes, "is the source of all wealth. All private ownership in land is usurpation, and the sooner it ceases the better."

"Stuff and nonsense!" said Silvertongue. "What the mischief do you want to nationalise the land for? Look at my little property in Ireland. How much in the last ten years do you think I have drawn from my patrimonial estate? Why, not a red cent. The whole of the rent paid by the tenants was swallowed up in the administration of the estate, and this year I have just had to send them a cheque for £500 to balance accounts. Precious little profit the State would get out of Ballymecarry if it were nationalised."

"Oh, well, Irish land, you know," said Wilkes, "is different."

"Different," said Lord Eastwell, "chiefly because the agricultural depression is less felt in Ireland than it is in England. In Ireland you can get rent; in England you cannot."

"What do you mean?" said Wilkes. "What do you say to the rent-roll of the Duke of Eastland, the Duke of Northumberland, and others who might be named?"

"I mean this," said Lord Eastwell hotly—"if you take the southern and eastern counties of England, with which I am better acquainted, you will find that purely agricultural land has no rental value at all. In short, agricultural land in England at this present moment has sunk to prairie value."

"I see!" said Wilkes sarcastically. "And what about the rent-rolls of the country, which, judging from statistics, do not seem to have fallen off very materially?"

"I don't know about your statistics," said Lord Eastwell, "but this I will say—if you take any estate in these eastern counties, and go into matters carefully, you will find that what is nominally called rent is nothing less than interest on capital—outlay by the landlord. You cannot strike at that without striking at investments of every kind."

"Oh, that is what is always said," replied Wilkes airily.

"It is true," retorted Lord Eastwell. "Who is going to sink money in rebuilding a farmstead or draining a bog, if the whole of his money is to be airily wiped out by you Radical fellows because it happens to be invested in land?"

"But," said Sir Artegal, "without discussing the morality of the question, will you explain to me how it is that any one is going to invest capital in land in the future, if it is once laid down that the only kind of capital which is entitled to no protection is capital invested in land?"

"Excepting capital invested in strong drink; that is also outlawed without benefit of clergy," interrupted Silvertongue.

"Oh," said Wilkes, "why talk like that? People will be keen enough to invest money in their own holdings when the great estates are broken up and the whole country is covered with peasant proprietors."

"Hum," said Lord Eastwell, "perhaps you have not had so much experience in dealing with peasants, or the labourers whom you are proposing to convert into peasants, as some of us. Take myself, for instance. I have done my best to develop small holdings on my estates. I have done this, not because of philanthropy, but because I think the landed interest has followed a suicidal policy in destroying those who ought to have been its most effective supporters. We certainly should not have had Free Trade, which is ruining us, if, instead of a few landowners, the whole country had been covered with small proprietors. If you doubt that, look at France. What is the invariable rule whenever I grant an allotment? I have always to advance the money. I have to drain the land or to fence it or to put up buildings. I do this, and do it gladly; but if you are to go through the county preaching the doctrine that capital invested in land is to bear no interest, you put the knife to the throat of all improvements."

"Now," said Silvertongue, "if you want to nationalise something, why don't you begin with a business that pays?

A Birthday Party at the "Radical Arms."

Why not nationalise railways, or banks, or pawnbrokers, or anything rather than the only industry in the country which is stricken to death by the fiscal system which you have deliberately adopted?"

"Yes," said Lord Eastwell, "and what is more, there seems to be no bottom to it. The fall in prices in agricultural produce alone this year represents a loss of twelve millions sterling to the British farmer."

"But look at the countryside," said Silvertongue. "Look at Kent, to say nothing of Blankshire here. They are all studded with empty houses, which stand like sepulchres of the deceased landed interest. Where are the owners? They cannot make lan'l pay, and do you think the State will?"

"That is all very well," said Wilkes. "These owners, where are they, and why are their houses shut up? Simply because they have outrun the constable. The agricultural depression is responsible no doubt to some extent, but the agricultural depression has much less to do with the reduction of our landed aristocracy to their present impecunious position than the reckless expenditure which was the result of senseless emulation. For one country house which has been shut up because rents have fallen, you will find two which have been closed because their owners spent 30s. for every twenty they received. The fact is that the struggle of the peers to outdo the plutocracy in expenditure has finished the ruin which the democratic movement of our time brought to their order. Beaten from one stronghold after another by successive reform bills, they entrenched themselves at last in their social position. They would still flaunt it with the best. Then the new men came in, and just as the Radicals had ousted them from a monopoly of the representation of the House of Commons, so the brewers, the bankers, and the millionaires from across the seas have ousted them from that posi ion of social pre-eminence which is due to the expenditure of money. As one of their number said recently, the pace was set by the *nouveaux riches*; and the landed nobles, instead of taking refuge in a proud but honourable poverty, eagerly accepted the challenge, and have gone under, exhausted by their own folly and extravagance. And England is now studded from end to end with the castles of splendid paupers."

"And supposing all this is true," said Sir Artegal—"and no one can deny that there is much truth in it—why should you select this broken interest, weighed down with mortgages and hopelessly crippled with debt, as that of all others which you propose first to nationalise?"

"They have had their day," said Wilkes, "and must now make room for men who will bring business instincts to the management of their estates."

"Commercial instincts, you mean," said Milman; "and I wish you joy of the exchange. The old aristocrat may have been a fool—no doubt he often was—but so far as the people in the midst of whom he lived are concerned, they will find the new plutocrat will chastise them with scorpions, whereas the old noble but scourged them with whips."

"What I don't see," said Lord Eastwell, "is where you are going to get the margin with which to carry on. You talk about allotments, but if you had had any experience with land at all you would know that only a fractional part of the land is capable of being cultivated as allotments."

"Oh," said Wilkes, "what we propose to do is to constitute a commission in every county, which will be empowered to ascertain how much land there is that is available for allotments, and then proceed to divide it up."

"And how do you expect," said Lord Eastwell, smiling, "to cultivate the remainder? For the land which can be cultivated as allotments constitutes what we farmers would call the 'eyes' of our farms. Only the other day I let a farm which had been lying vacant for two years, and I was only able to do so by adding to it a field, without which, the tenant declared, it would be impossible to make it pay. In a few days my labourers came to me and asked that they might have that field for allotments. But if I divided that thirty acres among them as allotments, I should have three hundred acres thrown on my hands without a tenant. They saw how the land lay, and did not press their application. You will find in Blankshire, and elsewhere," he added, "that while the labourer is anxious to have a garden, he will not say, 'Thank you' for a small farm."

"I am of the same opinion," said Sir Artegal, "as the late Lord Derby, who used always to put this riddle, which no one seems to have answered: Who is it wants land in this country? Here, in Blankshire, we have 20,000 acres of land lying derelict, which will not pay rates and taxes. There seems to be no land-hunger in Blankshire now. In Ireland, yes; in the North of Scotland, yes; but here—no. So far from hungering and thirsting after land, it seems to me people will not have land as a gift."

"Try," said Wilkes, savagely. "See what a paradox it is. Look at Holland. The Dutch, one of the most thrifty people in the world, are beginning to pump the Zuyder Zee dry, spending £12,000,000 sterling on that transaction. Why? To reclaim from the ocean depths, as it were, some 100,000 acres of land. Here we have farms which are drained, fenced, with roads and farmsteads, near to the greatest market in the world, and you cannot find any one to take them! Is it possible to frame a more terrible indictment of the system under which this is possible?"

"You may indict the system as much as you please, but that does not affect the fact," said Lord Eastwell, "that you cannot get people to cultivate the land. The system which renders it impossible is not the system of which you complain. The system which is really to blame is that by which you crush the land by a ruinous burden of local taxation, and at the same time keep your markets open for India and Australia to undersell all that your land produces. That is the system which is ruining English agriculture, not the landed interest which is your *bête noire*."

"Tell me, Wilkes," said Dick Milman, "do you really doubt that English agricultural land at present is a drug in the market?"

"Under the present system, of course."

"Never mind about the present system," continued Milman. "Will you believe me when I say that one of the most prominent peers in the country said to me only the other day, 'If any one were to offer me as a free gift agricultural land with a nominal rental of £100,000 a year, I would refuse it. It would cost me more than £100,000 to keep the estate up.' He illustrated this by telling me a fact in his own experience. 'My estate,' he said, 'in Buckinghamshire, has a nominal rental of £12,000 a year. Supposing you reckon that to keep up the house and grounds cost £3,000 a year, I ought then to have a rental of £9,000. But how much do you think I got last year? £6,000, £3,000, £1,000? No, instead of receiving anything, I had to send a cheque for £6,000 to meet the deficit on that estate.'"

"But we all know cases like that," said Silvertongue, "I could mention nobleman after nobleman who this year has received nothing, and has to face a reduction of the November rents."

"I have never been able to see," said Sir Artegal, "why you should object to land going out of cultivation in England. If wheat can be grown more cheaply in India, why should you lament that land in Blankshire, which is only capable of growing wheat, should have gone out of cultivation? From the point of view of Free Trade it is very illogical."

"So it is," said Silvertongue. "But even your most

D

vehement Free Trader knows that men do not live by bread alone, and no healthy State can exist which has all its population crowded in great cities, and no human reserve in the country to renew the vigour of its population."

"Oh, but you are not a Free Trader, Silvertongue," said Sir Artegal.

"Yes I am, up to a point," said Silvertongue, "and every one is—up to a point. Take the Cobden Club for instance; it would not be in favour of allowing the land to go derelict if it knew that we should have war with France next year."

"Your argument points then," said Milman, "rather to the relief of the land than to an increase of the burdens upon it, whereas Wilkes, I understand, is anxious to tax the landlord out of existence."

"Precisely," said Wilkes; "we have begun with the death duties, and we shall more and more saddle the land with the whole cost of local administration."

"And yet," said Sir Artegal, "the landlord is the only capitalist in the country who corresponds in any way to your socialist ideal."

"How do you make that out?" asked Wilkes.

"He receives the smallest interest upon his investments to begin with, and of the proportion which he does receive he returns to the general community a far greater proportion than any of those who are engaged in trade or who have money in Consols."

"I will give you a case in point," said Milman. "I know two brothers—two of my uncles, in fact—who, fifty years ago, came into possession of £100,000 upon their father's death. The elder brother took his £100,000 in the shape of the family seat, which yielded him, after paying cost of administration, about £3,000 a year. The other uncle had his £100,000 in Consols. This was fifty years ago. The uncle who had the estate has lived on it ever since. He was a frugal man, and was able to keep his expenditure down to about £2,000 a year. The other thousand he devoted, year by year, to the improvement of the estate. It was his ambition to have his labourers well housed; to have a good water supply for the villages; to furnish them with reading-rooms, and generally to make the life of the labourers on his estate as happy as possible. Out of the £2,000 a year which he allowed for living expenses, he contributed at least £200 to schools and churches and local institutions. Besides this, his park, which is not very large, but is very beautiful, with a fine herd of deer, was as much at the service of the public as any of the royal parks in the neighbourhood of London. His house was the centre of all efforts for the improvement of the condition of the people, and was the common meeting-place for rich and poor in the country-side. Now, after fifty years, my uncle is an old man of seventy. The fall in the value of produce has brought down his net rent-roll from £3,000 to £1,500 a year, which is only three per cent. on the £50,000 he has invested in the estate since he came into its possession. That is to say, the whole of his £100,000 is wiped out, and he is living upon the interest of his savings.

"Contrast this with my other uncle. He put his £100,000 in Consols and lived in a house in Kensington, spending about £2,000 a year. His money came to him punctually every quarter-day. He had no responsibility for its col'e.tion, nor did he feel any personal obligation towards those who paid him his income. Living in Kensington, he had no local responsibilities. He was neither a Justice of the Peace, nor a member of the Quarter Sessions, nor an *ex-officio* Guardian. His time, like his money, was his own. He was not expected to subscribe to schools, churches or charities, and all the other local institutions which tell so heavily upon the purse of the landlord. Instead of being rated, as his brother was, upon the full value of £3,000 a year, he paid rates upon his house rent, which was not more than £500 a year. For every penny one paid in rates the other paid a shilling. At the end of fifty years this uncle has a secure fortune of £150,000 in Consols, with no encumbrances, no obligations. He has spent twice as much upon himself, and has but given one-tenth the amount of thought to his neighbours that the other brother has done. Yet according to your scheme of the universe, Wilkes, it seems that the one who ought to be held up to execration as a tyrant, and whose property should be confiscated, is the one who owns land, while you do nothing at all with the man who owns Consols."

"Oh, yes, we do; we propose to get at that gentleman through the death duties," said Wilkes.

"Yes, you have begun to try your hand in that direction, but even then you have hit the landowner as hard as you have the other man; and the worst of it is that the landowner cannot run away, and the other man can. Did you ever hear the story of Mr. Jones of New York?"

"No," said Wilkes; "what is it?"

"The other day he proposed to Lord Rothschild that he should take the custody of securities valued at £800,000, and collect the interest on them without deducting the income-tax, which had been collected by the Bank of England. Rothschild replied that as long as Jones remained in this country and enjoyed the protection of its laws he must pay the income-tax like other people. Whereupon Jones in great dudgeon withdrew his securities from the Bank of England and from Rothschild, and transferred them to Paris, where, up to this time, they have not attempted to levy income-tax upon non-French subjects."

"The scoundrel!" said Wilkes. "We shall have to tar and feather some of these millionaires before we have done with them."

"I wish you joy of your task," said Silvertongue.

"Come," said Sir Artegal, "it is getting late, and we must break up now. I think we have pretty well arrived at an agreement of what may be called the fundamental facts of the controversy. Firstly, agricultural land in the East and South of England is at the present moment valueless; therefore it is the property of all others which should be taken over by the nation. Secondly, the landlord differs from the fundholder in recognising personal obligations of neighbourhood and service to those whose labour earns the interest on his investments; therefore the landlord must be hunted down as a monster. Thirdly, as English land with the present rates and taxes cannot be made to pay, even when ample capital is placed at the disposal of the agriculturist, therefore let us hand it over to the men who have no capital and no skill, and let us saddle it still more with increased rates and taxes."

"Well, you cannot expect me to accept that as a fair summing up of our conclusions," said Wilkes. "I should rather say that what we have agreed upon is that the existing landed system has hopelessly broken down, that land which in every well-governed country is a source of profit and is eagerly competed for, has in England, under the present management, become a drug in the market. Therefore the time has come to change all that, to abolish the old system, and raise up another on its ruins which will give the virtual ownership of the land to——"

Lord Eastwell interrupted. "To men without experience, without capital, and with neither the buildings, the implements, nor the skill with which to cultivate the land."

"Come, come," said Milman, "you will only get vexed if you carry on like this. Good-night, Wilkes, and good luck to your candidature, despite all your heresies!"

CHAPTER IX.
EXIT LORD BLADUD.

ETHEL MERRIBEL'S illness was more serious than Ænid at first imagined, when, in the flush of friendly sympathy, she undertook to relieve her, thinking that in the morning she would be well again. In the morning Ethel was far from well. When she tried to get up she fell back faint and helpless, and uttered a despairing little groan which brought Lady Ænid to her side at once. "What can I do?" she moaned—"what can I do? I am so weak, I cannot move!"

"Never mind," said Lady Ænid; "lie still for a time, and you will soon be better. We will get a nurse down to relieve you."

"Yes," said Ethel dreamily; "but in the meantime—in the meantime, what will become of them? There is so much to do, and you have no help."

Lady Ænid, for the first time confronted by the sterner duties of life, rose unhesitatingly to the occasion. "Ethel," she said firmly, "lie still. It is simply a case of utter nervous collapse with you. I will stay here until the new nurse comes. In the meantime you must be quiet and rest."

When Dr. Glogoul came in the morning, Lady Ænid told him with brief peremptoriness what had happened. "Now," she said, "you have promised on your honour that there will be no experiments on the patients while I am in charge. Although I shall be here longer than I expected when you gave me the promise, that does not matter."

The doctor bowed. "Certainly, Lady Ænid. Having promised, I keep my word; but it is a positive sin to allow such a beautiful chance to pass. With that lone orphan I could have inoculated half the village."

"No," said Ænid, "even if there had been no other objection, you have come too late. The little thing died last night within an hour of its mother. They will both be buried to-day in one coffin."

"But, Lady Ænid," he said, "what are you going to do?"

"I am going to telegraph to the Sanitary Authority to send down a nurse. Until she comes I hope you will regard me as acting in Miss Merribel's place. I know I have no experience," she said, somewhat pathetically, "but Ethel will give me general instructions, and if you will tell me exactly what to do I will carry out your directions implicitly."

Dr. Glogoul was touched by the appeal for help made by this strong, self-reliant young woman, and he made light of difficulties which would otherwise have seemed to him almost insurmountable.

"You may rely upon me, madam," said he, "neither to vivisect my patients nor to neglect the instruction of their nurse. I hope," said he, with a little laugh, "that the virtue of the latter part of the promise will atone for the sin of the former. For a doctor to neglect to practise experiments upon his patients is to be false to the first duty he owes to medical science."

"I know nothing of science," said Ænid simply. "But there must be no vivisection while I am here; and now will you take me round and tell me exactly what to do."

So matters were arranged, and Lady Ænid took charge of the temporary hospital at Garlam. It was not found so easy a matter to provide a substitute for Ethel Merribel. The Rural Sanitary Authority was slow to realise that their nurse had broken down, and adjourned the question till the next meeting of the Board. Meanwhile Lady Ænid became more and more engrossed in the work of the hospital.

"Ethel dear," she said one night, when sitting by the bedside of her friend, "you have no idea how interesting I find this nursing. I think there is a great deal of the hunter in my blood. From the time of the Conquest down to the Repeal of the Corn Laws, the male Belsovers at least have spent a third of their life in the pursuit of game. When such a habit is persisted in for centuries, the taste seems to be wrought into your very bones, and you get to look at everything more or less from the point of view of the hunter."

"Really," said Ethel, somewhat drowsily, "I do not understand what you are driving at."

"Well," said Lady Ænid, "I feel as if you and I and Dr. Glogoul were three hunters stalking wild beasts. All the diseases of our patients present themselves to me as wolves and bears and tigers and other carnivorous beasts. They are prowling all around us, watching for an opportunity to strike us down, while we, on our part, are constantly endeavouring to drive them away from the prey which they have already seized. How tame deerstalking seems to me beside fever-stalking! It is what cub-hunting is to tiger-shooting. This hospital sport becomes all-engrossing. It possesses every element of romance. There is personal danger, there is the need for constant vigilance, and there is the great reward of possible success. I feel as proud of every patient who goes out of the hospital cured as my father did when he brought in the great elk's head which he had shot in the Far West."

"Yes," said Ethel, fairly roused, her eyes glistening with excitement, "I have never quite looked at it in the light of a hunt. I dare say you will get more sport out of it than I should. But I also visualise diseases. To me they seem to be unclean spirits, and, as I go round the ward at night when everything is silent, save the moan of a patient or the muttering of the delirious, I see the diseases, like shadowy spectral vampires, draining the lifeblood of the poor people or stifling their breath. Twenty beds in a ward, and every bed occupied; in every bed beside every patient there are these loathsome things. Ah! how I have often longed for the power of some ancient saint, by which I would make the sign of the cross, and compel all these phantoms to flee away and leave their victims at rest. But charms don't work nowadays. It is a life and death combat between us and these powers of evil. That text has often come to my tired brain while I have been lying here helpless: 'For we wrestle not with flesh and blood, but against principalities and powers, against the rulers of darkness of this world, against spiritual wickedness in high places.'"

"Oh," said Ænid cheerily, in her practical matter-of-fact way, "I am not mystical like you, but it is a constant exhilaration to regard this Garlam as a kind of Indian jungle full of all kinds of fierce beasts which we are stalking, Dr. Glogoul and I. Sometimes they get the better of us, but oftener we get the better of them. And what tricks they play, these maladies. I declare they are as cunning as the cleverest old dog-fox that ever baffled the hounds in the hunting-field."

"I never can understand the difference," said Ethel, "which you make between the spiritual and the material world. I suppose it is because you don't see the things which I see. They are all real to me; and it is not the so-called invisible which are the worst. By the way," said she, "did you hear whether the Earl of Bladud took any notice of the death of his little child and its mother?"

"Not the least," said Ænid. "I got Dr. Glogoul to write to Sloane Hall and report the death of the girl and her child, but no notice was taken of the letter."

"I suppose," said Ethel, "he is having one of his drinking bouts, or possibly enough he may be in London. Not that he would care, anyhow. It is he and Mr. Faulmann who seem to me to be so much worse than all the diseases which we have to keep at bay. They seem to dwell in the hospital, the lords of the unclean spirits, who torture and slay according to their sovereign will and pleasure."

"Did you ever see Lord Bladud?" said Ænid. "I have never met him in flesh and blood, and pray God I never shall. He is not the kind of man any woman would care to meet."

"I don't know," said Lady Ænid; "the same instinct which leads you to go in a howdah when the elephants are beating the jungle for tigers, makes me feel that I should rather like to see this Lord Bladud. It is not likely that he would do me any harm."

The day after this conversation Ethel had recovered sufficiently to insist on Ænid taking a couple of hours relief from nursing. She had been a week in the hospital without having had a breath of fresh air, and the confinement and unaccustomed work had told upon her considerably. She was looking a little haggard, so in the evening Ethel insisted upon her taking a long run on her bicycle in the moonlight. Satisfied that the patients were sleeping quietly, and that her friend was well enough to stand two hours' vigil, Lady Ænid mounted her cycle and rode off into the country.

Down in the village she could see the lights of the "Green Man," at the door of which some loafers were standing, but with that exception the streets of the little town were deserted. The moon was bright, the road fairly good, and there was no wind. Very soon, Lady Ænid had left the squalid little town behind her, and was rushing along between the high hedges which lined either side of the road, and whose shadows marbled the moonlight on the ground before her wheel. Lady Ænid went in the direction of Coleford, determined to have a ride of about twenty miles. Presently she saw the lights of Sloane away in

NEARER AND NEARER HE CAME TO THE FLYING GIRL.

the west. The gas-lamps on the outskirts of the town appeared like pin-holes of light against the darkness. She then turned to the north, along the main road, which led to Sloane Hall. She slackened her pace and was dreamily pedalling along, thinking of the strange experiences of the last fortnight when she was suddenly startled by the sound of horses' hoofs not far behind her.

Looking back along the road she saw four or five men following at a smart trot. They were apparently market-merry, or worse, for they were shouting and swearing and laughing loudly. It was—although Lady Ænid did not know till some time after—Lord Bladud and some of his boon companions, who had been out hunting, and having dined and wined at Coleford, were now returning to Sloane Hall. For a moment Ænid felt the awkwardness of her position. Here she was, alone in the country roads, it was almost midnight, and within a hundred yards of her was a party of drunken horsemen. Her only chance was to outdistance them by her superior speed. She silently increased her pace, hoping to gain a turn in the road before they noticed her, in which case she could easily outdistance them, as they were only coming along at a trot.

Unfortunately, the moon was shining very brightly in a cloudless sky. The foremost horseman spied her, and gave vent to a wild yell. "Tally-ho!" he shouted, "Tally-ho!" and spurring up his horse he came galloping down the road, followed by his companions, shouting drunken curses as they came thundering behind her. Lady Ænid sent her cycle forging ahead at its utmost speed. Fortunately, after two or three hundred yards the road began to descend, and

THE DEATH OF LORD BLADUD.

dropped by a pretty steep decline into the valley below. The road was clear and free from loose stones. Down such a hill a bicyclist can go at a rate which no prudent horseman can follow. Lady Ænid, without pausing for a moment, dashed down the hill.

By the time she had reached the bottom of it she had gained a clear lead of several hundred yards. Rested by the momentary relief from constant pedalling, she shot forward with renewed vigour. But it was evident that her pursuers found the chase of a flying cyclist quite as exciting as a fox-hunt. As soon as they reached the level ground they began to gain upon her. One of the men, mounted on a light chestnut, led the others by at least a couple of hundred yards. His horse was either fresher or its rider was not so drunk as his companions.

Nearer and nearer he came to the flying girl. She had a moment's horrible consciousness that he would ride her down, and then she suddenly became perfectly calm. She was flying along the level road with the horse hardly a length behind her. The rider swerved slightly to the right to pass her and then compel her to stop. Stooping down, Lady Ænid unfastened the clasps of her air-pump, and the moment the horse's head came level with the seat, she struck the animal with all her force across the nose. As she struck she almost reeled over, but the speed with which her cycle was going enabled her to regain her balance before she dashed into the ditch on the other side of the road. As she did so she saw that her blow had succeeded beyond her hopes.

The horse, on receiving the blow, had shied violently to the right, falling into a deep ditch and throwing its rider into a mass of briars and brambles, from which, with imprecations deep and loud, he was endeavouring to extricate himself. She had only time for a momentary glance, as the other horsemen, paying no attention to the mishap of their companion, came galloping after her. She had dropped her air-pump in the effort to recover her balance, and was now without that resource.

Although they gained upon her, it was but slowly, and judging from the sound of the hoofs one had abandoned the chase. The third horseman, she thought, must have gone back to the aid of his dismounted companion. The second horseman, too, began to lag behind. Not even the excitement of the chase could prevent her from feeling that her strength was giving out, and the labouring of her breath warned her that if the struggle between horse and cyclist were prolonged much longer she would be at the mercy of her pursuer. Hot as she was, a cold shudder came over her as she thought of this eventuality, and of all that it might mean.

Suddenly she saw a man ahead. Another glance, and she saw he was carrying a red flag, a sign that he was preceding a traction-engine, to give warning to approaching vehicles. The puffing of the engine was heard round the turn of the road, which was bordered on either side with sloping banks. For a moment she thought of stopping and appealing to the man with the red flag for help, but at the rate at which she was going she could not hope to dismount until she was carried considerably beyond him, and her pursuer would by that time have her in his grasp, regardless of what any dismounted man might attempt in the way of rescue.

So she went on with a kind of wild despair. The man with the red flag waved it frantically, and shouted, but neither she nor her pursuer paid any attention. On they went, the bicycle about twenty yards in front of the hunter. As Lady Ænid swung round the corner she saw the lights of the traction-engine which apparently blocked up the whole of the road. More by instinct than by calculation, she swerved to the left, and attempted to force her way between the sloping bank and the wheel of the engine. She passed the front wheel all right by riding through the little ditch at the side of the road. But to pass the second wheel she had to mount the side of the slope. I was a desperate chance, for as the cycle rose on the bank it was almost certain to fall. Still, there was no other way of escape, and she dashed at it. The pedal revolved once twice, and carried her just past the engine. Then the front wheel slipped, her pedal caught in a briar, and Lady Ænid had barely time to spring from her machine before it fell heavily into a ditch.

All this happened in a much shorter time than it takes to describe it. She pulled the machine from the ditch, and in the mad passion to escape mounted and rode off without a moment's pause. Her machine was damaged, but on, on, she went.

She rode more than a mile along the road before it occurred to her that there was no longer any pursuit. She could neither hear the clatter of horses' feet nor the snorting of the traction-engine. But still she rode on, and it was not until she had covered another three or four miles that she discovered that she had punctured her hind wheel, and that almost all the air had escaped. She had lost her air-pump, and so there was nothing for it but to get off and walk the remainder of the way to Garlam. Fortunately it was not very far distant. She could see the glimmering of the light on the lightship which lay off Garlam three or four miles ahead.

It was almost two o'clock when she arrived at the hospital. By that time she had recovered from her fright and from her exhaustion. She was able to reassure Ethel, who had been very anxious at the excessive prolongation of the midnight ride, with the explanation of the punctured tyre and the lost air-pump, which were sufficient to account for her delay. She easily persuaded Ethel Merribel to go to bed, and resumed her post as night nurse.

About the same time that she resumed her duties at the hospital, two men were carrying on an improvised stretcher the mangled remains of the Earl of Bladud up the avenue which led to Sloane Hall. Lord Bladud had been drinking heavily, and being moreover somewhat heavier than his companions, he had fallen behind in the race with the cyclist. But when his companion had been flung, he took the lead in the race with the dogged pertinacity of his character, and was steadily and speedily overhauling his flying game when the traction-engine blocked the way. He was too keen in pursuit of his prey to draw rein, even if he had been aware of his danger, which he was not. Hence he galloped full speed round the curve, and his horse, on seeing the lamps of the traction-engine, halted so suddenly that the Earl was flung from his saddle right under the wheel of the lumbering monster. The driver shut off the steam and reversed the engine, but it was impossible to bring it to a standstill before the heavy wheel had crushed Lord Bladud's skull level with the road. It was all over in a moment. Lord Bladud's horse galloped riderless homeward. As for Lord Bladud himself, he also had gone to his own place.

CHAPTER X.

THE RADICAL CAMPAIGN.

NOW it fell out upon a day, the very day after the birthday-party at the "Radical Arms," that a mustering of discontents took place at the Temperance Hotel, where the worthy Brassy held council with his cronies about the prospects of the election.

"I don't like it," said Brassy; "my suspicion is that we are being sold. Wilkes, they said, was the man for our money. Wilkes, they said, would go as far as any of us; but, confound it, he is a stuck-up snob who will hardly speak to an honest working-man like me."

"Why," said Bob Greenacre, whose features were picturesquely decorated with a long strip of plaster, covering a gash he had received recently in a poaching affray, "thou'rt getting mighty perticker, old man. This 'ere Wilkes be as thorough as they make 'em, and my cousin who works in the printing-house where they are striking off his address, says it's real stingo and no mistake. He makes 'em sit up, he do."

"Oh, writing's one thing," said Brassy, "but doing's another. We don't want any of your blooming snobs coming round here hobnobbing with duchesses, and then standing as a regular Democrat. It won't do, boys—it won't do."

"What do you mean?", asked Bill Dawkins, who was sitting on the table, filling a very dirty pipe with twist tobacco. "Who's been hobnobbing with duchesses? I don't believe it on him, no, not if you say it yourself, Joe Brassy."

"Don't you," said Brassy; "and what would you say if no later than last night this precious Radical candidate of ours had a birthday party at the 'Radical Arms'; and who do you think he invited? Why, a set of aristocrats from the West-end of London, that snivelling peer, Lord Eastwell, being the chief of the party."

Bill Dawkins seemed to admit that this looked ugly, so he said no more.

"But a lord ain't a duchess," said Greenacres; "you don't mean to say he has been up at Eastland? That would be too much."

"Why," said Brassy, with a malignant scowl on his unprepossessing features, "I don't say he has been at Eastland, but I do say on unimpeachable authority that this 'ere blessed Radical candidate of ours actually arrived in this 'ere town of Rigby in a castle carriage."

"That he didn't," said Dawkins, recovering himself, "for I seed him mesel' getting out of an old cab at the 'Radical Arms.'"

"Which is true," said another, "for I was downstairs having a pint at the bar when I seed him being carried in. It was a cab, I tell you—Jim Ostler's cab; for when Jim had got his fare he came and joined me in another pint."

"And who says no," said Brassy. "I didn't say that he came to the 'Radical Arms' in a castle carriage. No, a conspirator and a traitor don't play such a game so openly. But now as you have mentioned Jim Ostler, I will tell you that it was Jim himself who saw Wilkes get out of the carriage which set him down at the cab-stand at the entrance of the town,

THE RADICAL CANDIDATE.

and if ye doubt my word, Dawkins, you can go and ask yer friend."

After this Dawkins ventured no further protest, and Brassy had it all his own way. "We are in for it, however," he said, "and we have to fight with this here Wilkes or with nobody; but he's not a gamecock, he's a craven. I'll put none of my money on him, anyhow. It will surprise me if at the meeting to-morrow night, which is to open the campaign, he will say so much as a hot word about his friends at the castle. However, we will all turn up and draw our own conclusions."

The Radical campaign was to be opened the following evening by a large meeting in the town hall of Rigby. The word had been passed round by Mr. Wirham among the Conservatives that on no account was any attempt to be made to break up the meeting. That sagacious agent had not been in Rigby many hours before he discovered that the true policy was to lie low, and allow the heterogeneous forces of discontent to develop their differences free from all menace from without.

Mr. Wilkes was in blissful ignorance of the mutterings of discontent at the Brassy headquarters. He had drawn up an electoral address which, as Greenacres had described, was "real stingo." In it he had rung the changes upon all the notes of Radical oratory. It was an impassioned appeal to the millions to rise up in their might and possess themselves of the acres now monopolised by aristocrats whose titledeeds, obtained by fraud and violence, were besmeared with the people's blood. The address concluded with a glowing picture of the time that was coming, when the landed aristocracy would have vanished into limbo, and the whole country would be covered with small cultivators, under whose spades the derelict land of Blankshire would bloom as a garden and blossom as the rose.

Wilkes, who had penned this address with great care, regarded it with the affection of a mother for her first-born. He was particularly pleased with the reference to the derelict farms. He stole out in the evening and joined as an unknown stranger a group of Rigby citizens who were studying the address as it was displayed outside the "Radical Arms." They read it without much comment beyond an occasional grunt; but when they came to the end, a rough-looking labourer somewhat disconcerted Wilkes by observing, "If that chap had a try with a spade on the clay lands of Blankshire, he wouldn't be so glib with his gardens and roses, I reckon, eh, Bill?"

Bill had not quite finished the perusal of the address, and made no answer. When he had finished he turned on his heel and said, "Aye, but you can't expect townfolk to know aught about it."

This was not very comforting.

Wilkes's satisfaction was still further damped the following morning by receiving a brief, business-like letter, which ran as follows:—

Dear Sir,—I have read your address to the electors of Blankshire. I am at the present moment the unfortunate owner of several of the derelict farms to which you refer with so much feeling. As I take you to be a man of your word and to believe what you say, I would very gladly offer you one of these farms as a free gift. You can have one hundred, two hundred, or three hundred acres, as you please. All that I ask is that you will pay me the present cash value of the farm buildings and other improvements, in which I have sunk a pretty penny in the last thirty years. I shall be very glad to show you the land at any time. And if you have among your friends any labourers whom you think can be trusted to turn any of these farms into a garden by spade culture, the land is at your disposal, free gratis and for nothing.

The letter was signed by one of the smaller landowners in the neighbourhood. When Hopton, who was completing the arrangements for the evening meeting, and who had taken a day off for the purpose, looked in, Wilkes was reading the letter for the second time. He threw it over to Hopton and asked him what he thought of it. Hopton read it, and then said, "Don't you wish you might get it! They must think that you are very green."

"Why?" asked Wilkes.

"Why, to think that any sane man would take a farm as a free gift if he had to pay for the buildings. Why, there is hardly a farm in Blankshire that is paying interest on landlord's capital sunk in buildings or improvements—hardly one. Well, I never," continued he, "but he must think townspeople are very green."

Wilkes said no more, but asked what were the prospects for the meeting.

"I know," said Hopton, "there will be no opposition, so you will have it all your own way to-night. But——"

"But, what?" said Wilkes, looking at him.

"Well, I hardly like mentioning it, but as you have asked me, I will tell you. Some of my friends have been talking rather curiously about your being an aristocrat in disguise."

"Really," said Wilkes, somewhat interested to know on what the accusation was based.

"Well," said Hopton hesitatingly, "that you have been dining with lords and driving in carriages with duchesses."

Wilkes smiled, and Hopton went on, "And they say, moreover, that the orders which have been given from the Conservative Club not to disturb the meeting are a clear proof they are right in their suspicions. The Radicals of Rigby have never been allowed to hold a meeting without broken heads. There must be a reason, some of our people are saying, that they should have made an exception in your favour."

"What drivelling nonsense!" said the young man. "But we will let them see."

"I hope so," said Hopton cheerfully, and departed to complete the arrangements for the meeting.

It went off very well. The Conservatives had obeyed orders from headquarters. Wilkes made a very good impression. He was young, eloquent, earnest, enthusiastic, and at the close of the meeting a vote accepting him as the Radical candidate was passed with acclamation. But after the meeting was over Brassy observed significantly to Greenacres as they walked down to the Temperance Hotel (where more beer was drunk than in many a beershop): "Didn't I tell you? Never a word against the Duke, not a single word, only compliments, as if we wanted a Radical candidate to come here and compliment Tory dukes. He soon showed the cloven hoof."

"Why," said Greenacres, "I thought his speech had a good ring in it. No one said a word agin 'im."

"Greenacres," said Brassy, "thou'rt a fool. Who was to say a word against him? But mark my words, he won't be a week in the field before there will be a split in the camp." Saying which, Brassy turned into his hotel, meditating moodily over the disappointment of his hopes. What vexed him most of all were not the compliments to the Duke, which it must be admitted were of the most perfunctory nature, but the ferocious attack which the candidate had made upon the owners of slum property. Brassy had not bargained for this, and he saw with disgust, from the cheers which greeted this portion of the candidate's speech, the beginning of an agitation which boded him no good.

Wilkes was in high spirits. Hopton, to whom the success of the meeting was largely due, was also very well satisfied; and the minister, when he retired to his room that night for prayer, thanked God with exultant heart that at last a young David had been raised up to smite with sling and stone the Goliath of landlordism. The campaign which had been opened at Rigby was to be prosecuted at Coleford, which was the centre of the division, by a meeting to be held in the Corn Exchange. It was to be presided over by Mr. Faulmann, the president of the Liberal Association, who had been unavoidably prevented from taking the chair at the Rigby meeting.

Wilkes, who was accompanied by Hopton, Brown, and a contingent of Rigby Radicals, dined before the meeting with Mr. Faulmann at the "Boar's Head." Among the members of the Radical executive Wilkes saw Brassy, but ignored him. When he shook hands with Mr. Faulmann his heart somewhat sank within him. He was in the presence of a man of great force of character, with keen dark eyes which seemed never to be at rest. There was the soul of a Jew behind the mask of the Teuton—a powerful combination, Wilkes thought. But there was in his somewhat passive and sphinxlike features a negative element which chilled and repelled him. His hand was cold, and there was no grasp in it. In conversation at dinner Wilkes found him somewhat reserved, but apparently well informed as to the business of the association. His utterances were cold but clear, and no one could have been more devoid of enthusiasm. Wilkes felt an instinctive repugnance to the chairman of his committee, and kept marvelling at the strange chance which had brought him into close political alliance with one towards whom he was utterly antipathetic.

The meeting in the Corn Exchange was crowded and enthusiastic. The same tactics were employed by the Conservatives at Coleford as had been used at Rigby. There was a great muster of all the Radical elements in Blankshire. Conspicuous on the platform was the Rev. Jedediah Jones, the Methodist tub-thumper whose invectives against the Earl of Bladud had been mentioned by Mr. Holdem. There were several Dissenting ministers, a great muster of trade unionists and of agricultural labourers, several Radical shopkeepers, and a large contingent of ladies. On the whole, it was a good gathering of the elements of revolt which exist more or less in every English county, and seeing that the division had never been contested in the present generation, it is not surprising that the mere novelty of the gathering brought together a large and interested crowd.

As the crowd was gathering at the doors of the Corn Exchange, a rumour ran from mouth to mouth that there had been a terrible accident, and that the Earl of Bladud had been killed. No details were given, but the news was confidently repeated. The death of a leading opponent added a certain tragic interest to the assembly. The news, however, had not been published, and apparently no whisper of it had reached the platform, for when the Rev. Jedediah Jones opened the meeting with prayer he did not omit a single syllable of his impassioned appeal to the Lord of Hosts to avenge the innocent and to smite the oppressor, which all his hearers knew had reference to the evil earl of Sloane Hall.

A suppressed hush ran through one part of the hall, but it passed unnoticed, and Mr. Faulmann arose amid prolonged cheering to introduce the candidate.

He spoke with precision and with a slightly foreign accent. He said they in Blankshire had groaned long under the dominion of the territorial aristocracy. Under their baneful rule the bread of the people had been taxed, the liberties of the people had been confiscated, and under the influence of the same upas tree the prosperity of the county was languishing. The land must be freed. They were there to inaugurate a struggle for the rights of man, to assert the obligations of property, and to declare that where these obligations had been neglected and ignored, the rights of property were forfeit to the sovereign people.

Mr. Brassy, who acted as fugleman, cheered and cheered again this declaration of war against the Duke.

Mr. Faulmann then proceeded to introduce the candidate to those whom before long he hoped would be his constituents. He said he was a young man, but a true man, whose principles could be relied upon, and who would go straight for the people wherever their interests led him.

When Mr. Wilkes rose to speak, and looked down upon the crowded meeting, which had risen to its feet, and was cheering him vociferously, he suddenly caught sight of a familiar face which startled him not a little. It was that of a young lady who was sitting almost immediately in front of him, and who was contemplating the scene with an amused interest. He recognised the face in a moment, but could not remember its owner. It was not until he had gone through the first sentences of his speech that it flashed upon him that it was the cyclist who had rewarded him for saving her life by spraining his knee, and whose subsequent kindly offices had given rise to an incipient revolt among the Radicals of Rigby. He felt pleased that she should have come to his meeting, and the consciousness of her presence inspired him to put forth all his powers. "She shall see," he thought to himself, "that although I am a Radical and a Socialist, I can be a gentleman, and treat my opponents with as much chivalry as if I had belonged to their own order."

Accordingly, he began his speech by disclaiming any intention of making a personal attack upon the territorial magnates whose domain he had invaded as the representative of the people's rights. There were landlords and landlords. They were men of like passions with themselves, and he had not come to the county to carry on a campaign of personalities. Brassy nudged Dawkins (who was sitting next to him) in the ribs, but said nothing.

"In the county of Blankshire," Wilkes continued, "they had the Duke of Eastland, an honourable and upright nobleman"—"Did I not tell you?" growled Brassy—"who was bearing to the best of his ability, and discharging according to his lights, the onerous responsibilities which he had inherited from his forefathers. Of the other peer, the Earl of Bladud, he could hardly speak in similar terms, but——"

At this moment, a tall, gaunt countryman, who was standing beside one of the pillars in the centre of the hall, exclaimed, "Young man, say no ill of the dead; Lord Bladud died last night."

A profound sensation thrilled the crowded audience, not one-third of which had heard the rumour of Lord Bladud's death.

Mr. Wilkes abruptly stopped, and said, "I had not heard the news, but it only adds another reason to those which I was about to mention as to why I should keep silent concerning the deceased earl."

Having thus, in his most courtly manner, shaken hands with his opponents on entering the political ring, he proceeded to show fight in the approved style. Possessed of a vivid imagination, Mr. Wilkes warmed up the audience, which for years had never heard the existing system roughly handled, except with bated breath and whispering humbleness. Even Bill Dawkins plucked up courage to whisper to Brassy that "He's agoin' it, isn't he?" to which the only response was a growl.

He devoted the greater part of his speech to a denunciation of the landed system and of the ascendency of the territorial magnates. He merely referred in a few sentences to such political issues as Home Rule, Employers' Liability, and the Welsh Church, all of which he seemed to think were only of importance as they helped out the indictment of the Lords. But when he came to the exordium, he declared that his candidature was no personal matter,—it was a means by which the great democracy was going to break down the system which had so long cursed the land in order to establish on the ruins of an effete social system the social millennium.

"Remember," he said, in warning tones, "that our foes are many and strong. If we had merely to deal with the mediæval and bankrupt peers who are perishing, stifled by the mortgages incurred by their extravagance, and smothered by the unpaid bills of their unfortunate tradesmen, we could win the battle almost without a fight. But behind the battered and broken ranks of landlordism we can see rallying already to their support the serried legions of plutocracy. Behind the peer stands the sweater; behind the landlord, whose broad acres are lying desolate as the result of the banishment of the people from the soil, stand the owners of slum property, the jerry-builders, and all the unclean crew who are heaping up wealth by poisoning the life and ruining the health of the people."

It was now Dawkins's turn to nudge Brassy in the ribs. "One for thee, old man, I reckon!" said he.

"Hold your mouth," said Brassy savagely. "Did I not tell you he was a traitor in the camp!"

"Nay, but he speaks true," said Dawkins.

Mr. Wilkes' peroration, which brought down the house in a tumult of applause, was an impassioned invitation to all the oppressed and down-trodden people to rally round the standard of liberty and reform and follow his lead against the enemies of the people. "I am not rich or famous, neither do I own a single acre in this country. I have nothing to offer you but the devotion of a heart and a life that is dedicated to the service of the people. Far before us gleam the camp fires of the vanguard of the hosts of liberty ; I follow where they lead. They are already on the point of triumphing over the broken and helpless forces of those splendid paupers, our territorial peers; but the real struggle of the future will be with the cruel and grasping hordes of that capitalism which ruthlessly exploits the labour of those who fill its coffers, and is already rearing a more hateful tyranny upon the ruins of the territorial aristocracy. In that struggle you may at least depend upon me not to falter, not to flinch. Whoever goes back," said he proudly, "I at least press on!"

When he sat down, and his audience had also resumed their seats, among all the confused crowd of faces around him he distinguished only two. One was that of Lady Ænid, who seemed to be carried away by the enthusiasm of the meeting. The other was that of his chairman, who, somehow or other, did not seem particularly happy.

One or two other speeches followed, and then the chairman said, "I am told that there is some one here who can give us some information concerning the sudden death of Lord Bladud. As we are all near neighbours and interested in the news, will he come forward and tell the meeting what he knows?"

A sturdy, stout little man came forward with difficulty through the crowd and mounted the platform. He was evidently labouring under the influence of deep feeling. As he passed on to the platform, Lady Ænid thought she had seen the face before; but the impression was vague, and she could not connect it with any definite time or place.

She had come over to Coleford with Ethel Merribel. The relief nurse had arrived, and Lady Ænid had driven Ethel over to Coleford on her way home. When her friend had been carefully put to bed at the "Boar's Head," Lady Ænid, finding that Wilkes had to speak at the Corn Exchange, and that this afforded her an opportunity of hearing him speak without being recognised herself, she had joined the crowd, and found herself seated immediately in front of the platform, where Mr. Wilkes had seen her as soon as he rose to speak. She had no idea as to the tragic sequel of her adventurous midnight ride, nor had she the least idea as to who they were who had hunted her so savagely a few hours before. The whole incident was to her more like a nightmare memory than an actual occurrence. It was only when the man began to speak that she suddenly linked on her own experience with the story which he told.

"I am no scholar, and not much of a speaker," said the man, as soon as he was hoisted upon the platform; "but so be as the chairman asks me to tell what I know, I will do my best. It was last night, in bright moonlight, that I and my mate that drives the traction-engine was coming along the main road through the cutting which lies between Sloane Hall and Garlam."

Lady Ænid started, and in a moment remembered where she had seen the man. He was the man who had waved the red flag in order to announce the approach of the engine.

"We were coming along," the man continued, "at our usual pace, when suddenly I see a bright light coming down the road as swift as lightning, and behind I hears the clatter of horses' hoofs and some shouting. I waved my flag and shouted, but before I had time to say two words the light flashed by me, and a bicyclist passed me riding as for dear life. He was by me in a flash and round the corner, and how he got past the engine I don't know. My mate saw the light for a moment as if it was climbing up the hill, then it vanished, and we have never seen it since. After the bicyclist, galloping as hard as a hunter after a fox, came the Earl of Bladud on his grey mare. He was swearing and cussing and spurring his horse like mad. He took no more notice of me than if I hadn't been there. He dashed past, and in a moment he was right upon the engine. The horse gave the most awfullest shy that I ever seed in my life. I heard the Earl shout 'Damnation!' quite loud, and he fell heavily on the ground, right in front of the wheel. My mate shut off steam and reversed engine, but it was too late. I heard a sickening noise as if a cart-wheel was crunching a rotten turnip. I turned sick-like, and sat down on the roadside. We found that the engine-wheel had just stopped at the shoulders; there was no head left, only a mass of blood and brains, all mixed up with hair. He was quite dead. Afterwards some of his friends came up, and we carried the body to Sloane Hall, where it lies now. It was not our fault. Neither me nor Jim could have done more than what we did."

The man then sat down on a chair, took a drink of water, and buried his face in his hands. There was a profound silence throughout the hall. Lady Ænid was breathing hard, clenching her hands, almost overcome by the sudden and horrible tragedy in which she had played so prominent a part.

Then, suddenly, the silence was broken by a long-drawn-out cry, half moan, half an exclamation of exultant joy. The sound came from a woman plainly dressed, with strongly marked features, who seemed to be as it were in a trance. Her lips were moving, but there was no sound beyond the first exclamation. She swayed silently to and fro, and then rising to her full height—and she was very tall—she cried out, "Lord, now lettest thou Thy servant depart in peace, for mine eyes have seen the coming of the vengeance of the Lord." A shudder of horror passed through the meeting, which, however, speedily died away as the tall form sank back insensible upon her chair.

"Good God!" said Wilkes to his neighbour, "what a horrid thing, to exult over such a death!"

"Perhaps," said his neighbour, in an unsympathetic whisper —"perhaps if your sister had been walking the streets of London, as Deborah Jinks's sister is, through the dead Earl's devilry, you would understand."

CHAPTER XI.

AN UNEXPECTED MEETING.

NEXT morning, while waiting for breakfast, Mr. Wilkes was turning over the pages of the hotel register, when his attention was struck by the name of Miss Ethel Merribel.

"What, Ethel—my cousin Ethel!" he said. "What in the name of wonder has brought her to this part of the world? I thought she was nursing in a London hospital." Then turning to a waiter who was standing near he asked if Miss Merribel was still in the hotel.

"Yes, she arrived yesterday with another lady. They are leaving to-day. We are just taking up breakfast."

"What is her number?"

"Number 32," replied the waiter.

"Your breakfast is served, sir," said another waiter, hurrying from the coffee-room. On taking his seat the waiter handed him a note. "The other gentleman has gone, sir," he said. Wilkes tore open the envelope. It was a brief memorandum from Faulmann, informing him that pressing business had summoned him to London at once. He begged Wilkes to excuse him.

"Humph," said Mr. Wilkes, "I wonder what is behind all this? He seemed to be very cool last night. He hardly exchanged a word with me, although the meeting was an immense success; of that there can be no doubt." And thereupon the complacent candidate applied himself to his breakfast with the appetite of a man whose conscience and whose digestion were both of the best.

Upstairs, in Number 32, Ethel Merribel was pouring out her tea, and wondering what could be the matter with Lady Ænid. Ethel was feeling the first glow of returning health. She had had a sound sleep, and was feeling better than she had done for a long time. She had called Lady Ænid half an hour ago, and she wondered much why her companion had not made her appearance. "Strange," she thought, "she is usually up so bright and early. I must really go and see what is the matter."

Leaving the table, she went to Lady Ænid's bedroom, and knocked at the door. There was no answer, so she quietly opened the door and entered. Ænid was asleep, but in very restless slumber. Her eyes, although closed, seemed red and swollen. Ethel saw in a moment that her friend had

An Unexpected Meeting.

been passing through some very trying experience. Stooping over the bed, she kissed the girl gently on her lips.

Ænid started, opened her eyes, looked wildly round her as if she were a hunted thing, and said, "Oh, it is you, dear! I am so glad you have come." And stretching out her arms she pulled her friend down towards her, then raising herself on her pillow she burst out crying.

"Oh, Ethel, Ethel, it is too dreadful! It has haunted me all night."

"You poor child, what is dreadful? Everything seemed to have gone so well."

"Oh, you do not know!" Ænid said. "You could not know, you were asleep when I came in. The thought of it has nearly driven me mad."

"Come, tell me what it is all about, dear," said Ethel soothingly.

But Lady Ænid having at last found some one to cling to, simply buried her face in her friend's bosom and sobbed as if her heart would break.

It was only after a long time that Ethel was able to extract from her the terrible story of Lord Bladud's fate. As she heard it come, syllable by syllable, from the lips of her trembling and sobbing friend, Ethel could hardly resist a feeling of stern delight that the man whose misdeeds had haunted her so long had at last met with so terrible a doom. She said nothing, however, until her friend had told her story to the close.

"Now, dear," she said, when the poor girl had ceased, "it is very terrible, no doubt. Still I do not see why you should torment yourself about the doom which has overtaken the Earl. But, come, I will not say anything more to you now. Compose yourself, take a cold shower-bath, and come to breakfast. I am afraid the tea will be ice-cold by this time." So saying, she left Ænid, much relieved by the mere fact of having communicated her trouble, to her bath and her toilet.

As she had said, the tea was ice-cold, and when she rang for some fresh tea the waiter who came up said, "Please, mum, there is a gentleman below who says he knows you, and wants to know if he may come up. Here is his card, mum."

Ethel took it. "Edmund Wilkes!" she said. "Why, it is my cousin. Show him up at once. Has he had breakfast?"

"Yes, mum, he has just finished."

"Tell him to come up directly," she said impulsively, "and bring up some fresh tea."

In another moment Wilkes appeared in the doorway, and holding out both his hands to his cousin, said, "I thought you were tied by the heels nursing in London."

"So I was; but how do you come here?"

"Don't you know? I am Radical candidate for the representation of Blankshire at the coming election."

"Never heard a word of it," said Ethel. "So you are really going to Parliament?"

AND GENTLY KISSED THE SLEEPING GIRL.

Wilkes smiled. "Not by this road, I am afraid, but we shall make a fight for it. The rest will come hereafter. But do sit down and get your breakfast and tell me all about yourself."

Ethel sat down, and while pouring out the tea she explained how she had been sent down as provisional nurse to take charge of a fever hospital at Garlam. The moment she mentioned Garlam, Wilkes started.

"What," he said, "you have been there?"

"Have I not, and nearly stayed there for good in a grave. I never saw such a God-forsaken place in all my life. In fact, I should have died had it not been for Lady Ænid. But here she is," she exclaimed, as Ænid entered. "Let me introduce you to her. Lady Ænid Belsover—my cousin, Edmund Wilkes."

Lady Ænid had come in looking pale and feeling still the effects of the storm which had raged through the whole night, unrelieved even by her feverish sleep, for she had seen in her dreams all the passages of that tragic chase with the vividness of reality. But when she saw standing before her the man who had already been associated with her in her first but much less serious cycling adventure, she blushed crimson.

"Lady Ænid," said Wilkes, looking at his cousin inquiringly, "we have have met before, but I did not know that you were Lady Ænid," and advancing he shook hands with the girl with a frank, unaffected friendliness that soon put her at her ease. "I was glad to see you at my meeting last night, Lady Ænid. Yours was the first face I saw on rising to speak."

"Yes, I was there. I thought it a good opportunity of hearing you without compromising either you or myself."

"You are quite right," said Wilkes gaily. "Do you know that I am threatened with the defection of some of my supporters on the ground that I have been riding in carriages with duchesses?"

"Who has told?" she asked impulsively, much to Ethel's amazement.

"It was the cabman, I think, to whose care you left me when we arrived at Rigby. After he had deposited me at the 'Radical Arms,' he had a drink at the bar with some of my supporters, and the whole story leaked out."

"But the cabman did not know who I was."

"But he recognised the carriage as belonging to the castle, and so the story got about that I was driven to the Radical stronghold by a Conservative duchess."

Lady Ænid laughed. "Well, you can deny that, anyhow. But how is your campaign progressing?"

"Oh, we have just begun," said Wilkes. "But tell me, what did you think of the meeting last night?"

"It was splendid. I enjoyed it immensely. The conclusion of your speech was magnificent."

Wilkes smiled. He had thought so himself, but, of course, could not say so. Nothing is so pleasant as to find your own sentiments expressed with enthusiasm by the lady in whom you have already begun to feel a certain sympathetic interest.

"Well, you see," said he, "my father is a very wealthy man, and all but a very small portion of our money is invested in stocks and business enterprises. About a tenth of it, however, was spent in buying a small estate in Gloucestershire, and upon my word we have to spend more on the people's cottages and the like from the proceeds of that estate than we have to spend from the proceeds of all the other investments, which are nine times as great. Of course, I am against territorial interests and all that; it is played out, and the time has come to make an end of it. But our own experiment in Gloucester has been sufficient to prove to us many times over that of all forms of property, land is that which returns least to the owner and involves the largest obligations to those employed about the place. Hence, I could not in honesty, after having said so much about landlordism, conclude without speaking one plain strong word as to the much greater evils of capitalism."

"You certainly spoke strongly," said she. "You will think me very rude, but do you know what thought came to my mind when we were all standing up and cheering you?"

"No," said Wilkes; "what was it?"

"Whether you would dare to be as good as your word," said Lady Ænid shortly.

Wilkes flushed slightly. "Oh, really, Lady Ænid," said Ethel, "you are too bad for anything!"

"May I ask what reason you had for doubting me?" asked Wilkes, after a pause.

"Forgive me," Lady Ænid said, "for my rudeness. It was only because I seemed to realise more than you did what it would cost you to live up to your declaration."

There was an awkward pause. Then by way of changing the subject, Wilkes remarked, "What a terrible affair that was of Lord Bladud's death!"

"Yes," said Lady Ænid, doing her best to look unconcerned. "I have never heard anything more awful than that woman's cry; although I think, Ethel, you at least would have said 'Amen.'"

"Really," said Wilkes, "was the Earl in reality such a bad lot?"

"You had better not ask," Ethel said. "Ever since I came to Garlam, the thought of that man has haunted me like an evil demon. No one can imagine what a curse he has been to the country-side."

"There was one thing in that signalman's story," said Wilkes, "which I could not understand. I cannot say I altogether disbelieve him, but it was very improbable, all that tale he told concerning the pursuit of a flying cyclist, who strangely and mysteriously disappeared into space. I confess," he went on, not noticing the embarrassment of Lady Ænid or the self-conscious look of her friend, "that the probability is that the men in charge of the traction-engine were drunk, or keeping no look-out, and invented this tale in order to conceal their crime."

"But," said Lady Ænid, "what motive could have induced them to invent the story?"

"Motive!" exclaimed Wilkes. "You do not know, then, that both the men were arrested last night, and will be charged with manslaughter."

"You don't say so!" said Lady Ænid in genuine alarm. "Why, it is monstrous! They could not help it."

"My dear Lady Ænid," said Wilkes, "pray don't excite yourself. Justice will be done, depend upon it. For if they can produce their cyclist it will be all right. If not, it will be a case of hard labour for both of them. It is a serious business killing an earl in the public highway, even although he may be as big a scoundrel as Lord Bladud seems to have been."

Lady Ænid was silent, and again there was an awkward pause.

"Are you going back to Garlam?" Wilkes asked of his cousin.

"Never, I hope," she replied. "It is one of those places to which one never willingly returns."

"What was the matter with the place?" Wilkes asked.

"Garlam," said Ethel, "is the latest and most authentic illustration of the policy of unrestricted commercialism, with its policy of *laissez-faire*, and the devil take the hindmost. Lord Bladud had been bad enough in one sense. His personal character was scandalous, but even he, scoundrel as he was, had a higher sense of the obligations of property and the responsibilities of life than has Mr. Faulmann."

Wilkes drew a long breath. "Is it really so very bad?" he asked.

"Bad!" said Ethel; "no one who has not lived in the midst of those poisoned, fever-stricken people can possibly form any conception of how bad it is! I have frequently said to myself, when I have seen them come into the hospital all cankered with lead and groaning with disease, that the most malignant tyrant we ever read of in history could not have contrived a more horrible arrangement of human torture than that which results almost automatically from this man's cynical neglect of his duty towards his workmen."

Wilkes looked across the table at Lady Ænid. She did not seem to be listening to the conversation, but was gently applying herself to an egg.

"Lady Ænid!" said he.

She did not hear.

"Lady Ænid!" he repeated, more earnestly.

"I beg your pardon," she said, starting.

"I begin to understand," said Wilkes, "somewhat of the reason for the doubt which you expressed just now."

"Oh, forgive me!" Lady Ænid said. "It was very rude of me, and I am the last person in the world who should have said such a thing to you."

"What do you mean?" said Ethel.

"I mean," said Lady Ænid, "that I must have been judging you by myself when I doubted whether you would flinch, because I have in myself the coward soul which would flinch under similar circumstances. If you fail, you will only be following my example."

"You speak in enigmas," said Ethel. "What do you mean, both of you?"

"I mean," said Wilkes gravely, "that Mr. Faulmann is the chairman of my election committee, and that he presided over my meeting last night, and introduced me to the audience."

"And I mean," said Lady Ænid, as if impatient to get the painful confession out—"I mean that I was the cyclist whom Lord Bladud hunted when he came to his death, and I shrank like a coward from coming forward to confess the fact. No one knows of it, no one would suspect me of riding about at that time of night; and think what a scandal it would cause! It would nearly kill my poor mother. As for the Duke, I do not think I could ever enter Eastland again."

At that moment the waiter knocked at the door and said that a gentleman named Brassy wished to see Mr. Wilkes. He was waiting below.

"Brassy!" said Ethel; "can that be the man who put up all the slum property in Garlam?"

"Very likely," said Wilkes gloomily. "I will go and see him anyhow." So, bidding the ladies good-bye, he went downstairs.

Sure enough it was the redoubtable Brassy. But whatever might be his motives, there was not the slightest trace of animosity on his smirking countenance. "I just called to congratulate you, Mr. Candidate, on the effect you produced last night. Quite wonderful. I walked down with Mr. Faulmann to the station, and he declared that he had never seen anything like it before; but," continued Brassy, "it has just occurred to me that it would be friendly like on the part of one of your committee to give you a hint that you have said quite enough about capitalists. There are precious few capitalists in the county excepting landlords."

"And Mr. Faulmann," observed Wilkes, rather bitterly.

Brassy was pursing up his lips for a whistle, but he checked himself. "Yes," said he, "excepting Mr. Faulmann, and, of course, a candidate ain't going to quarrel with his own chairman, leastwise not if he hopes to make any show in the fight. But a nod's as good as a wink to a blind horse," added Brassy sententiously. "Good-day, Mr. Wilkes."

Hopton came running in. "Won't you go across to the court?" said he. "Those traction-engine drivers are coming up before the magistrates directly, and they will be remanded. Decent fellow is Jim, the driver, as ever stepped, but I am afraid it will go hard with him."

Wilkes put on his hat and walked across to the court with Hopton. It was crowded in anticipation of the opening of the magisterial inquiry into the death of Lord Bladud. Almost immediately one of the justices of the town and another of the county took their seats upon the Bench. The prisoners were brought up and charged with having caused the death of Lord Bladud. The Inspector who conducted the case produced a policeman who deposed that he had on the previous night arrested both the driver and the signalman, and after duly cautioning them that anything which they might say would be used as evidence against them, read out the statements which they had made. They were substantially the same as that made at the Radical meeting. The driver merely said that he heard the tramp of horses when approaching the turn of the road; that he heard the signalman shout, and a moment after the bright light of a bicycle lamp flashed past him, the bicyclist almost brushing against the wheel of the engine. Then he heard no more, for his attention was immediately directed to the horseman, who was apparently chasing the bicyclist. He described the shying of the horse and the death of the Earl as the other had done.

"I have now to ask," said the Inspector, "that the men be remanded till to-morrow. The coroner's inquest will be held to-day at Sloane Hall, and to-morrow I hope to have sufficient evidence to justify you committing these men for trial."

The magistrates conferred for a moment, and then remanded the two men in due form, ordering the prisoners to remain in custody until next day.

"Cannot you bail them out?" asked Hopton.

"I am afraid not," said Wilkes. "Otherwise it will be supposed that I had a hand in the killing of the Earl." So there was no question as to bail raised. The two men were to appear as witnesses at the coroner's inquest two hours later at Sloane Hall.

After leaving the court, Wilkes returned to the hotel and sent up his card to his cousin's room. The answer came down that the lady had gone out, but that the other lady would be glad to see him. He went up and found Lady Ænid alone. She was looking very distraught, but there was a grim determination about her face.

"Well?" she said.

He told simply and briefly what had happened. He proposed to go to the coroner's inquest, but it was evident that unless the cyclist could be produced, and some confirmatory evidence brought forward that the signalman had warned the unfortunate Earl, the men were certain to be committed for trial at the assizes. Lady Ænid sat still for a moment. Then, looking up, she said, "I was very rude to you just now when I said that I doubted whether you would keep your word. I little thought that I should so soon have personal knowledge of the bitterness of sacrifice."

"There is no need for apology, Lady Ænid. I understand too well how just was your doubt."

"But," said Lady Ænid, with a radiant light of determination in her bright eyes. "I want to tell you that I see my duty quite plainly, and I am going to do it," she added, "and I hope you will do yours."

"It would be a shame," said he slowly, "if I were to be less faithful to my public pledge than you to a duty of which no one knows but us three. If you don't fail, how dare I flinch?"

She stretched out her hand and grasped his. "That strengthens me to do my painful task," she said.

"What are you going to do?" asked Wilkes.

"Ethel has just gone out to order a carriage, and we are going to drive over to Sloane Hall, to the inquest," said Lady Ænid.

CHAPTER XII.

AN INQUEST AT SLOANE HALL.

LADY ÆNID'S trials were by no means over with her resolution to appear before the coroner, and give evidence on behalf of the engine-driver. When Ethel Merribel returned, announcing that the trap had been engaged, and would be round in an hour, she brought with her a telegram, which was addressed to Lady Ænid. She opened it hastily, looked at its contents, and cried, "Oh, Ethel, father is ill, and they want me to return home immediately. What can I do?"

Ethel glanced at the telegram. It was from the Duchess of Eastland, and simply stated that bad news had arrived from Belsover; that Lord Belsover was dangerously ill, and in a state of such prostration that any excitement might be fatal, and that Lady Ænid must return home immediately, as the worst might happen at any moment.

"Of course, you must return home at once. How about the trains? My poor child," she said, "this is a terrible blow."

Lady Ænid's eyes were filled with tears. "My poor

father," she said. "He was always so good to me. Now if I go to this inquest there will be a scandal in all the papers, and who knows what the consequence might be?"

Her companion was already turning over the pages of "Bradshaw." "Now," she said, "it is eleven o'clock. The next through train to Belsover is—let me see—does not leave Coleford until four. You have time to go to the inquest. What will you do?"

If Lady Ænid had not spoken about it to Mr. Wilkes, the chances would have been ten to one that she would have said that she would not go, justifying her sacrifice to the interests of justice by the paramount consideration of the life of her father; but she had said she would not flinch, and the additional strain to which her resolution was subjected strengthened rather than weakened her resolve.

"I will go," she said. "Meanwhile, leave me alone for a time."

Ethel caressed her tenderly, and left her in her own room, where, in an agony of prayer, Lady Ænid sought for strength from on high to do her duty without flinching.

Mr. Wilkes asked his cousin if he might accompany them to Sloane Hall.

"Better not," said Miss Merribel. "You know what trouble came from riding with a duchess before," she added, with a shrug.

So it was agreed that Ethel and Lady Ænid would drive by themselves, while Mr. Wilkes and Hopton would precede them in a cab, and arrange for their accommodation.

The inquest was fixed for one. It still wanted ten minutes to that hour when Wilkes and Hopton drove through the gates and up the avenue of the beautiful Elizabethan mansion which had so suddenly lost its owner.

Sloane Hall was one of those famous country places which were built towards the close of the Elizabethan era. It stood on the site of an old priory which had been dismantled and condemned in Henry VIII.'s reign, and the Church lands passed into the hands of a courtier who was the founder both of the Sloane Hall mansion and the earldom of Garlam.

It was a long drive from the lodge gates to the house, through the beautifully laid-out park. The carriage-drive passed some charming artificial waters in which swans were sunning themselves in the bright noonday sunshine of October, and the water from the lakes fell in miniature cascades into the stream, which formed a thread of silver at the foot of the ravine. Herds of deer browsed quietly on either side of the drive. The long-legged herons sailed lazily overhead. Now and again the drive passed a copse into which rabbits ran in scores, bobbing their white tails as they went.

In the drive Wilkes and Hopton overtook a cart laden with wine-cases, which the Coleford spirit-merchant had been ordered to send to Sloane Hall only the day before Lord Bladud's death. The Earl had issued invitations for a great dinner party that night, preparatory to the annual slaughter of the pheasants that was to take place the following morning, and, although telegrams had been sent to many of the guests, others who had heard nothing of the catastrophe were arriving at what they expected to be a house of mirth, only to find it full of desolation and death.

Approaching the mansion, they passed a waggon piled high with boxes and trunks of every conceivable variety. Some one was evidently leaving the house, who had either made or intended to make a long stay.

"Halloa!" said Wilkes. "There she is! I had forgotten she was here, although it was notorious enough."

As he spoke, an open carriage and pair dashed by. Seated alone in the carriage, half buried in luxurious furs, sat Mrs. Longton, one of the most notorious of courtesans of the Victorian era. Wilkes recognised her in a moment. He had seen her on the stage, where she posed but could not act, and her well-known face, with the smooth regularity of its features, and the absolute lack of any expression other than that of a somewhat stupid sheep, enabled him to identify at once the harpy who, having battened on the lives and fortunes of many lovers, was now hastening with her gains from the last man who had called her mistress. These were her boxes, which were going away, and with her in the carriage she had her jewel case. She had taken good care to stow away every precious stone the late Earl had ever placed within her reach. There was no trace of emotion upon that wooden and impassive face, as little as there was of passion in its owner, for Mrs. Longton was one of those women who, from the very lack of all feeling, seemed the better able to play the fatal game of rousing the passions of those whom they seek to plunder.

The sound of the wheels of the departing leman had already died away in the distance when they drove into the spacious quadrangle of Sloane Hall. It seemed as if half the county were there. Every one had his own version of the strange and mysterious death of the fast Earl. Men gathered together in little groups, discussing the matter. One held that it was a Radical plot directed by the Anarchists, and that the Earl had been as surely done to death as if he had been blown up by dynamite bombs. Others held that it served him right, and the only wonder was that it had not happened long ago. Between these two opinions the conversation ebbed and flowed, but the one thing on which all agreed was that there was a great mystery about the cyclist. The majority flatly refused to believe that there was any such person. It was the invention of the driver. But all these effusions were cut short by the arrival of the coroner, who at once proceeded to empanel the jury.

Mr. Wilkes was uneasy. Lady Ænid had not yet arrived, but the inquest had been formally opened, and as the jury, together with some friends, were already on their way "to view the body," he joined the little gathering of visitors who streamed through the house to the chamber of death.

Everything about Sloane Hall bore testimony to the luxurious magnificence in which its late owner had lived.

Lord Bladud was an illustration of the truth of the old saying that one generation makes money, the second keeps it, and the third spends it. Lord Bladud was the third, and there was no doubt that he had made money fly with both hands since his accession to the earldom.

If the aristocracy are "splendid paupers," the Earl had splendour for his share; leaving pauperism to those who came after. The Sloane estate was in splendid order, and it had come to him on the death of his father unembarrassed by any encumbrance; but its net rental of £20,000 a year was far too little for the extravagant tastes of the new Earl. In addition to his ancestral seat in Blankshire, he had a shooting-box in a deer forest in the Highlands, a mansion in Berkeley Square, and a floating palace of a yacht, the maintenance of which cost him considerably more than the income of a Cabinet Minister. He prided himself on his kennels, which were the best in the eastern counties. He had a most valuable stud of racehorses; and wherever he was, to use his own phrase, "he went the pace." Wine, women and play soon exhausted his immediate resources, and he resorted to borrowing recklessly and lavishly, but to his credit be it said, he did not reduce the outlay which had been the condition of the estate, nor the management of the farm and the affairs of labourers' cottages. In another year or two, even these resources would have failed him, but up to the very moment of his death the Earl had always been able to lay his hands upon as much cash as he needed either to spend or to give

MRS. LONGTON LEAVES SLOANE HALL.

away, and Sloane Hall, from garret to basement, simply reeked with evidence of the luxury and extravagance of its owner.

There was about the late Earl a certain popular sympathy which made him anxious to emulate the openhanded and unostentatious hospitality which used to distinguish the English nobility. The tenantry were always welcome to Sloane Hall, nor were any restrictions placed upon the number of times they might come to regale themselves at the hospitable table which was set apart for their use, and abundantly furnished with foaming tankards of ale and vast sirloins of roast beef. He was no niggard, and when he had money he spent it as freely upon others as upon himself. No more generous host ever lavished the resources of his mansion upon his guests. He was very fond of flowers, was by no means deficient in natural taste, which found expression in the choice of pictures and statuary, and his halls and drawing-rooms were veritable treasure-houses of art.

Through the hall, through the drawing-room, past the library, which was converted into a billiard and smoking room —for the Earl and his boon companions cared little for any books but those they made at races—the jurors made their way to the Earl's bedroom, where the body lay waiting identification.

There was a strange contrast between the voluptuous beauty of the fittings of the Earl's room and the figure which lay stretched upon the bed. Immediately opposite, looking down, as it were, upon the mutilated corpse, was a picture of Bacchus and Bacchantes, full of life and colour and a certain shameless immodesty which the Earl in life had always affected. One or two of the still more pronounced pictures of the French school had been draped. Luxurious settees, piled high with the softest of cushions, stood near the fireplace, and there was everywhere a profusion of mirrors which, when the great electrolier was turned on, gave a wonderful brilliance to the room, a brilliance that could be converted into utter darkness by the turning of a button.

On the bed there lay a figure covered with a sheet, around which the jurymen grouped themselves, waiting for the coroner. They had not long to wait; they heard his quick step and authoritative voice.

"This way, gentlemen, please, to view the body. Uncover the corpse," said the coroner, upon which the attendant drew back the sheet that concealed the body from sight.

The Earl was a man of somewhat gross body, and the spectacle that was presented of an almost headless trunk, was sickening indeed. Identification of the remains was almost impossible; but there was no doubt that it was the Earl.

Having viewed the corpse, the sheet was replaced over the Earl's remains, and the jury returned to the library.

The evidence was clear and to the point. The Earl, with three of his companions, had been dining at the "White Hart." They had dined generously, and had partaken freely first of champagne, and then of some hot whisky-and-water as they got into the saddle. They were all mellow, but none of them were much the worse for drink. Two of the Earl's companions, who were summoned as witnesses, testified that, after having gone some two or three miles from Coleford, the Earl had suddenly raised the cry of "Tally-ho!" and had begun galloping after a cyclist. They had believed it was a race between horse and machine. They followed to see the sport. That was all they knew. They had not seen the cyclist, and could not identify him; had seen nothing of the accident until they rode up to find the Earl crushed to death by the traction-engine.

Their evidence was given reluctantly, and they seemed to be considerably confused.

"We have had in evidence," said the coroner, "that there were three companions of the Earl. Where is the third?"

There was no answer.

"Call the landlord," said the coroner.

"Now, Boniface." said he, "who were the three gentlemen with Lord Bladud?"

"Two of them have just been called. The third was Lord Skeppy."

"Where is Lord Skeppy?" said the coroner; "let him be brought."

"Lord Skeppy," said one of the servants, "is ill in his bedroom."

"If he is too ill to leave his bed," said the coroner, "we will take his evidence where he is, but carry him down, if it can be managed."

After a short delay it was announced that Lord Skeppy would be brought on a chair, and that he was anxious to testify what he knew. When he was carried into the library he made considerable sensation. His face was fearfully scratched, one of his arms was in a sling, and he looked ghastly and ill; but the sensation produced by his appearance was nothing to the sensation produced when he stated that the cyclist whom Lord Bladud had chased was a lady.

"Lady!" said the coroner incredulously. "Ladies do not go about cycling at midnight."

"I assure you it was a lady, and a very pretty lady as well, otherwise she would not have been worth the chase."

"Then you chased her as well as the Earl?"

"Certainly," said Lord Skeppy. "I was a lighter weight, and better mounted than he, and I was the first to come upon her. I was going past her to hedge her back, so that Lord Bladud could pick her up, when she struck my horse over the head so violently that it shied into the ditch, flung me off, dislocated my shoulder and scratched my face, as you see; after that I know nothing."

The engine-driver and signalman were then called. They repeated their former story, but neither of them could say anything as to the sex of the cyclist. They swore they had seen no petticoats—only a flashing light, and some one rushing past them like the wind. Upon the vital question as to whether or not due warning had been given, they could produce no further evidence.

"I do not see what can be done," said the coroner, "unless that cyclist can be found. Shall we issue a reward for her appearance, or shall we adjourn this inquest until at least we have time to make inquiries? It ought not to be difficult to discover what lady cyclists there are in the county."

The Superintendent of Police here stepped up to the coroner and said that he believed the lady was in attendance and was willing to give evidence.

"Let her be called at once," said the coroner.

Wilkes drew a long breath when he saw Lady Ænid make her way to the witness's stand.

After being sworn, she began her evidence.

"What is your name?"

"Ænid Belsover."

The coroner and those present looked as if the ground had suddenly opened before their feet.

"Lady Ænid?" said the coroner. "Address, please?"

"Six Elms Castle, Belsover Park."

Then the examination began. Lady Ænid told her story very simply. She told how she had cycled over to see her friend Ethel Merribel, who was present, and could be produced. Finding her knocked up with nursing at the Fever Hospital, she had taken her place for a few days, until she recovered strength; that, after being in close confinement for more than a week, a fine moonlight night had tempted her to take a ride, when the roads would be free from traffic, and she could get a breath of fresh air before returning to duty.

THE PLUTOCRATIC MICROBE. 49

Then she detailed all that followed. On the vital question of the warning her testimony was perfectly clear. She was about a hundred yards off when she caught sight of the signalman waving the red flag, and shouting repeatedly. It was only because she was in mortal terror of her pursuer, and found it impossible to stop at the rate she was going in time to claim the protection of the signalman, that she had ridden on. The distance between the signalman and the engine was, she thought, about a hundred yards, but there was a turning in the road, and she could not speak certainly about the distance. She was, however, quite sure that everything had been done to warn herself and her pursuers of the approach of the traction-engine, and it was because she knew this to be the fact that, at considerable inconvenience to herself, she had come forward to bear testimony.

When she had finished her evidence, Ethel Merribel was called merely to confirm the statement as to Lady Enid's departure from the hospital, and her subsequent return, with a damaged machine, and in a condition of exhaustion and excitement.

The coroner then summed up, and the jury returned a verdict of "Accidental Death," entirely exonerating the driver and signalman from all responsibility for the accident.

After the verdict, Lady Enid hurried back to her carriage. At the door, Mr. Wilkes met her, and handed her into the carriage.

"Good-bye," she said, in a tone that told volumes as to the intensity of the strain from which she was suffering. "I have not flinched!"

"Good-bye," he said. He held her hand for one moment in his. "Lady Ænid," said he, "you have done bravely indeed, and the memory of your deed will help me when my turn comes.".

She looked at him gratefully—just one wistful look of gratitude mingled with a sense of weariness and pain, and then she was gone.

HE HELD HER HAND FOR ONE MOMENT.

CHAPTER XIII.
THE PLUTOCRATIC MICROBE.

WHEN Mr. Wilkes was turning back to the Hall, in his abstraction he almost walked over Dr. Glogoul, who had come over from Garlam to attend the inquest.

"I beg pardon," said Mr. Wilkes.

"On no account," said Dr. Glogoul. "I am glad to make your acquaintance, sir, if you are the gentleman who is standing as the Radical candidate for Blankshire?"

"I am," said Wilkes. "Are you an elector?"

"I am not—at least, not in this county. My voting place is some thousands of miles away from here, in the American Republic, but I was anxious to make your acquaintance, and if you have no objection, and you are not particularly busy, I should like to accompany you around Sloane Hall."

Wilkes did not exactly know whether to resent the liberty which his new acquaintance was taking, but thinking it would be following the line of least resistance to assent, he languidly assented, and the American marched him off over the grounds, through the conservatory and the vineries, talking glibly as he went about many things, to which Mr. Wilkes, absorbed in his own thoughts, paid little attention.

Suddenly he was aroused from his brown study by hearing the word "Faulmann." He listened, and marked Dr. Glogoul's words—"I should not be surprised if Faulmann were to take this place. He is on the look-out for a well-preserved property that can be had cheap; told me so himself, and Bladud's place might have been made for him. It is not more than half-an-hour's drive to his works."

"You mean Mr. Faulmann of Garlam?" said Mr. Wilkes incredulously.

"That same gentleman, and no one else," said Dr. Glogoul blithely. "I was talking to him this very morning."

E

"This morning," said Wilkes. "Why, I understood that he had been summoned to London."

"I know nothing about his being summoned," said Dr. Glogoul. "He was at the Patent White Lead Works at Garlam this morning, and in a very bad temper too. He is not a beauty at the best of times, but to-day something seemed to have vexed him beyond his wont. Still, he was evidently bent upon getting possession of Sloane Hall, and, if so, the Lord have mercy upon the tenants and the peasants and dependents. It is a bad time they will have when Faulmann comes to the fore."

They had wandered now into the picture-gallery, which was deserted by all but themselves.

"Sit down," said Mr. Wilkes. "I want to speak to you. You know this man Faulmann?"

"Rather," said Dr. Glogoul. "I have been physicking the people he has poisoned for the last three weeks, and I am about tired of it. Not all the drugs of the Pharmacopœia would cope with the wholesale murder for which Faulmann is responsible. I have told him repeatedly what it was necessary to do in order to diminish the mortality, but he said that life was cheap, and it was none of his business. He had to make money and pay wages. If they did not, like the conditions of work they could go elsewhere; and, of course, I recognised that it was business. In our country that is the way in which we run things. 'Each man for himself, and the devil take the hindmost.' What interests me is to see the way in which the substitution of this kind of thing for the doctrine of *noblesse oblige* seems to find favour with Radicals in this country."

Mr. Wilkes winced slightly, and only said, "Are you going back to Garlam to-night?"

"I intend to go there as soon as our conversation is ended."

"Will you take me over to your place?"

"You will have to put up with short commons and miserable accommodation, I am afraid; but if you care to come I shall be delighted."

"I will come," said Wilkes. "I want to see with my own eyes what you have been telling me. Do you know," said he suddenly, "that this man Faulmann is the chairman of my election committee?"

"I heard so," said Dr. Glogoul, in a matter-of-fact kind of way. "What of that? Business is a thing outside politics. A man can be a good Radical, but a bad employer of labour. There is no necessary connection between private life and public policy, is there?"

"There ought to be," said Mr. Wilkes.

"Well, if you think so, come to Garlam," said Dr. Glogoul, "and test, if you like, your chairman's public professions by his business practices. It is a dangerous experiment, and I do not advise you to make it; but if you are bent upon it, I am very much at your service."

And so it came to pass that the Radical candidate for Blankshire accompanied Dr. Glogoul to the village of Garlam to visit *incognito* the Patent White Lead Works of Mr. Faulmann, and the town which had sprung up around those works.

As Wilkes drove through the unpaved streets and over the open gutters, Glogoul asked him to notice a low, straggling building standing a little on the right hand side of the road. "That," he said, "is the latest achievement in jerry-building. By-the-bye, do you happen to know anything of Brassy, the jerry-builder?"

Wilkes asked, "Do you mean Joe Brassy, an oily, sinister-looking fellow, with a hare-lip and a curious bald patch at the back of his head?"

"The same," said Glogoul.

"Know him?" replied Wilkes. "I should think I do; he is one of my committee!"

Glogoul smiled grimly, and said, "We had better look into your committeeman's shed, if you are not afraid of infection."

"No," said Wilkes, "where you can go I can go; and if my committeeman keeps this house, I had better see what it is like."

They got out of the carriage and made their way to the door. Dr. Glogoul opened it without ceremony, and they entered. Wilkes was almost overpowered with the nauseous stench. Bunks were arranged round the room, at the end of which were the sanitary conveniences, so-called because they were the most insanitary that could be contrived, and filled the shed with a fœtid smell. By the light of two paraffin lamps there were dimly visible groups of frowsy men and women sitting round tables, at one of which they played cards, and at the other dominoes. In the middle of the room, before the fire, some herrings were frizzling, adding a flavour all their own to the aroma of mildew and sewage which filled the shed.

"Well, Tom," said Glogoul, addressing the deputy, "how's Nance?"

"Worse, doctor," was the reply. "I don't think she will last the night. Her cough is something fearful, and the moment she dozes there is some drunken row, and she is waked up again."

"You don't mean to say," said Wilkes, "that a poor woman is dying in the midst of this crowd?"

"Come and see," said Glogoul. They passed the two groups of players, and made their way to the farthest end of the room. In one of the bunks, with her head not more than a foot or two from the open cesspool which served as a lavatory and retiring-room for the lodgers, a poor woman lay in the last stage of consumption. Her cheeks were sunken and her eyes had an unearthly glitter, while from time to time a hacking cough was followed by a pitiful spitting of blood. When Glogoul approached she raised herself slightly on her elbow, but failed to do more than turn herself slightly in the bed.

"Doctor," she said, in a hollow whisper, "could you not take me to some quiet place to die? Here it is too——" Her hacking cough interrupted her sentence.

"I will do what I can," said Glogoul; "meantime I will give you some medicine which will give you a little sleep."

"Thanks, doctor," she said, "oh, thanks so much!—it is too horrible here."

"Bring me a glass, will you?" said Glogoul to the deputy. The man brought a tin pot. "Now," said Glogoul, "a little water and a spoon to mix this medicine with. Nance is suffering a great deal, and I am going to give her something to make her sleep." He mixed a potion and put it to her lips, she swallowed it eagerly, and lay back with closed eyes. In a few minutes she seemed easier, and appeared to fall into a quiet sleep.

"She is all right now, I think," said the doctor, "until the morning. I will call to-morrow; do not send for me during the night."

So saying they left. "Is she the only patient you have here?" asked Wilkes.

"Oh, no," replied Glogoul; "there are two or three others, but they will last a little longer. She has been here for a week or more, and it is very interesting to notice the development of consumption among the other lodgers."

The doctor spoke in a cold unsympathetic tone, as if the communication of the virus of consumption to healthy persons was an interesting experiment provided for his observation by kindly Nature.

"Won't you have to come and see that woman again?" asked Wilkes.

"Certainly not," said Glogoul; "I am going to spend the evening with you."

"But," said Wilkes "she is a dying woman!"

"She will be dead before midnight," replied Glogoul calmly.

"What!" exclaimed Wilkes.

"Dead," said Glogoul. "I arranged for that. If I had not given her that medicine she would have lingered for another day, continuing to poison the atmosphere of that overcrowded shed, suffering miserably, as you saw, because she cannot get a quiet place to die in. The opiate which I gave her has secured her all that she needs. She will never wake again."

Wilkes, who was of a hot temper and unaccustomed to discuss the problems in the midst of which Glogoul spent his life, exclaimed wrathfully, "Do you mean to say you poisoned her?"

"My dear sir," said Glogoul calmly, "I have given her a sleeping draught. There is not a doctor in the profession who would not justify its administration under the circumstances. But," he continued grimly, "if you wish to prolong her life, you have only to return, wake her up and give her this emetic, and she will suffer horribly for another day and then die in agony, whereas now she will sleep peacefully off at midnight."

Wilkes was silent. When he entered Glogoul's lodgings and noticed the skulls and jars of specimens which lined the walls, he said to the doctor, "After hearing your defence of a murder, one feels almost as if one were entering the den of a poisoner."

"So you are," replied Dr. Glogoul coolly. "All medicine is poison. The most successful physician has to poison or to murder—if you prefer the word—the microbe which is destroying the vital tissue of his patient. Hence the study of medicine is the study of poison. Do you see these jars ranged round my laboratory? In every one of them I am cultivating some bacillus or other. I am making great progress here. Never could I have had more admirable or more willing subjects for pathological experiments. I am cultivating, as you see, the bacilli of all the diseases, and at each successive stage I test their virus upon one or other of the inhabitants of Garlam. The progress of each patient is carefully noted, until at last I arrive at a sufficiently attenuated sample to be used for purposes of general inoculation."

"But do you mean to say," said Wilkes, "that you are absolutely inoculating healthy persons with disease in order to test the imperfect results of your experiments?"

"Certainly," said Dr. Glogoul; "and we all do it."

"But it is a species of human vivisection," said Wilkes impatiently.

"Of course," replied Glogoul. Then assuming a more confidential tone he went on. "My dear sir, I perceive that you are labouring under a great delusion. You call yourself an advanced politician, but you are in reality a very reactionary philosopher. You do not seem to have mastered the fundamental doctrine of the philosophy or religion of the future—namely, that men are automata, and that the doctrine of moral responsibility is a figment of the imagination. The laws of force and energy act with undeviating uniformity throughout the whole of life. Metaphysicians have imagined they could slice off a small fragment of existence and assume that the law of necessity which dominates the whole of physical nature ceases at an arbitrary frontier line which they draw. It does not cease. There is no frontier line. We are all creatures of necessity."

"THERE IS NO MORAL LAW," SAID GLOGOUL.

"Then," said Wilkes, "on that doctrine what becomes of the moral law?"

"There is no moral law," replied Glogoul, "any more than there is any religion. What is right to-day may be wrong to-morrow, and what is wrong to-morrow may be right the day after. The welfare of society in the future will rest as a foundation upon what, if we may use old mythological phrases, may be described as the moral obligation to murder."

"You talk like an assassin in the jargon of a philosopher," said Wilkes bitterly.

"You will not offend me," said Glogoul calmly; "nothing can offend a man when he has once firmly grasped the fundamental principle of the new philosophy. An unfamiliar idea, when first propagated, always produces its natural reaction in the social organism which is always conservative, and rightly so. Your martyrdoms and crucifixions, what were they but the reflex action of the self-preserving instinct in society? You may call me an assassin now, but the assassin of to-day is the philanthropist of to-morrow. Modern civilisation is rapidly securing the survival of the unfit, with the result that the whole race has run to nerves. The modern man, but still more the modern woman, is becoming a hopeless neurotic, and if it were not for cholera, war and similar beneficent agencies I should despair for the future of the race.

"Now, for instance," continued Glogoul, handing a cigar-case to Wilkes and lighting his own cigarette, "you consider that your democratic socialism and humanitarian enthusiasm are the finest outcome of the civilisation of the past. That it is a product of the past, and that it will work out certain results, I do not doubt; but these results are not what you anticipate. Your maudlin philanthropy with its revolt against the decrees of Nature, what is it doing? It is creating a neurotic population which flies from the country, in which alone healthy manhood is possible, and crowds the cities, which are hotbeds of mental and physical deterioration. Having destroyed the monarchy, you are now waging a holy war against the aristocracy, and what is the result? Bladud has gone and Faulmann rises in his stead. The tendency of the neurotic civilisation is to establish on the ruins of all dynasties and hierarchies and religions the despotism of the dollar, the sway of the plutocrat, which will be as ruthless as Asiatic cholera and a great deal less speedy in its beneficent surgery."

"A truce to theorising," said Wilkes. "You may be right or you may be wrong, but what about Faulmann?"

"All right," said Glogoul; "don't be so impatient. Let me finish what I have to say. In this old country you have succeeded in preserving, how I do not exactly know, nor need we inquire, the principle of *noblesse oblige*, which has played its part and has contributed its fair share to the welfare of the social organism. It has even succeeded in teaching ten per cent. of your moneyed men that if *noblesse oblige* is a good doctrine, *richesse oblige* has also something to say for itself. But if you want to see the plutocrat freed from the swaddling-clothes of aristocracies, you must come to my country. There you will be told that Democracy is Triumphant, with the result that capital is king—king by right divine of the almighty dollar, with a power which disdains the limitations with which your philanthropic sentiment has crippled the capitalists in this country. But your sentimental socialism is saturating the American working man with its dreams of an impossible Utopia, and capitalism, even in the States, has occasional nightmares based upon the memories of the Christian mythology which it learnt in its childhood. To see the true ultimate of the power of plutocracy freed from the trammels of mythological scruples or humanitarian prejudices we must go to China. There alone the pathological student can make experiments without fear of consequences. There alone is the right divine of money sanctioned by custom and recognised as the highest law, by a population laborious and ingenious enough to dominate the world."

Glogoul paused, and for a few minutes the two men smoked on in silence. Then Wilkes looked at his watch. "You have not told me a word about Faulmann," said he.

"No," said Glogoul; "I have all the material ready, and you can read it at your leisure." Thereupon he handed him a portfolio, in which were arranged with the careful pedantry of a university professor all the documents relating to the "type Faulmann." There was, to begin with, the copy of the original prospectus on which the White Lead Company was founded; lists of the shareholders, of the officers, and reports of all the annual meetings held since the company was founded. There was a list of the dividends paid from the year of its commencement. There was a portrait of the man Faulmann, with a biographical sketch as complete as could be made, showing that he was the son of a Jew pedlar in Germany, and commenced life by helping his father to wheel his barrow. He had gradually accumulated a little capital, with which he had speculated luckily, and again speculated until he had been able to start business as a small moneylender. It also stated how his business had grown and thrived; that he had excited much animosity in the district in which he lived; that he had been obliged to realise his investments and come to London. There was also the scandalous story of the obtaining of the monopoly for the supply of white lead to the Turkish Empire, which he had procured by bribing a pasha high in office at the Sublime Porte, together with notes of the conversations which the doctor had had with Faulmann on various occasions. The gist of all these was the same, that business was business, money was money, and that—

"Dollars and dimes, dollars and dimes,
To be without money's the worst of crimes.
To keep all you get, and get all you can
Is the first, the last, the whole duty of man."

Then followed a series of extracts from blue-books which contained the reports of the inspector of factories as to the condition of the lead works. They began from the year after the works were opened, and continued down to the last published volume. They were an unbroken series of condemnations. They pointed out that the machinery was left unfenced, that the necessary provisions for cleanliness were not made, that the workpeople were allowed to eat in the works, and that, in short, every precaution which sanitary science showed to be necessary to render innocuous the prosecution of such an industry was conspicuous by its absence.

There were also one or two cases in which actions had been brought in the neighbouring police and county courts against the White Lead Company, but always with one result—namely, that after the first hearing there was a remand, and then nothing more was heard of the case. The Company always found it better policy to square the individual than to provoke a public scandal.

As Wilkes read on and on with a sinking heart, he turned to another bundle of documents. They were extracts from the reports of the medical officer of the Union in which Garlam stood. From these he learned that the whole of the ground on which Garlam stood had been leased to the White Lead Company by the Earl of Bladud. The Company was the sole ground landlord, but almost all the houses in which the workmen lived had been put up by Joe Brassy of Rigby. These reports to the Local Sanitary Authority were varied by an occasional report by the medical inspector of the Local Government Board when an epidemic had broken out. They all told the same tale, and showed the absolute neglect of everything which would not bring the Company a profit. There was neither water supply nor drainage system, no provision for cleanliness, nor for the education or the civilisation of the unfortunate workman. In short, if the condition of the Patent White Lead Company's works were deplorable, that of the village of Garlam was still more detestable. It was a scandal to a country calling itself civilised that such a population should be found in such a condition of squalor, filth and disease.

Glogoul had gone on smoking without saying a word. When Wilkes had finished reading the last document he looked up at his host. His cheeks were pale and his lips compressed.

"Well?" said Glogoul.

"Well, indeed," said Wilkes bitterly, "the infernal scoundrel!"

"My dear sir," said Glogoul, blowing a ring of tobacco smoke, which floated slowly up to the ceiling—"no impatience. Remember Faulmann but acted according to the law of his being. He is a very good specimen of—what should I call it?—the plutocratic microbe, whose virus has not yet been sufficiently attenuated by civilisation."

"But," said Wilkes, "this twenty-per-cent. fiend is a thousandfold greater curse to the country than a scamp like Lord Bladud."

"And yet," said Glogoul, with a slightly malicious humour gleaming in his eye, "it is under the auspices of Mr. Faulmann of the Patent White Lead Works, and Mr. Brassy, landlord of Garlam, that Mr. Edmund Wilkes has come down to wage war to the death against the territorial magnates in order to promote the well-being of the people."

CHAPTER XIV.
DEFEATED BUT TRIUMPHANT.

EDMUND WILKES slept little that night. When he came down to breakfast he found that Dr. Glogoul had already gone on his rounds. On his plate lay a card, on which the doctor had written as follows:—

"Excuse my absence, but I have to start early to arrange for a successor. I forgot to tell you last night that I am going by the next mail to China. That is the country of the future, for it is the country of the logical ultimate of materialism and money. It will take your Faulmanns and your Walled-offs another generation before they can develop the type of man whom I am seeking, and whom I shall find in the Celestial Empire. By-the-bye, Nance died last night."

Wilkes finished his breakfast and went out into the village. The men were all at work, and the frowsy women were standing gossiping in the streets. A swarm of dirty urchins were sailing chip boats in the gutter. Overhead the sky was bright and clear, for a land wind drove the smoke of the works far away over the sea. As he stood at the doorway, looking about him, Wilkes noticed a man who appeared to be a cross between a bill-sticker and a gamekeeper, coming down the street, handing what seemed to be tracts to the people. Wondering what phase of social or religious propaganda this distribution might represent, the man rapidly approached him and offered him a couple of handbills. He took them mechanically, without looking at their headings, and said to the man, "Are you distributing them everywhere?"

"Yes," was the reply, and the man hurried on. "Election business! Couple of these to be delivered at every house in the county before to-morrow night!"

Wilkes glanced at the bills, and as he did so his heart sank within him.

HE GLANCED AT THE BILLS, AND HIS HEART SANK.

He entered the house, closed the door, and sat down. He saw in a moment their significance, and he paid unwilling homage to the ingenuity and adroitness of Mr. Wirham, whose hand he at once recognised. The two bills resembled each other in shape and size. Each was headed on one side, "WHAT THE RADICAL CANDIDATE SAYS!" Wilkes recognised with a groan the peroration of which he had been so proud when he delivered it at the Corn Exchange at Coleford. On the other side of one of the bills was printed, "WHAT THE RADICAL CHAIRMAN DOES!" which was followed by a most scathing extract from the report of the Local Government Inspector as to the scandalous neglect of every precaution for preserving the health of the employés of the Patent White Lead Works at Garlam. At the bottom of the bill was printed one line: "The dividend of the Patent White Lead Works last year was 20 per cent." The second handbill was also headed, "WHAT THE RADICAL CANDIDATE SAYS!" and on the opposite side was the heading, "WHAT THE RADICAL LANDLORD DOES!" then followed an extract from the Rural Sanitary inspector's report as to the condition of Mr. Brassy's house property at Garlam. At the bottom of this leaflet was printed, "How can the Radical Candidate keep his Word?"

Wilkes remained in the doctor's room for ten minutes, staring at these two bills, the bearing of which on his candidature he saw in a minute. He had taken the field with a generous enthusiasm and an honest belief that the cause of social democracy demanded a revolt against the influence of the territorial aristocracy, and now he was confronted with incontrovertible evidence that the chairman who was bringing him out, and one of the leading members of his electoral committee, were guilty of infinitely more heinous offences against humanity and the working-people than the worst peer in Blankshire. What was he to do? Retire? He shrank from that alternative. He had pledged his word to the electors to fight the battle through without flinching. He honestly believed that the ascendency of the Duke of Eastland was prejudicial to the best interests of the county. The broad features of the political and social situation were in no way altered by the fact that he had a scoundrel for his chairman and a rascally jerry-builder among his supporters. Yet what hope was there of making even a semblance of a fight if at the beginning of the campaign he were to quarrel with Faulmann and Brassy? What was he to do?

His first and foremost impulse was to have it out with Faulmann there and then. He put on his hat and coat and walked down to the offices of the Patent White Lead Works and inquired for Mr. Faulmann, only to be told that he had left the place and would not be back for two or three days. Garlam was hateful to him, and Wilkes felt he could not remain there another hour. As it was only about ten miles to Coleford, he came to the conclusion that he could not do better than walk off his spleen. By the time he arrived at Coleford he would probably have made up his mind as to what course to adopt. Pulling his hat over his eyes he strode sullenly down the street, past Joe Brassy's facetiously designated "Model Lodging House," and out into the open country. He was relieved to have left that pest-smitten village behind him. There was a fine autumnal crispness in the air, and before he had gone a couple of miles his spirits began to rise.

Seeing that a winning game was out of the question, could he not play the grand game? He had taken the field against the territorial system; it was now time for him to fulfil his pledge to defend the cause of the people against the capitalist scorpion. He had a meeting that night in Strouwich. Hopton would be there, and Brown would support him in whatever he did. He would show the county what his candidature meant. There should be no flinching. He would fight the Duke, and Faulmann, and Brassy, and the whole crew. With which valorous resolve he fell to preparing the speech in which he would declare this new departure, and proclaim to his supporters that their chairman was to be henceforward regarded as the enemy.

On arriving at Coleford he bought a special edition of the Liberal weekly paper, which contained a full report of the proceedings at the inquest at Sloane Hall the previous day. There was a short editorial, in which the writer commented somewhat sarcastically upon the modern young woman who went cycling at midnight, apparently in search of adventures, and who was attending Radical meetings at the time when her father was dying. "There must be some strange attraction in Blankshire at the present moment," continued the leader writer, "to induce Lady Ænid Belsover to leave her home and indulge in such vagaries as these."

A telegram in another part of the paper announced that Lord Belsover had died at three o'clock the previous day, almost exactly the same moment that Wilkes had handed Lady Ænid into a carriage at Sloane Hall. He realised as he had never done before the sacrifice which she had made, and the cruel misrepresentations to which she had laid herself open on his account. A fierce impulse seized him to go to the newspaper office and flog the editor within an inch of his life. A moment's reflection convinced him that this would only make matters worse, more especially as, glancing down the paper, he came upon a significant paragraph, which ran somewhat as follows:—

Grave dissatisfaction was expressed at the Radical head-quarters at the extraordinary utterances of the young man from London, Mr. Edmund Wilkes, at the meeting in the Corn Exchange last night. He went out of his way to compli- ment the Duke of Eastland, and was preparing an elaborate attack upon the deceased Earl of Bladud, who had been doue to death by the vagaries of a fair cyclist who appears to have a singular fascination for the Radical candidate. Checked in the delivery of this attack upon a dead man by the indignation and horror of the audience, this "Radical" candidate brought his speech to a close by making what all present regarded as an attack, no less monstrous because it was cleverly veiled, upon the chairman of the meeting. Well has the Tory D. lilah played her part! The Philistines are upon thee, Samson!

Flinging down the paper in disgust, he went to the "Boar's Head" and ordered something to eat. While waiting for lunch to be served he took up the Conservative paper. It contained a picturesquely written description of the meeting in the Corn Exchange, not inaccurately done, but at the close of his peroration, which was reported in the first person, the descriptive writer said:—

The meeting rose and cheered vociferously, but there was one person who showed no inclination to join in the enthusiasm of the crowd. That person was the chairman. He seemed as uncomfortable as a toad under a harrow, and no wonder. Mr. Wilkes is a young man, and is unacquainted with the story of the Patent White Lead Works of Garlam.

The leading article complimented him upon the intrepidity with which he had stated his opinions, and expressed a hope that he might be as good as his word, and carry the war into the camp of the capitalist who, out of a dividend of twenty per cent., left his workmen to rot with disease, while the hard-hit landlords, who were scarcely drawing two per cent. upon money invested in improving the land, were expected to supply the labourers with healthy cottages and to look after their sanitary needs.

Here was but cold comfort for Wilkes. One or two people at the market ordinary, who had been at the meeting, came over and shook hands with him. Others who had been very enthusiastic at the Corn Exchange passed him without seeming to notice his existence. As soon as he had finished his lunch he took the train to Strouwich.

On arriving there he found a pretty state of affairs in his committee-room. Brassy had been there all the morning declaring that Wilkes was a traitor; that he had sold the cause; and that he was the lover of Lady Ænid Belsover, who had been used as a decoy to lure the impulsive young Radical into the Tory fold. He said that Mr. Faulmann was determined to have nothing to do with his candidature, and that he himself was convinced that Wilkes was a wolf in sheep's clothing, and that the campaign must be abandoned unless another candidate could be found at once. The local committee were in session when he arrived. Brassy had left, having sown the seeds of suspicion and distrust with both hands. Wilkes was a stranger and alone, without any person even to introduce him to those who were present.

"You are Mr. Wilkes, I suppose," said a burly beer-house keeper, who had turned Radical because of being severely fined by a Tory magistrate for some offence against the Licensing Laws. "Mr. Wilkes," said this worthy, whose name was Peter Philpot, "we ain't Londoners, but plain countryfolk, who say what they think and don't beat about the bush. What is the meaning of all this talk that is in the papers this morning about you and the lady cyclist who killed Lord Bladud?"

"Sir," said Wilkes, with difficulty restraining an inclination to throw the man downstairs, "I am perfectly ready to answer any questions which you may care to ask me, but I would beg of you as a gentleman to refrain from insulting a stranger whom you have invited to address you."

A quiet-looking man who was sitting near the door said, "Philpot, sit down; that is not the way in which to open this business, which is delicate and difficult, and with your permission, sir," he said, turning to Mr. Wilkes, "we would like to ask you one or two questions."

"Ask as many as you please," said Mr. Wilkes.

"We have heard, sir," said this man, who was in a thriving way of business, "we have heard you called a traitor, and there be those who have said all manner of evil against you behind your back; but as they are not here to say it before your face, we do not need to take any account of them. But, Mr. Wilkes, we are uneasy about one thing: do you mean to fight this thing out, or will you sell us to the enemy?"

"Hear, hear," said Philpot; "that is the question, and let us have a straight answer, young man."

"Gentlemen," said Mr. Wilkes, "I am going to fight this battle through to the bitter end, whether or not I have the honour of your support. I was asked to come here as the only man you could find who would be independent enough —and, shall I say, reckless enough—to raise the standard of revolt against the enemies of the people. Personally I had nothing to gain, and much to lose. I had a safe seat offered me in more than one northern county, but the forlorn hope attracted me, and I came here to fight to the last. There will be no flinching on my part, gentlemen."

The frankness of his speech disarmed a good deal of the suspicion with which he had been regarded. "I see now," he continued, "that the fight will be much more serious than we had anticipated when I came. For, gentlemen, what we have to contend against is not merely the influence of the landlords, which will be used without mercy now that they are threatened in the very stronghold of their power, we have to encounter a much more dangerous and more insidious foe. As you know, I came here a stranger. I was introduced to the meeting at Coleford by Mr. Faulmann, the chairman of the Radical committee of Blankshire. I knew nothing about Mr. Faulmann excepting as the chairman of your committee, and I had been told that he was a sound Radical, who was willing to support energetically the struggle we were to make for independence. I spoke, as some of you who were at the meeting may remember, with great emphasis as to the need for fighting the foes of the people wherever they were found; whether they were the broken-down tyrants of territorialism, or the new tyranny of the plutocrats. I did not know then what I know now."

There was a stir in the committee-room, and every one bent forward to catch his lightest word.

"I spent last night at Garlam. I have had the opportunity of studying the official reports concerning the way in which Mr. Faulmann fulfils his duty as an employer, and the reports of the local officer of health as to the sanitary condition of the village which he has allowed Mr. Brassy to build on his land, at his gates. Gentlemen, I do not disguise from you for a moment that, bad and hateful as the dominion of the squire and parson has been, and great as is the dereliction of duty on the part of many of the peers who have lorded it over this free democracy, there is nothing that I have either read or heard to equal for infamy the condition of misery which has come into existence in the last few years under the direct authority of Mr. Faulmann."

A profound sensation followed this emphatic utterance. Committeemen whispered to each other, and Philpot audibly snorted, "Didn't I tell you so?"

"Now," said Mr. Wilkes, "let us be perfectly plain and above-board. If I am to head the revolt of the people against their tyrants and taskmasters, that revolt must be directed equally against all tyrants and taskmasters, whether they call themselves Radicals or Conservatives. We stand for the people. It is their cause that I came to Blankshire to fight, and it is nothing to me whether they suffer from a plutocrat or a peer. Wherever wrong is done, that wrong must be righted, or we will know the reason why. Now, gentlemen, I have told you where I stand; it is for you to decide what you will do."

Mr. Wilkes resumed his seat. Peter Philpot jumped up instantly and declared, "It is all very well for the young man from London ——"

"Hush!" said a companion; "keep a civil tongue in your head, anyhow."

"Well, will the candidate tell us," he continued, "how we are to fight this battle without a chairman? Where is the money to come from?"

Another member of the committee asked more civilly how Mr. Wilkes proposed to carry on the campaign, if he were to begin it by adding Mr. Faulmann to the list of the enemies against whom they had to fight?

"Well," said Mr. Wilkes, "all this has come on me as a surprise. What I propose is, to meet the people, in the Town Hall to-night at Stronwich, and put the case before them fully and fairly. If they support me, well and good; we shall replace Mr. Faulmann as chairman of the committee. If they refuse to support me, I shall prosecute my candidature without regard to the Radical organisation. I cannot go back. I have nailed my colours to the mast, and I am going to the poll."

After considerable discussion, and some acrimonious animadversions, it was agreed that no better course could be suggested. Mr. Wilkes, therefore, that very evening, met a crowded and boisterous assembly of the electors in the town-hall. There was a great deal of prejudice against him at first, and for a time it seemed as if there would be some difficulty in obtaining a hearing. His composure, his good humour, and his quiet determination triumphed at last, and soon the crowded assemblage was listening intently to his words. Discarding all pretence of making a regular political speech, he told the whole story of the state of affairs at Garlam, and appealed to them whether, as honest men, they could declare war against the landlords, while in their own ranks they cherished a jerry-builder whose lordlordism was far worse than that of the most despotic peer in the county; or whether they could go forth to battle under a leader whose works were a byword for his cynical neglect of all care for the well-being of his people.

Long before he had reached his peroration Wilkes felt that he had the audience in his hand. When he sat down there was no whisper of opposition. Philpot was cowed, and even Brassy, who had slunk into a corner where he could hear and not be perceived, did not venture to dissent. It was decided to prosecute the campaign on Mr. Wilkes' lines, and a general meeting of the party was summoned to meet at Rigby on the following Monday.

When that committee met the first business was to read a letter from Faulmann resigning his chairmanship. There was no explanation, nor was any needed. Mr. Brassy also resigned his position on the committee, but with these exceptions the committee stood firm. The Rev. Ebenezer Brown was appointed chairman in the place of Mr. Faulmann, and the campaign was fought out on the lines laid down by Mr. Wilkes at the meeting in Stronwich.

"It is magnificent," said Mr. Wirham, as he read of Mr. Wilkes' doings, "very magnificent, but it is not war. We may dismiss half our canvassers at once, as it is useless to go to any unnecessary expense. As for myself, I will go back to town. Lord Bulstrode's return is a certainty."

The experienced wirepuller was right. But for a time Mr. Wilkes and his supporters, full of the energy and enthusiasm of youth, deceived themselves by the mere reflection of their own energy into believing that they had a chance of success. They had enthusiastic meetings everywhere. Lord Bulstrode hardly ever opened his mouth, and when he did, as one of his followers candidly admitted, "he always put his foot in it." The clergy, with two or three exceptions, canvassed their parishes ostensibly on behalf of the Welsh Church, but in reality in the interests of Lord Bulstrode. Of Mr. Faulmann nothing was heard or seen. Mr. Brassy laid low, feeling that he was in imminent danger of being crushed between the upper and the nether millstone; but what influence he could exert he used against Mr. Wilkes, and he gave his vote for Lord Bulstrode. When the polling day came Lord Bulstrode received 3,600 votes, while Mr. Wilkes had 1,300.

The election had been a long one, for the contest had not taken place until six weeks after the death of Lord Bladud. After hearing the declaration, Wilkes, weary and worn under the blow of his crushing disappointment, retired to the "Boar's Head," excusing himself from his committee by saying that he wished to be alone for a little time. He entered his room, locked the door, flung himself on a couch, and was just giving way to a series of bitter self-reproaches, when there was a knock at the door. He jumped up in a moment and opened it.

"Did I not tell you that I wished to be alone!" he exclaimed, when he saw standing behind the apologetic waiter the figure of a young lady in deep mourning.

"She would not give her name," said the waiter, "but said that she must see you."

"May I not see you, Mr. Wilkes?" said the lady, in a voice which thrilled him like an electric shock.

"Certainly," he replied. "Waiter, it is all right."

The waiter, marvelling at this sudden change, closed the door, leaving Mr. Wilkes face to face with Lady Ænid. She threw back the veil with which she had concealed her identity. She was in deep mourning.

"Mr. Wilkes," she said, "I came to thank you for the gallant fight you made. You promised me you would not flinch, and nobly you have kept your word."

The candour with which the girl addressed him was as frankincense and myrrh to the wounded and mortified self-love of the defeated candidate.

"YES, MR. WILKES, YOU MAY!"

"It is very good of you to say so, he said. "I have often wondered if you ever thought of it all."

"I have been," said she, "through deep waters. My poor father was dead before I could reach home, and my mother, who was in weak health, never survived the shock of my father's death. Both my parents are dead," she said. "Knowing what the result would be, I hurried over to be with you at the declaration of the poll, and to assure you how grateful I feel for the splendid manner in which you have redeemed your pledge. Now it will not do for me to stay here any longer. Good-bye," she said, extending her hand.

He took it in both of his, but did not let it go.

"Lady Ænid, I cannot tell you all you have been to me during this struggle. Whenever I felt inclined to flinch, it was your example that steeled my resolution and carried me through the whole of this campaign. But," he added with a bitter smile, "it has all ended in nothing, as you see. A majority of over two thousand for Lord Bulstrode. How the enemy will jeer!"

"Nay," said Lady Ænid, "was it not better to have fought and lost, as you have done, than to have fought and won with Faulmann?"

"Forgive me, Lady Ænid," he said. "Do not go yet; as you have been my only inspiration, you are now the only consolation that I have. I cannot tell you what your words have been to me until this day. I was in the depths of despair when you entered, and now your friendship has given me a new hope, and even," he added, "an aspiration of which, if I might——" He hesitated.

Lady Ænid, who had never looked more charming in her life, laughed a merry little laugh. "Really, Mr. Wilkes, I must be going. I cannot stand here all day."

Then there came into his eyes a wondrous look of yearning tenderness and almost despair; and as she was leaving the room he cried after her, "Oh, Lady Ænid, may I not——"

And Lady Ænid, who was just closing the door, looked in for one moment, and with a twinkle in her roguish eyes, said demurely, "Yes, Mr. Wilkes, you may!"

She closed the door, and in another moment was gone.

PART II.—THE YELLOW MAN WITH THE WHITE MONEY.

CHAPTER I.
A SHOOTING PARTY IN THE HIGHLANDS.

"SO the Duke has really sold Chatsworth at last!" said Dick Milman to his companion, as the two threw themselves down on the heather to rest after having climbed a rugged brae.

"Yes," said his companion, Rawton Silvertongue, now somewhat older and greyer; "I heard the report at White's just as I was leaving London. It made a great sensation. Five years ago, when it was first talked about, every one said it was a bit of bluff, but it seems that he has really been and gone and done it, as the cockneys say."

"I wonder why?" said Milman. "He cannot be so hard up as that would imply."

"I don't know that," replied Silvertongue. "The Duke has been pretty hard hit lately. One of his watering-places on the south-east coast has been nearly empty for the last year or two, owing to an alarm—a false alarm, I believe—about the drains; and the manufacturing town in the north, on which he and his father had spent a little fortune, has turned out to be a white elephant. His Irish estates, too, have been a cause of endless trouble, and, on the whole, I am not surprised that he should have jumped at the offer."

"Who is the buyer?" asked Milman.

"Oh, heaven knows!" said Silvertongue; "and we shall too, I suppose, in time. At present, all that is known is that it has gone into the hands of the well-known wreckers who for some time past have been picking up all the valuable derelict mansions and bankrupt estates of our aristocracy. Quite a flourishing business they have at present—one of the few businesses which are flourishing nowadays. I remember," he continued meditatively, "when Christie's was the great resource of the impecunious peer. Their famous auction-rooms were a kind of aristocratic pawnshop, by which many a splendid pauper was kept on his legs. But Christie's business has been badly hit lately, as you might expect, from the working of that law which we have borrowed from Italy, forbidding owners of art treasures to sell them out of the country."

"Yes," said Milman, "and a pretty pass things have come to to require such a law. I know at this present moment a peer who sits shivering in the midst of half-a-dozen Raphaels which he is not allowed to sell, and which he cannot keep from mouldering on the walls from sheer lack of pence with which to buy the coals necessary to heat his castle."

"Well," said Silvertongue, "something had to be done; there was such a drain of curios to America and the colonies that it would not have been long before we should have been cleared out. It is owing to this law that our country places are still tolerably well furnished with articles of vertu."

"Yes," said Milman, "and what is the result of that? In place of Christie, who sold jewels, treasure, and curios retail by auction, we have got this firm of wreckers (an American and a German—'Glogoul and Faulmann'), who are doing so wholesale, not by auction, but by private treaty. Chatsworth is only their latest acquisition; there is not a property of historic interest or of residential value in the country that they have not offered to buy up. They pay good prices too. How they do it I don't understand."

"But I do," said Silvertongue. "'Glogoul and Faulmann' have branches all over the East. Glogoul lived somewhere in China and is in the confidence of the whole Hebrew tribe in Europe. They seem to have an unlimited supply of capital, and wherever there is an ancient castle, or modern treasure house, or stately palace, or charming estate in difficulties, anywhere in the three kingdoms, they are the first to hear of it, and it is very seldom it escapes their clutches."

"They are really," said Milman, laughing, "a kind of liquidators of the British aristocracy, the unofficial receivers of the estates of our ancient nobility. So the old order changeth, giving place to the new."

"Unfortunately," said Silvertongue, "it can hardly be added that 'God is fulfilling Himself in many ways.' It is playing the devil with the old social system, and I confess I don't like the outlook."

"Neither do I," said Milman; "but we had better be moving; we have a long way to go before dusk."

The two men rose to their feet and stood for some time admiring the scenery which stretched around. They were on the slopes of the hills overlooking Glen Affaric, in the Western Highlands. In all the Highlands there are few more romantic glens than that over which they were looking. The popularity of the Trossachs will never be impaired as long as "The Lady of the Lake" forms part of the favourite reading of the English-speaking world. But some day another poet may arise who will make Glen Affaric and Loch Duich as famous as the Wizard of the North made Loch Katrine and Ellen's Isle. Then it will only need the extension of the railway to Strathglas for the glens and lochs of Inverness to take their rightful place as the crowning glory of Scotch mountain scenery. After a long lingering glance over the valley they began with rapid steps to descend the mountain side.

They had not proceeded far when they were joined by an old Highlander, wearing the picturesque garb of his clan. He was evidently an acquaintance, for he gave them both friendly greeting, and the three proceeded down Glen Affaric towards Glen Cannich.

"We were talking," said Silvertongue, "of the way in which the old landed estates in England are being bought up by the Jews and Gentiles."

"Ay, ay," said the old Highlander, "the curse is coming your way now. It is no new thing with us; and maybe that now you see the misery and the curse of it at home, you will have more sympathy with the Gaels, who have suffered the same curse for more than a hundred years."

"Dash me!" said Silvertongue; "it never struck me before. But old Chisholm is right; the Highland lairds all went the way our peers are going. Here in this very district we are in the heart of what used to be Harmer's country."

"Harmer?" said Milman. "You mean the man of the flying-machine?"

"That very same," said Chisholm. "It was not so many years ago that over 400,000 acres of this mountain land, stretching from sea to sea, there was no lord, or monarch, or emperor who had more absolute power than this same gentleman of whom you speak. Never was there such a chase as that which lay under the shadow of his guns. Our poor penniless lairds were very glad to let the forests to him or to any other man who had the siller, and Harmer, they say, had enough to have rented the whole of the forest land in the Highlands, and still to have more money in the bank than he could count. At one time over these hills, from which all the children of the mist have been driven to make room for the stage, there roamed herds of deer which they counted not by the tens, or the hundreds, or by the thousands, but by the tens of thousands. Where the deer roam, no man must put his foot. What are the rights of man to live, compared with the lust of sportsmen to slay?"

"But he paid for it, I suppose," said Silvertongue, "and liberally? From all that I have heard, I believe that your

GLEN AFFARIC.

"THEN THESE STRATHS AND GLENS WERE PEOPLED WITH A BRAVE AND HARDY RACE."

Highland lairds taught Mr. Harmer that it was not only in Aberdeen where a Jew cannot make his living. A pretty penny he must have paid for lawyers' bills and costs; and all for what?"

"They do say," said Chisholm, "that first and last he must have dropped more than a quarter of a million of money in this country; and with all his drives, he never shot two hundred head of deer in any single year. His deer must have cost him about £100 a head—a deal of money for a stag!"

"Yes," said Silvertongue, "but it was his fancy, and if he once set his mind upon a thing he would get it if money could purchase it. He used to say that he had never met a woman whom he could not buy; and as it was with women, so it was with land or with any other mortal thing."

"Was he much of a stalker?" asked Milman.

"He a stalker!" replied Chisholm contemptuously. "Can an elephant stalk? He could no more stalk than the Prince of Wales—for the same reason. As the Prince had his drives in the Mar Forest, it was Harmer's ambition to do as his Royal Highness. That, they say, was at the bottom of all his work up in these parts. He used to say, 'The Prince has a drive once a year, but I shall have a forest big enough to have a drive as good as the Prince's every day in the season;' and so he did. The Prince, poor man, was not rich enough to afford such a luxury; and as it was with the Prince, so it seems to be with your nobles. They tried for a time to keep up with the rich bankers, and traders and millionaires from America, with the result than that one after another they have gone down like our Highland lairds, and the Lowlands will have to bear what the Highlands have borne —the curse of the coming of the plutocrat."

"Oh, come, come!" said Milman, "it's all very well to talk about him as being a curse, but he pays his way, and very liberally too."

"He has money enough," said old Chisholm, "and he is liberal with it, no doubt; but has not one of your own poets said—

Ill fares the land, to hastening ills a prey,
Where wealth accumulates, and men decay.

Time was when these straths and glens were peopled with a brave and hardy race; where are they now? Still you can mark the site of their little crofts on the hillsides by the superior verdure of the grass to which the deer come down in the winter time. Here and there you may see the ruins of their humble shielings and traces of their gardens. But the flowers of the forest are a' wae'd awa', and the brave men and fair women who for a thousand years peopled the glens have vanished like the mist of the morning."

The party now reached the "Strathfarrar Arms," where they halted for refreshment. After a brief rest they turned to the left, up the hill which leads to the road through Glen Cannich. On the hillside they met a gillie coming down, whom Chisholm accosted. "Have you English?" he asked.

"Yes," said the man, "but I prefer Gaelic."

While the two were talking the younger men pursued their journey. They admired the solitude and sombre magnificence of the silent waste. With the exception of the gillie's cottage, which they had just passed on their right, there was no sign of habitation visible. They pressed on until they came to where the stream running through the glen widened into a miniature lake, which lay like a mirror in the heart of the valley. It was difficult to realise that it was water, for the mountain on the further side was reflected in the tranquil depths with such verisimilitude that the reality could hardly have been more vivid. They sat down by the roadside to enjoy the spectacle until such time as old Chisholm should overtake them. In a few minutes he came striding along.

"Oh," said he, "you are looking at the eye of the glen, and you do well! Isn't it a pity, now, that a place so beautiful should have been given over to the wilderness? Time was when in this solitary glen there were no fewer than forty-five families living, and living comfortably, where that gillie alone is left. Thirty-three farmers there were in easy circumstances, and twelve cottage families besides. It was a Catholic glen when there was any one in it, and at one time there were as many as nine priests in the Catholic Church who were reared and educated in the glen. Now the deer come down in the winter time to nibble the grass around the deserted crofts. I can remember the time," continued the old man, as they resumed their walk up the glen, "when there were no fewer than twenty-six Glen Cannich men holding commissions in her Majesty's army. I sometimes wonder whether, if the war clouds gathered round the cliffs of Albion, and her enemies were to encompass her around, it may not come to pass that Britain may look and long for her Highlandmen, and look and long in vain. The recruiting sergeant would find small business in Glen Cannich to-day," said he, with a bitter smile, "unless he could enlist red deer and corby crows as soldiers."

"It is astonishing," remarked Milman, "how you come across traces of these Highland officers all over the Empire."

"There would have been no Empire," said Chisholm proudly, "without the Highlandmen. A man from this glen died as Governor of the Gold Coast in Africa, and half-a-dozen Macraes and Chisholms died in Gambia and Sierra Leone, the white man's grave. One died at Quatre Bras in the last days of the great Napoleon. Very few have laid their bones to rest among their native hills. These glens are rough and rude, and the Highlanders were not brought up on feather beds or with silver spoons in their mouths; but you will search in vain the crowded slums of your teeming cities for as stalwart a breed, and one as ready to maintain the honour of their country and the safety of their fatherland."

The friends were silent for a time, brooding over the memories which the old man's narrative had awakened.

"And now," said Milman, "to whom does it belong?"

"The forest," replied Chisholm, "is divided. There is no longer any lord among the deer like Harmer, although he still keeps a trifle of 50,000 or 60,000 acres as a kind of preserve for the deer on the western coast, but he shoots no more here, and the deer are free to live and breed as they please. A couple of rich brewers take a large handful of the land between them, a Jew baron has just taken 100,000 acres of forest on the east, and an American millionaire is building a shooting-box a little further to the north. They are only here for a few weeks in the year; for the rest of the time the land is given up to the wilderness and the deer, with a few idle keepers and gillies sauntering about to see that no child of man sets his foot where red deer roam. And if I may ask you," said old Chisholm, looking up suddenly, "where may you be going this afternoon?"

"Oh, we are going through the glen," said Milman. "We are going to Westlands Castle, but it will take us all our time, for it is some miles from here."

"It may be," said he, "they will be sending horses for you. And so you are going to Westlands? Then maybe you know the fair leddy who brought Westlands as her dower to her husband—Lady Muriel Eastland that was."

"Oh, yes," said Silvertongue. "I knew her before she was married."

"Lady Muriel," said Chisholm, "has a sweet face and a good heart, and who knows but through her the curse may pass that has hung for four generations over her family."

"Nousense!" said Milman. "You don't mean to say that the Eastland family is under a curse?"

"Oh, I suppose you are like the rest of this sceptical generation; but we of the older race, who were cradled among the glens and learned our creed among the mountains, know that many things of which you in the Lowlands make light, and even deny, do exist. But ever since the fatal day when, more than a hundred years since, the then Duke of Eastland made the clearance in Western Inverness, which to this day glows like burning fire in the memory of every Highlandman, there has been a curse on that family. As in the days of the exodus, when Pharaoh would not let his people go, the firstborn was slain, so it is to-day. No Duke of Eastland has ever been succeeded by his firstborn for a hundred years. Heaven forbid," said the old man devoutly, "that I, a sinful man, should speak lightly concerning the workings of God's providence; but he would be worse than a heathen and an infidel who could not see the awful workings of Divine justice. When the Duke contemplated the clearance by which he made a wilderness of this country, he began by inducing the firstborn to enlist in the king's service; and he promised them, if they would go with their claymores and their muskets to fight the battles of the king, their families should aye remain in secure possession of their little crofts. But no sooner did these brave lads march off, with the bagpipes playing and their eyes filled with tears for the dear ones they left behind them—no sooner were they scattered far and wide over many a distant land, than the Duke forswore his solemn word, and turned the grayhaired grandsire and the widowed mother and the helpless child out of their homes, and drove them aboard the ships which carried them, the exiles of despair, far across the sea to Canada and Australia. From that time to this the curse has never left the family of the Eastlands, and never will until there shall arise in Eastland Castle someone who will put the people back upon the land from which they were driven, and once more reclaim those glens from the sheep and the deer, and gladden the sight of the wayfarer with the blue peat reek rising from the crofter's cottage."

"Really," said Silvertongue, "have the firstborn always died for a century?"

"No Duke of Eastland has ever been succeeded by his firstborn for a century," said Chisholm; "but it may be that Lady Muriel, bless her bonny face, may break the evil spell. I am a man of peace," said the old Highlander thoughtfully; "all war seems to me murder, but for us in the Highlands there is such a thing as the curse of peace. In the olden times, when clan was making war against clan, and when every Highland chief for safety, as well as for honour and glory, was bound to rear as many fighting men as the land could raise, there was no fear of depopulation. War peopled these glens and kept them full of a sturdy breed; but when peace came, and the claymore was put into its sheath, and men cared more for the yellow gold than they did for their fellow man, then the curse fell upon the land, and it was discovered that the land which could rear and feed soldiers could not provide sufficient food for cultivators. Then the clearances came, and whole glens were made desolate, and one shepherd tended sheep where a dozen farmsteads had found room enough and to spare. Then the sheep made way for the deer. It is as the prophet saw it in other lands: 'the cormorant and the bittern possess it; the owl also, and the raven dwell in it; and He has stretched out upon it a line of confusion and the stones of emptiness. They call the nobles thereof to the kingdom, but none are there, and all her princes are nothing. And thorns come up in her palaces, nettles and brambles in the fortresses thereof; and it is an habitation of dragons and a court for owls. The wild beasts of the desert meet with the wild beasts of the island, and the screech owl also rests there and finds for herself a place of rest. There the vultures are gathered, every one with his mate.'"

Chisholm stopped abruptly. "And as it has been with us," he said, "it will be with you. Of the curse which has eaten into this land you also are to have your share."

CHAPTER II.
MESSRS. GLOGOUL AND FAULMANN.

IN a luxuriously-furnished suite of apartments in Pall Mall we have the well arranged firm of Messrs. Glogoul and Faulmann, wreckers, as they describe themselves, of the social system. It was in accordance with Glogoul's cynical humour that he chose this term. In reality, he used to say, "We ought to be called salvors. We did not wreck the system. It was a crazy old craft, and nothing could have saved it from the breakers to which it had drifted."

Certainly the firm of Glogoul and Faulmann had done nothing to bring it there. All that they did was to endeavour to save as much out of the wreck as they could, and to this laudable purpose they were devoting the whole of their united wits.

Dr. Glogoul had aged somewhat since we left him as *locum tenens* of the medical adviser at the hospital in Garlam. He had carried out his intention, and had made his way to China very shortly after the outbreak of the war between China and Japan. He had not been three days at Shanghai when he met an old college chum, who introduced him to a young Chinese Mandarin of great repute and of immense wealth, who was believed to be the coming man under a new *régime*.

Ping Yang Yaloo—for that was the name of the high functionary to whom Glogoul was introduced—was a man after Glogoul's own heart. No man could be more destitute of those disagreeable impediments which people who are still in their mythologies are fond of labelling moral scruples. Ping Yang Yaloo was a Materialist of the most uncompromising type. It did not even occur to him that right and wrong, immortality and duty, were other than mere phrases as meaningless as the names of the gods of ancient Greece. They were pretty playthings, invented by Western knaves for the purpose of cheating Western fools. He was not a pure-bred Chinaman, but there was a strain in him of a Portuguese half-caste, who had been the concubine of his grandfather during his sojourn in Macao. His eyes were not quite so oblique as the pure-bred Mongolian, and the European strain in his blood allowed him to assimilate Western ideas with greater facility than would otherwise have been possible.

Such a man Dr. Glogoul was delighted to recognise as the type for which he had been seeking. Ping Yang Yaloo was equally pleased with Glogoul, although, being a man of few words, he contented himself with appointing the American specialist as medical director of the cotton factories which he was then beginning to build. Ping Yang Yaloo's authority at Court was considerable, but it was nothing compared with the absolute power he possessed as proprietor and millionaire in the province in which he lived. Ping Yang Yaloo's word was law. Whom he would he slew, and whom he would he saved alive. In the two years during which Glogoul served the Mandarin as medical inspector, he treated the whole of the unfortunates of the province as raw material for his pathological experiments. On only one occasion had he any trouble with his master. After a considerable number of experiments, conducted with inexhaustible patience, Glogoul succeeded in identifying the bacillus of cholera, and then introduced it into the well from which the village of Cheekin drew its water supply. The result was an epidemic of cholera, which carried off about one-third of the population. Glogoul was in ecstasies; but when Ping Yang Yaloo found that his rents had fallen off by one-third, he gave orders for the instant decapitation of the doctor. Fortunately for Glogoul, his college chum, who

PING YANG YALOO.

was acting as private secretary to Ping Yang Yaloo, explained that difficulties might result if Glogoul were beheaded, and he further pointed out the immense advantage that would accrue to Ping Yang Yaloo in the future, now that he had a physician sufficiently skilful to poison a whole village without incurring any responsibility. Ping Yang Yaloo was mollified, recalled his order, but intimated to Glogoul that experiments of such a wholesale nature had better be conducted on neighbouring estates, not on those which paid him rent. Glogoul took the hint, and there was no further hitch.

He succeeded in discovering methods by which the bacilli, not only of cholera, but of many other deadly diseases, could be preserved in ice for an indefinite period, and when thawed out show no loss of vitality. It was therefore perfectly easy for him to introduce an epidemic wherever the population became too dense, or wherever it was necessary to diminish the over-pressure of the beds in any public hospital.

His zeal, however, for pathological research somewhat cooled, and after a time he began to think that the Western specialists, whom he had previously held in such sovereign contempt because they had forsaken research for money-making, were, after all, wiser than their own generation.

"Pathology," he said to his friend one day, "is all very well, but there's no money in it. I have arrived at a perfect knowledge of the way to poison human beings in twenty different methods, without any risk of detection; but, thanks to the stupid prejudices of mankind, what use can I make of this knowledge? There is no millionaire or philanthropist, as far as I have seen, sufficiently emancipated from prejudice to pay me millions for producing an epidemic in some great over-crowded city, although it may be demonstrated that such an epidemic would contribute more to human progress and social welfare than any other means devisable by man."

"Well," said his friend, "if poisoning bodies does not pay, poisoning minds is profitable. When I left England, the only investment that paid 70 per cent. was the Empire Theatre, which made its dividend by providing a prostitutes' promenade and drinking-bar; but a flinty-hearted County Council refused its license, so that avenue of money-making is closed. But what do you say to the Stock Exchange?"

"I never was a gambler," said Glogoul. "Besides, I should like to utilise the aptitude I have obtained by my study of human criminology in whatever profession I take up. The dream of my life is to invent a new drink that would be pleasanter to taste than champagne, but would intoxicate as rapidly as brandy, and would be as fatal as opium. If I could discover that nectar of the gods, and could hold it to the parched lips of poor, hard-driven humanity, I should become as rich as a brewer, and, at the same time, enjoy the exquisite satisfaction of knowing, as I watched the increase in the death-rate, that I was appreciably diminishing the sum total of human misery."

"Get out with you!" said his companion. "Precious little you care about the misery of the world, and although cant may answer on the small scale, there is not enough money in it to make it worth your while taking it up at your age."

Ping Yang Yaloo's factories, meanwhile, were growing apace. He had all the latest machinery brought from England and America. He had almost at his back door a great mountain of coal that simply required quarrying. A whole province in the south was planted with cotton, under the supervision of the ablest experts that could be procured in the Southern States; and Glogoul could see plainly that with the continued fall in the value of silver, and the enormous advantages in the shape of inexhaustible and costless fuel, of soil almost virgin for the production of cotton, and labour which could be had at a penny per day, Ping Yang Yaloo was destined to become the great cotton producer of the world. As he watched the factories going up, one after the other, and observed the finished product which issued from the mills at prices far lower than that at which it could be shipped for export from Manchester or Liverpool, Glogoul saw daylight.

Shanghai would burst up Lancashire. Ping Yang Yaloo would be the cotton king of the world. In five years, Chinese cottons would dominate the English market in the same way that Indian wheat rules the price of corn in the English market. Lancashire mills would become as profitless as Essex clay lands.

"The Yellow Man with the White Money," said Glogoul to his friend, "is the coming king. The White Man with the Yellow Money cannot stand against him for a moment. Asia is going to be avenged on Europe. Already the Indian Ryot is avenging the conquest of India by compelling his conquerors to starve for want of employment in what used to be the granary of England; and to-morrow it will be the turn of our pig-tailed friends. What with opium wars and the like, we have a tolerably long score to wipe off before their account is cleared. As India has ruined Essex, Shanghai will crack up Lancashire, and when Lancashire is burst up, the industrial supremacy of England vanishes. Henceforth, that tight little island will have to reconcile itself as best it can to its altered destinies. Its Imperial strength depends upon its economic position. On the day that Ping Yang Yaloo undersells Manchester, and undersells her in the neutral market, the British Empire will have gone up the spout. It is all as plain as the nose upon your face, and there will be the greatest scramble the world has ever seen for the assets of John Bull and Co., who will have to go into liquidation."

"Well," said his friend, "what are you going to do about it?"

"Have you not read," said Dr. Glogoul mockingly, "where the carcase is there the eagles are gathered together?"

"I should have thought," said his friend, "the text would have suited you better had it said vultures."

"The translation may be wrong. Anyhow, I think I see my way."

The next mail brought him a letter which convinced him that he was right. It was from his old acquaintance, Faulmann, of the Patent White Lead Works. Faulmann had been much impressed with Glogoul's smartness, with the quickness of his perception, and his absolute lack of scruple. When, therefore, the scandalous Turkish monopoly was cancelled, and the Patent White Lead Company closed its works, Mr. Faulmann found himself with ample capital at his disposal, and without any opportunity, calling or profession in which to utilise his restless energies. His observations in Blankshire had convinced him that the landed interest was practically on the verge of liquidation. What with mortgages, settlements, encumbrances of all kinds, it was impossible with wheat at 16s. a quarter, and tending downwards, for the landed aristocracy to keep their heads above water. The wreck of the whole system was only a question of a very few years.

At the same time, the astute Faulmann was not blind to the immense residential advantages of these immense estates which were certain to be thrown on the market. The idea struck him that if he could find a partner it would be possible for them to form a salvage syndicate for the purpose of buying up all the possessions of the landed interest as they came upon the market. Faulmann had extensive connections on the Continent and in the Republic among rich Jew financiers, who regarded this country as a new and better Land of Canaan, owing to the absence of any social prejudices and the justice of our laws. But Faulmann was quite cute enough to see that the money power of the future was to be found, not in the West, but in the East, where China and Japan, at a bound, had reached a leading position among the great powers, and were competing keenly on equal terms in the markets of the world. India had long commanded the wheat market, and her producers were already beginning to make their influence felt in America and Europe. The African trade Bombay had almost entirely annexed, but the great power of the future was China, with its vast and undeveloped resources. This great colossus had been rudely awakened from the sleep of ages by the thunder-hammer of war, and the millionaire of the future, in Faulmann's opinion, was much more likely to be found on the banks of the Yellow River than by the side of the Hudson, or on the shores of Lake Michigan.

"Nothing can stand against us," said he, "as long as silver stands at its present ratio to gold. The Yellow man with his depreciated silver will beat the White man with his appreciated gold clean out of the field. If, therefore, I have to undertake the liquidation of the landed interest, I must have, as a partner, some one who knows the Yellow World."

Suddenly he remembered his old acquaintance, Glogoul. Glogoul had gone to China. Glogoul, he had reason to know from occasional items in the papers, had found a domicile in the country of the greatest of all Mandarins of the new school. Glogoul, then, was the very man he wanted.

It was Faulmann's fashion to lose no time when he had made up his mind, and the very next mail carried out to Glogoul a long letter, setting forth the financial advantages which lay within the grasp of a syndicate which was placed *à cheval* of the two continents, in touch with the moneyed Semites of Europe, and the coming millionaires of China, India and Japan.

When Glogoul got the letter he read it through, and then went down to his friend.

"Thompson," he said, "you do not believe in Providence any more than I do; but, if we were still in our mythologies, what would you say to that as a Providential sign-post?"

Thompson read the letter carefully, glanced at the signature, and handed it back to Glogoul.

"Smart fellow that," said he.

"Yes," said Glogoul. "Got a telegram form?"

His friend handed him a blank cablegram, which Glogoul filled in.

"What are you saying?"

Glogoul read out—"Accept. Leave next mail."

And thus it came to pass that the great firm of Glogoul and Faulmann was established, and, as might be expected, considering the character of the partners, it flourished exceedingly. A very lucky deal with two or three heavily encumbered estates, which were desired by a certain baron of the Bourse with whom Faulmann had dealings in old time, enabled them to start in business, with a prestige, and a capital which they very soon multiplied many times. To them the impecunious noble and heavily mortgaged landlord went as their only hope. The "Splendid Paupers" cursed them in their hearts as a couple of villains, but were compelled to admit that no native firm would pay them anything like the price that they could get from Glogoul and Faulmann. They did business with high and low, rich and poor, and it was a standing joke of Faulmann's that he would never be content until he had bought Sandringham. He had a friend in Constantinople, he said, an Armenian Pasha, who had taken a great fancy to the place, and as soon as His Royal Highness was ready to part, he had a purchaser ready. Indeed, it might be said that this was true concerning almost every country house in the kingdom. Famous old castles like Alnwick, lordly pleasure-houses like Dunrobin, romantic halls like Haddon, and famous historic palaces like Warwick Castle, were all marked in the record list. They had purchasers ready waiting for all those properties, and more besides. Famous picture galleries, libraries which had been accumulated by the patient labour and lavish expenditure of generations; priceless heirlooms, and all the innumerable treasures which wealthy nobles had been accumulating for centuries, were disposed of beforehand in anticipation. Hence, the moment it was announced that the Duke had sold Chatsworth, every one knew that the sale must have been effected through Glogoul and Faulmann.

And so it was; at this moment Messrs. Glogoul and Faulmann were the undisputed owners of Chatsworth Palace; and not of Chatsworth merely, but of all the Duke's estates in Derbyshire. Hardwicke Hall went with Chatsworth; of all the broad acres which the Duke owned in Derby there did not remain to him one, with the exception of the narrow plot which lay behind the church on the hill at Edensor where the Cavendishes lie buried.

CHAPTER III.

A DINNER-PARTY AT WESTLANDS CASTLE.

WESTLANDS CASTLE was always full of visitors in September. Sir Artegal Haddon and Lady Muriel—for Sir Artegal had married the only daughter of the Duke of Eastland, and by her had come into possession of the Highland property of Westlands—kept much company then. Westlands Castle was charmingly situated on the western coast of Inverness. At first sight the castle, with its quaint turrets and picturesque contour, suggested to the observer that Abbotsford had suddenly been caught up from the banks of the Tweed and set down perfect and complete on the edge of the Atlantic surge. A closer examination showed that Westlands had a beauty all its own, and an antiquity to boot to which Abbotsford could lay no claim. From of old the castle had been the central citadel of the feudal aristocracy in northern Scotland.

The traditions of the aristocracy, of ancient nobles linked to the soil by the close ties of tradition and of service, had lingered longer in Westlands than elsewhere in the island. The laird and his lady were for all practical purposes the king and the queen of the district in which they resided. For generation after generation the Highlander tending his sheep or tilling his little croft in the west could see no personage on the horizon that loomed more largely than the proprietor of Westlands. Although of late years the spirit of unrest and of revolt had spread among the crofters in the district, and they had signified their independence by returning a candidate of their own in opposition to a scion of the noble house, there was nevertheless deep in the hearts of the people a conviction that in times of stress, or when duty called, or danger there was no living man around whom they would rally with such confidence as the heir to the traditions and the glories of Westlands.

Sir Artegal Haddon, who by marriage had entered into the circle of this curious survival of mediævalism, preserved beneath a somewhat cynical demeanour a keen susceptibility to all that was romantic and glorious in the associations which surrounded his new position. Although Conservative and aristocratic by lineage and conviction, he had a perfectly open mind. To him all governments were more or less a *pis aller*—necessary evils of which the wise man would make the best. There was a certain dash of the Prince of Denmark in his character, but only a dash, for nothing was further from his resolute and chivalrous character than the habitual indecision of Hamlet. If we must look for his prototype in the fields of poetic romance, we shall find the original rather in the splendid picture which Spenser has given of Sir Artegal, the Knight of Justice, in the deathless pages of the "Faerie Queen." There was a frank simplicity about his noble nature which endeared him to his friends, and even his political opponents admitted grudgingly that, although he was horribly mistaken in all his political opinions, they always knew where to find Sir Artegal, and that his devotion to the public welfare was never affected by a single thought of his own personal interest.

In Lady Muriel Sir Artegal had found a partner well fitted to supplement his character and to redress the balance which in his own case was somewhat overweighted by a philosophic scepticism. Lady Muriel was young, beautiful and enthusiastic. Although born in the south country, she was always in sympathy a daughter of the Highlands. Just as Lady

Aberdeen, transplanted to Ireland, became more Irish than the Irish, so Lady Muriel, transplanted from Blankshire to Inverness, became more Gaelic than the Gaels.

She was young, but frail, for her physique was the very antithesis of the *flamboyant* vigour and rude health of her friend Lady Ænid, whose marriage with Mr. Edmund Wilkes had taken place in 1896. Born to great possessions, she exercised her queenly prerogatives with the unconsciousness of nature. Not a cotter in all her broad domains was less affected than she, nor did any one make friends or acquaintances feel more instantly at their ease than the chatelaine of Westlands. Although barely out of her teens, she discharged all the delicate and arduous duties as head of the numerous household which, with guests, servants and retainers, seldom fell short of a hundred persons, with a skill and an absence of strain which is the crowning distinction of the experienced matron. The wheels of all the business of the castle ran exceedingly smoothly, and an atmosphere brooded over the place, pervading its almost regal hospitality with a sense of simple comfort often lacking in such establishments.

Of all her innumerable guests there were few whom she did not make to feel that their coming was a separate and distinct pleasure to herself; and within a narrow circle, mostly among the young men who were coming on, she exercised a subtle influence of inspiration which to many of them was almost as a spell from another world. But it was in her county, among the clansmen and crofters whose ancestors had formerly followed the Dukes of Eastland to battle, that she appeared at her best.

Half unconsciously, led by a divine instinct, she set herself to realise the prayer of the Nazarene for His disciples that they might have life, and have it more abundantly, for the humble and industrious population which lived in frugal independence on the Westland hills. To vary the monotony of their existence, to increase their material resources, and to give them a fresh interest in life, she founded the Rural Industries Society, which brought her into close and human relationship with almost every crofter and crofter's wife in the county. She sympathised with their aspirations, and was the common nerve centre through which they all communicated with each other and learned to understand that they all were members one of another. It was with Westlands under Lady Muriel as it was in the Vision of Sir Launfal :—

The castle gate stands open now,
And the wanderer is welcome to the Hall.
* * * *
The meanest serf on Sir Launfal's land
Has hall and bower at his command :
And there's no poor man in the North Countree
But is lord of the earldom as much as he.

LADY MURIEL, SEEING HIM ENTER, AT ONCE CAME FORWARD.

On the night on which Silvertongue and Milman arrived at the castle after their long walk, there was a miscellaneous assemblage of guests, chiefly young people, whose talk was of stags and of the delights of outdoor life. At first, Lady Muriel had been somewhat pained by the continual talk about stags killed; but she had overcome that pardonable weakness of human nature, and listened with the apparent ardour of a schoolgirl to the thousandfold variant of how some noble stag was brought down by the bullet of his pursuer. Yet sometimes a far-away, wistful, yearning look would creep over her features, until, as one of her enthusiastic admirers declared, you could see an angel look out from her lambent eyes. Sir Artegal was a deer-stalker with the best of them, and it cost him no effort to keep up his interest in the conversation.

A Dinner Party at Westlands Castle.

Sterling, who was one of the party, had never fired a gun in his life, and found some difficulty in concealing the fact that the continual talk of slaughter bored him. He remarked on the opposite side of the table a lady of great vivacity and of striking features, whose high spirits and pleasant chatter seemed to diffuse an atmosphere round her end of the table which did not derive all its glow from the zest of the chase. When dinner was over, and the ladies had retired, Sterling took an early opportunity of leaving the table, where the conversation was now almost entirely devoted to deer, in order to follow the ladies. Lady Muriel, seeing him enter, at once came forward.

"Oh, Mr. Sterling, I wish particularly to introduce you to Madame Olga. To tell you the simple truth," added Lady Muriel in an aside, "I do not think I could have prevailed upon her to come so far north excepting to see you. She is political to her finger-tips, and when she heard you were coming she put off all other engagements."

"I shall be delighted," said Sterling. "In fact, I came in purposely to ask you this favour."

In a few minutes Sterling and Madame Olga were merrily chatting as if they had known each other from childhood. They had so many friends in common that it was a marvel that they had never met before.

"I really believe," she said, "that you must purposely have kept out of my way."

"Surely you do not think that I could be so foolish?"

"I don't know," she said archly. "Sometimes there is a greater compliment in avoiding than in seeking acquaintance. I know one of your Ministers who for years made it quite a duty to avoid meeting me. He seemed to find out by some kind of instinct whenever I was invited to a dinner-party he was asked to attend, for of course I was as anxious to meet him as he was to avoid meeting me. But, invariably, just before the dinner-party assembled, our host received a letter from the Minister saying that owing to the serious indisposition of his wife the dear man was regretfully obliged to ask to be excused."

"Wives are convenient sometimes," said Sterling.

"Yes," said Madame Olga, "especially when they recover as rapidly as they fall ill. But tell me, is it true that you are at last being devoured by the Jews? They have eaten up Austria entirely; there is not a morsel left. France is almost as bad, and in Germany they are in vain endeavouring to stem the tide. Now I hear that your country is disappearing down the voracious throat of the insatiable Semite."

"I don't know," said Sterling; "we are passing under the *régime* of the plutocrat, but all plutocrats are not Jews."

"No, indeed," said Lady Muriel; "have you heard the story about Chatsworth?"

"What," said Madame Olga, "that splendid palace in Derbyshire? It has not gone to the Jews, has it?"

"No," said Lady Muriel, "worse than that."

"That cannot be," said Madame Olga.

"What would you say to a Chinaman?"

"What, a yellow man with a pigtail! Well, come, that is rather worse. The Jew at least is a Theist, whereas your picturesque barbarian from China—well, what has he to do with Chatsworth?"

"I have just had a letter from my cousin the Duchess, who tells me that a horrible rumour is circulating to the effect that Chatsworth, which as you know was some time ago bought by Glogoul and Faulmann, the estate agents, has been sold by them to a Chinese Mandarin of immense wealth."

"With half-a-dozen wives, I suppose," said a lively young lady, who evidently found ten hours' salmon fishing in a mountain stream insufficient to exhaust her nervous energy.

"As for polygamy," said the Russian disdainfully, "that is a mere phrase. But a Chinese Mandarin as the lord of Chatsworth!—that will produce some interesting complications indeed. I declare," she added briskly, "it is a new argument in support of my favourite theme, the Anglo-Russian alliance. Ever since the Japanese took Korea——"

"And you the province of Manchuria?"

"Oh, well, never mind," she said; "but ever since that time it has seemed to me that the Chinese factor constituted a new and powerful argument in favour of the Anglo-Russian alliance. They will eat us up, these barbarians, unless we stand together. United, we conquer; divided, we fall. It is a good maxim, is it not?. And now that the Celestial has encamped himself in the very centre of England, the truth will begin to come home to you. Do you not think so?" she asked.

"I don't know," said Sterling gloomily; "it is an ugly development."

"But why," said the Russian, "why should the Duke have sold a palace which is not only an heirloom but a museum of heirlooms?"

"The Duke has been very badly hit of late. Ever since the new death duties were imposed in 1894 they seem to have preyed upon his mind, and the bad times through which we are passing seem to have convinced him that in justice to his heir he must rid himself of cucumbrances."

"We are talking about the sale of Chatsworth," said Lady Muriel to her husband, who now joined the party.

"Oh, yes," said he, "that is bad indeed. Have you heard who the purchaser is?"

"My cousin wrote and told me," said Lady Muriel, "that it was a Mandarin of some outlandish name—Ping Yang Yaloo, I think."

"Not the great Mandarin who has broken Laucashire?"

"I think so," said Lady Muriel. "Yes," she added, producing the letter, "Ping Yang Yaloo. But do you know anything about him?" she said, looking anxiously from her husband to Sterling.

"Oh, yes, he is the greatest millionaire in the world. Neither the Rothschilds nor the Vanderbilts can compare with him. He is the modern colossus of finance."

"And he has bought Chatsworth?" said Sir Artegal.

"Such is the report in London," said Muriel; "it has produced quite a sensation."

"Naturally," said Sir Artegal. "I wonder how our constitution will stand the strain of such a new element?"

"But," persisted Madame Olga, "why should the Duke sell Chatsworth, of all places in the world? It is good land close to great populations. If there was any land worth keeping, I should have thought that this was."

"No," said Sterling, "you don't know what Chatsworth means. Of course Ping Yang Yaloo will make it worth his while, for he will run Chatsworth on commercial principles, as he runs his cotton-mills, working his operatives eighteen hours a day, and feeding them upon a handful of rice. But Chatsworth has been a white elephant to the Duke."

"But how? I do not understand."

"I will tell you a story," said Sterling. "Some years ago an American and a Sheffield Radical were discussing the infamies of our present social system. They were abusing the landed interest, and the American, by way of giving point to his arguments, said, 'For instance, there is the Duke at Chatsworth; what an outrage for one man to own so many acres!' 'Stop! stop!' said the Radical;

F

'you mustn't meddle with him. That is another matter; the Duke keeps Chatsworth up for us.'"

"What do you mean by that?" asked Madame Olga.

"Simply this, that the general public has much more use out of Chatsworth than the nominal owner. Some time ago I was over in Derbyshire, and made some inquiries as to how things actually stood. I found that about fifty thousand people were yearly admitted to the house and grounds at Chatsworth. The total rent of the Chatsworth estate was £12,000 a year, and the outlay for keeping up the house and the general management of the estate was no less than £21,000. That is to say, Chatsworth at that moment represented an annual loss to the Duke of £9,000 a year."

Madame Olga shrugged her pretty shoulders. "A loss of £9,000 a year; that would be interest on half a million of roubles."

"Does your cousin say," asked Sir Artegal, "how much l ing Yang has paid for Chatsworth?"

"The actual sum is not known," said Muriel, "but it is supposed to be not less than a million."

"What madness!—a million sterling for property which yields £9,000 a year less than nothing!"

"Yes," said Sterling; "but you must remember that the new owner is not likely to maintain Chatsworth for the benefit of the public. He is not likely to be better in this respect than Mr. Walledoff showed himself to be in Berkshire."

"Oh, by-the-bye," said Wilkes, who had hitherto been silent, "that reminds me. Have you heard what Walledoff proposes to do?"

"No," said every one.

"He has bought up all the land on the other side of the Thames for about five miles—in fact, all the land which marches with Windsor Forest, and he declares that he will turn the whole country into a deer park. He cannot bear to see so much smoke from his windows, and tenant farmers, cottagers, and villa residents alike have received notice to quit."

"Upon my word," said Milman, "that Walledoff is a veritable William the Conqueror."

"Yes, and we unfortunate wretches," said Sterling, "are very much like the Saxons after the battle of Hastings, without even having had a fair stand-up fight for our Fatherland."

"Why are you so grave?" said Mr. Wilkes, as he noticed a cloud on Lady Muriel's brow.

They turned away from the group which had gathered round Madame Olga, and retired to a recess.

"I don't know," she replied; "it seems to me very cruel, this incoming of the money power. I suppose it is a vengeance for our sins. We have allowed the people to be divorced both from the soil and from their natural leaders, and now both are powerless before the money power. But bad as things are, men of our order have no reason to make them worse. I cannot understand great nobles degrading themselves to the level of hucksters, and selling their heirlooms to any pigtailed barbarian or American millionaire who may offer them a sufficiently splendid bribe."

"The principle of noblesse oblige will not carry too much strain," Wilkes said lightly, "and here is a great temptation to realise on part sufficient to save the rest. By-the-bye, have I ever told you what we have done on our estate at Six Elms?"

"No," said Lady Muriel, "I have often wondered how you reconcile——" She stopped with some embarrassment.

"You mean," he said, "how I reconcile my Socialistic convictions with my new position. I did not find it difficult at all; on the contrary, a landed proprietor in our day has better means of realising Socialistic ideas than any one I know. Ænid is enthusiastically at one with me in this, and we have every reason to be pleased with the success which has so far attended our efforts."

"Do tell me what you have done," said Lady Muriel.

"As you know, my father died very shortly after my marriage, and I was left with a very handsome fortune in the funds. The Six Elms estates, although yielding a net loss, were nevertheless comparatively unencumbered. As soon as we settled down we decided to see what could be done towards converting our tenantry into virtual proprietors, while at the same time we retained the advantages of the old system."

"That," said Lady Muriel, "is what we are all trying to do; but to eat your cake and have it is not even vouchsafed to the gods."

"I think we have done it," said Wilkes. "It is very simple. Our land is fortunately suitable for small holdings. They had been there in old times, but had been consolidated into large farms, and had mostly been thrown upon our hands, and were being worked by our bailiffs at an annual loss. We decided to cut them up into small holdings wherever the land was suitable for the purpose, and they were let to investors on the following terms:—We followed the American and colonial example in allowing the principle of free selection, subject to our veto. The land was let out in plots, varying from three to twenty acres. These were put up to public tender, giving preference to reputable men who lived on the estate. It was a condition of every such tender that the tenant must put up farm buildings and a house of a certain standard, the capital being advanced by rue for that purpose at five per cent. interest. If these buildings are not put up in twelve months the lot becomes vacant, and is again put up to public tender. Every tenant after having erected his buildings is given his lease, which practically gives him perpetual tenure of the land, subject to certain stipulations. The lots have to be kept up to a certain standard of cultivation. The leases run in terms of ten years, but are to be renewed, as a matter of course, unless there has been failure to comply with the conditions. Holdings are not to be mortgaged, nor are they to be used for harbouring poachers or bad characters, or for the sale of drink. Subject to these conditions, each of our tenants has an indefeasible title to his holding, without any fear of being disturbed."

"But," said Lady Muriel, sceptically, "did you find anybody to take your holdings on those terms?"

"Our only difficulty was the number of the applicants; and many of the tenders offered rents which we did not think that the land could bear, and which we refused to take."

"How did you provide for fluctuations?"

"Oh, it was stipulated that at the end of every year the rent should be re-arranged, in accordance with the average selling price of the articles produced on the estate. If the prices went up, the rents should go up pro rata, and if they fell, they should also fall pro rata."

"Supposing a peasant wished to leave, could he sell his lease?"

"In case of a change of tenure, the present proprietor could sell his interest in the land to any eligible successor to whom the lease would be transferred by the landlord on similar terms; but we reserve a veto on the incoming tenant. I must not omit to tell you, however, the chief feature of the new settlement. We calculated what the value of the land was at the highest honest estimate that could be put upon it when we succeeded to the estate. It was very low, for the land was not merely unletable, but entailed an annual expenditure in order to keep it from deteriorating into waste land. We had it carefully valued by three different valuers, and agreed to accept the mean between the three as the actual value of the land at the moment when it came into our hands. To these we added the total sum advanced for putting up farm buildings, lumping the two together. For the sum advanced for buildings the tenants pay us five per cent., of which at least one per cent. is spent in keeping the buildings in repair. That leaves us four per cent. If you take the value of a holding at £100, and the buildings upon it at £200, we receive on an average £7 10s. rent. this makes the total charge on a ten acre plot £17 10s. £2 10s. is spent on repairs, leaving us £15 a year. Now, we calculated that we could borrow £300 at three per cent. This leaves us £6 a year margin to be used as a sinking fund in paying off the capital. By this means we consider that we shall have realised the whole of our capital, both for rent and for improvements, in twenty years. At the end of that time it is arranged, instead of transferring the freehold of the land and the improvements to the tenants, that they shall continue to pay the £17 10s. as at present; but the whole of the money will be paid over to the Belsover Trust, which will consist of one person named by the landlord, one by the tenants, and another chosen by the other two. This trust will then take our place, and will be responsible for seeing that the conditions of the lease are maintained, and that the annual charge is readjusted every year, according to the rise and fall of agricultural produce, and that the revenue should be available for the common interests of the estate, such as the maintaining of pedigree stock, providing capital for creameries, co-operative estates, land banks, agricultural schools, etc., etc. In short, we hold that it is possible by such an arrangement to bind together the peasants on an estate in a self-protecting co-operative association that would have all the benefits of socialism and all the advantages of feudalism. The scheme has only been three years in active operation, but so far as we have gone we have been perfectly satisfied, and it has worked admirably. It is certainly better than the alternative scheme in Ireland, where the land remains in the hands of the present peasant proprietor, who mortgages it as far as he can and provides no common fund for the development and improvement of the estate."

The merry laugh of Madame Olga interrupted the conversation. It was getting late, and they rose to join the group of which she was the animated centre.

"Oh, your schemes, Mr. Wilkes, are very good—very good, and no doubt they will make some improvement; but if you think they are going to banish sin and misery from this planet, you forget one reason why it was created."

"And what may that be?" inquired Sir Artegal.

"It is a kind of penal settlement for the punishment of erring spirits who, in some other existence, have deserved being condemned to a life here; and if you make this world too comfortable you will simply shift the penal settlement to another planet."

"What a gruesome idea," said a young lady; "why, if that really

"THE DEVIL!" CRIED DR. GLOGOUL.

be so this world would certainly be a hell."

"No, not hell; purgatory," said Madame Olga.

CHAPTER IV.

A POLITICAL PLOT.

"THE Devil!" cried Dr. Glogoul, with a long whistle, as he threw a letter which he had just received from Shanghai over to his partner, Mr. Faulmann. Faulmann seized the epistle and began to read. Whatever its contents were, he was evidently intensely interested, for frequent exclamations broke from him as he turned over the closely written pages. When at last he came to the end, he laid it down on the table, and gazed into space.

"Devil it is," said he at last, "and no mistake! Who could have dreamed of that?"

"Oh, he has a level head!" said Glogoul—"a level head. I back him against any dozen. It is all as plain as a pike-staff. What fools we were not to see it!"

"Yes," said his partner enthusiastically. "He has got a head worth our two put together, and that is saying a good deal. How much is it that he intends to bring over?"

"Ten million pounds sterling," said Glogoul; "and that is a mere fractional part of the enormous wealth that he can realise when he pleases."

"Now," said Faulmann, "I begin to see why he bought Chatsworth. I could not understand him; neither did you, I think, Glogoul, exactly understand what motive this Chinaman could have in buying up the Duke's palace in Derbyshire. Now I understand—at last I begin to understand—

For ways that are dark and for tricks that are vain,
The Heathen Chinee is peculiar.

But how will this stand in with our business?"

"Why," said Glogoul, "it stands in this way, that we are absolved, and engulfed. Henceforth we are only a department of Ping Yang Yaloo's business. Instead of carrying on on our own account, we shall be his factotums. You will be his Prime Minister; I will be his Chief-of-Staff—but we must have a political adviser."

"Is it necessary?" said Faulmann.

"Absolutely necessary," said Glogoul. "I know all about pathology, especially the criminal side of it. You know all about finance; neither of us knows a cent's-worth of politics, and this scheme of Ping Yang Yaloo's carries us into politics at once."

"You are right," said Faulmann. "And I know the man."

"You do?" said Glogoul. "I hope you are right, because it may spoil everything if we choose the wrong man. Remember, first and foremost, can we trust him?"

"Yes,—if you pay him high enough."

"Ah, if money will do it. Money is not everything."

"Money is *not* everything. You sometimes have to pay in money; sometimes in power."

"Well, money and power; that is only two ways of spelling the same thing."

"What kind of power does he want?" asked Glogoul.

"He wants to be Prime Minister," said Faulmann.

Glogoul whistled. "It is rather a tall order."

"No doubt," said Faulmann cynically. "I do not think we need make him Prime Minister. We have only to talk to him and fool him to the top of his bent. We promise nothing. That is always safe."

"I agree," said Glogoul. "There is no dupe like the man who dupes himself. But who is this paragon of yours?"

"He is Sir Peter Patterson."

"Of course," said Glogoul. "How dull I am to-day, not to have thought of him at once! He is the very man."

"Yes," said Faulmann. "He is ambitious, but he is déclassé—a disappointed, disgraced politician. But he is smart; he used to know everybody. He has no character and an immense memory, and is the greatest coward that walks in shoe-leather."

"Humph!" said Glogoul. "That is true; but do you think that such an abject coward would be a desirable member of our team?"

"Why," said Faulmann, with a sneer, "that is his most valuable quality. You can intimidate a coward, especially when you have incriminated him. What we want is not a man, but a tool, and a better tool I defy you to find in all England."

"I daresay you are right," said Glogoul; "but the work in hand will require nerve."

"Of which we have plenty," said Faulmann. "We do not need to tell him more than what we choose."

"And that at present is very little," said Glogoul.

"Quite so. All that we need is to flatter his vanity and engage his sympathetic interest; the rest will follow in due course."

Whereupon each went his way to carry out the orders received from Ping Yang Yaloo. The letter which had unfolded such vistas of fortune before the eyes of the partners was written by Glogoul's friend, the great Mandarin's secretary. Its substance, in brief, was this. That Ping Yang Yaloo had already made a fortune of about £100,000,000 sterling, but it depended chiefly, if not entirely, upon two things. One was that silver should continue at its present depreciated value, and the second that he should be able to hold his own in the victory which he had gained over the looms of Lancashire. These were his two vulnerable points. In order to cover them, it was necessary for him to operate in England; and, as usual with Ping Yang Yaloo when any operation of great difficulty and delicacy had to be performed, he insisted upon being on the spot, and seeing after everything with his own eyes, for a long experience had taught him that no eye sees so clearly as your own eye.

He had therefore decided to take up his abode in England, in order that he might be in a position to use some portion of his enormous wealth in keeping up the price of gold, and in handicapping his Lancashire compatriots. For some time he had shrunk from the ordeal of taking up his abode in England, a country which he regarded as a barbarous land in the midst of turbulent seas, cursed with an atmosphere of fog and a temperature that was almost intolerable. Ping Yang Yaloo came from a semi-tropical climate in Southern China, and never wintered so far North as Shanghai. He had too much at stake, however, to be able to stand upon such trivialities as personal inconvenience, and when it was represented to him that money could create a little China in the heart of the British Islands, he made up his mind.

A telegram to Glogoul secured the purchase of Chatsworth. Formal instructions were at once drawn up to Glogoul and Faulmann to create around the palace a region in which the Mandarin could find nothing to remind him that he was living outside the Yellow kingdom.

To carry out his schemes it was obviously necessary, as Glogoul said, to enter into politics. It was necessary for them to master all the intricacies of local administration in order to take the utmost advantage of every privilege which the law gives to property owners. The first indispensable desideratum was the conversion of the Chatsworth property into a miniature China; but when Ping Yang Yaloo was domiciled in Chinafied Chatsworth he would not have secured his *pied-à-terre*. He would only be in a position to begin his great campaign, and at every step it would be necessary to exercise political influence, and to bring pressure to bear upon Governments and upon Parliaments. In order to do this, Glogoul and Faulmann felt instinctively that they were useless without an ally, and that ally, both agreed, must be none other than Sir Peter Patterson.

That night the two partners discussed at length how much it was necessary to tell Sir Peter of the scheme which had been unfolded to them. As yet they themselves had but an inkling of the great Mandarin's scheme. They could not approach Sir Peter without telling him something; but how much or how little to tell him, that was the question. Fortunately for them, Sir Peter Patterson was an enthusiastic monometallist, and it could not be difficult for them to approach him on that side. It was agreed that Faulmann, being the financier, should seek an interview with Sir Peter at his house in Kensington early the following morning, and sound him as to how far they could rely upon his co-operation.

Next morning, Mr. Faulmann was ushered into the study of Sir Peter. The latter received him with that half-brusque, half-hesitating manner which always gave those who saw him the first time an impression that he was receiving a possible blackmailer, and was never at his ease until he had divined the stranger's business.

Mr. Faulmann went straight to the point.

"Sir Peter," he said, "I have been reading with great admiration your last article in the *Nineteenth Century* upon 'The Idiocy of Bimetallism.' I am with you there, but I would not have come to tell you so if it had not been that a friend of mine, very extensively engaged in business, is anxious to co-operate with the English monometallists, in order to beat the attack which is being made upon their position by the United States of America. When I laid down your article, I said to myself, 'Sir Peter is the very man for my friend.'"

Sir Peter fidgeted rather uneasily in his chair, and said, "You are very flattering, but I do not exactly understand in what way I can co-operate with the friend of whom you speak."

"But you are already co-operating with him," said Mr. Faulmann, with a bland smile. "Your article indeed is one of the best methods of co-operation, however unintentional it may have been on your part. But I have nothing to conceal, and no object in making a mystery. I represent one whose name is familiar to you, but of the full scope of whose enterprise and ambition you are perhaps but dimly conscious. I refer to Ping Yang Yaloo, the Chinese millionaire."

"Oh!" said Sir Peter. "Of course, I have heard of Ping Yang Yaloo, the great Mandarin, whose cottons are at the present moment underselling those of Lancashire in the markets of London."

"That is my friend," said Faulmann. "Now, as you are well aware, the present ratio between silver and gold is one of the factors—only one, of course, but an important factor —in the problem which has enabled my Chinese friend to be a Napoleon of Asiatic finance. He may be wrong, or he may be right, but he has come to the conclusion that cheap silver is important to him, and any approach to remonetisation of the white metal in this country he regards as being detrimental to his interest, as you demonstrate in that article it would be to the best interests of Great Britain."

"Certainly," said Sir Peter. "I do not know how it affects Ping Yang Yaloo—that is his business; but as a compatriot, and as a British statesman" (Mr. Faulmann noticed the emphasis which Sir Peter placed on that word, and inwardly smiled), "I am certain that bimetallism is one of the most fatal crazes that ever gained possession of the public mind."

"Precisely," said Mr. Faulmann; "but although Mr. Balfour has, in his academic fashion, coquetted with this question, where is the statesman who will come forward boldly as an advocate of universal monometallism? If such a statesman there were, what an opening would lie before him!"

"Yes," said Sir Peter, "no doubt there would; but as for me, I have long since forsworn ambition. My only dream is to leave an unsullied name to my heirs, and those who will come after me."

"Ah," said Mr. Faulmann, "that is very noble, but it is not business, and you will excuse me, Sir Peter, for my time is precious, as I have no doubt yours is also. I came here to see a statesman, whom all we Radicals at one time hoped to see Prime Minister to the Queen, if, indeed, you had not converted this monarchy into a more rational Republic."

Sir Peter winced a little.

"But," added Mr. Faulmann, "if you have forsworn yourself, and have no longer a political ambition, I must go elsewhere for my man."

"Stay!" said Sir Peter. "It is true I have no longer any personal ambition—mark you, I said personal—but a mission to serve my country, even it may be in the arduous foretop of the Vessel of State; to that last infirmity of noble minds I am afraid I must still plead guilty. But what you say of your Chinese friend interests me hugely, and I am not sure but that you are right. It would be a great combination —a great combination. I suppose money would be no object?"

"Not the least in the world," said Mr. Faulmann; "and with money you can do anything in politics."

"Pray sit down, Mr. Faulmann. Sit down for a moment, and we will just consider what can be done."

"No," said Mr. Faulmann. "It must be enough for me to put the idea before you. I have implicit confidence in your honour. Your word is as good as your bond. I have only to ask you to treat this conversation as confidential."

"Certainly," said Sir Peter. "Not a word shall pass my lips; but if you will come again to-morrow I will think it over carefully and let you know in what way, in my judgment, your friend's object can best be obtained."

No sooner had Mr. Faulmann gone than Sir Peter summoned his wife. "My dear, sit down. You have so much clearer a head than I, and, besides, you really take an interest in this political game, which, I confess, rather bores me. I want your advice."

"Oh, Peter, Peter," said she playfully, "why do you endeavour to deceive even me? You can keep your hand in without practising on your wife!"

"Well, well," said he, "never mind that; let me explain what has happened. That fellow who has just gone out—a stranger to me—he came with a proposal which, if it be genuine, and he can produce credentials in support of it, will practically place the ball at our feet."

Lady Dorothy sighed. "I am afraid you are always too sanguine, Peter."

"Well, never mind," said he; "listen to what I have to tell you. Ping Yang Yaloo, the greatest millionaire in the world, is anxious to prevent any action in this country that may tend to raise the value of silver. As you know, I regard any interference on the part of Governments in the course of exchange as a pestilential heresy. This man Faulmann has seen my article in the *Nineteenth Century*, which he says agrees on all fours with his Chinese friend's position. He wants some one in this country who will work the oracle, not for him, but against the bimetallists, and the position is mine to take or to refuse. What do you say?"

"Bimetallism bores me," said her ladyship, with a yawn. "I could never understand any currency questions."

"But you have a precious keen scent for currency," he said, with a smile, "and I tell you, dear, there are millions in it."

"What!" she said, "millions?"

"Millions," he repeated slowly.

There was no longer any indifference on Lady Dorothy's part. "You mean to say, Peter, that you and I will have millions to dispose of, literally millions, as if they were our own?"

"Well," said he, "I will not say that; but so long as we could make our own policy coincide with the Mandarin's monometallism——"

Lady Dorothy sprang to her feet and took two or three quick turns about the room, the fingers of her clenched hand working convulsively.

"At last!" she said. "Peter, I shall see you Prime Minister some day." And crossing the room, she flung her arms round his neck and kissed him ardently upon the lips.

Sir Peter bore it as one who was used to it, and then said, "But how?—that is the question."

"Surely it does not need much discussion? We have many a time talked it over, and we have always had to abandon our scheme, because we did not see our way to the necessary cash."

"Well," said he; "go on."

"You know, about four years ago we had it all out, and if we had had £100,000 to spare in ready money, we could have upset the Government easily. I fancy that to-day, if we had £50,000, we could turn the Government out."

"Yes," said he, impatiently. "But what good would that do? To put out the Government whom you can bully, because it rests upon the support of a congeries of mutually warring factions, is possible; but if the only result of that is to put in a Government which you cannot influence, it seems to me very much like jumping from the frying-pan into the fire."

She looked grave for a moment, and then said, "Yes, it requires only a little money to upset a Liberal Government, but it would require a deal of money to break up the Conservative party."

"Therein," said Sir Peter, "has been our difficulty, and I am not sure whether this millionaire will be willing to incur the necessary expenditure."

"But even with half a million we could hold the life of the present Ministry in the hollow of our hands," added Lady Dorothy.

Sir Peter tossed his head impatiently. "Half a million!" he said. "I would ensure a dissolution in a fortnight if I had the free use of fifty thousand pounds!"

CHAPTER V.
BIMETALLISM IN EXCELSIS.

RAWTON SILVERTONGUE had spoken little in the drawing-room at Westlands on the previous evening, but he had thought the more. He was a man who did not care much for shooting; he had seen too much of it. When a man has shot tigers in the jungles of India, and stalked the great elk in the Rocky Mountains, he is apt to look with indifference upon the exploits of Nimrods who have never brought down anything more dangerous than a red deer. At dinner-time he had been seated in the midst of a group of young sportsmen, and his attention had been attracted by Madame Olga at the other end of the table, as a light in a cottage window attracts the belated traveller.

His attention was first excited by her star sapphire earrings, which shone like veritable stars in the electric light. When he learned who it was, he was naturally anxious to make her acquaintance. For the last twenty years she had been one of the best known and most liked of the international women of the Continent. Her mother had been one of the beauties of the Russian Court, and her father a patriot, whose lofty idealism puts that of Western Europe into the shade. Her brother's heroic and almost martyr death on an Eastern battlefield, when the issues of peace and war were trembling in the balance, decided the case in favour of the emancipation of the East. She herself was not unworthy such parentage and kinship, and during the Russo-Turkish War, when the London mob, possessed by the passions of all the nether fiends, smashed Mr. Gladstone's windows, and proclaimed with volleys of rotten eggs and dead cats their devotion to the Turkish alliance, Madame Olga held the fort on behalf of the liberties of the East and a good understanding between England and Russia. She was the only human being who had an audience in both countries, writing in two languages but speaking only one, and that was peace. More influential than many an ambassador, she was one of the few human links which united the great inarticulate mass of Slavdom with the more feverish and material civilisation of the Western World. Whether she was discussing theology with Dr. Döllinger, or politics with Mr. Gladstone, or history with Mr. Carlyle and Mr. Froude, she was equally vivacious and equally at home, and always intensely human. No one was less of a blue stocking, although she wrote in three languages and talked in four.

It was therefore not surprising that Silvertongue should have taken an early opportunity of sounding her upon the all-important subject of bimetallism. The Fates were propitious, and early next morning, when the sportsmen were off to the hills, Silvertongue found Madame Olga sitting on a garden chair reading the *Westminster Gazette*.

"Oh, it is you, Mr. Silvertongue!" she exclaimed; "pray sit down and tell me more about what we were talking of last night."

"Nothing would give me greater pleasure," said he, truthfully enough, for when once Silvertongue got loose on the currency question he would go on to the day of judgment. He plunged at once *in medias res*.

"The relation between the two precious metals——"

Madame Olga gave a little gesture of despair. "Ah, Mr. Silvertongue, it was not about that which I wished you to talk, but about the way the Jews and Chinese are eating up your country."

Silvertongue was for an instant disconcerted, but in a moment he saw his advantage and said, "But that is entirely a question of the currency. The ascendency of the plutocracy at the present moment is entirely due to the vital mistake by which silver was demonetised and gold made the single standard of value. Restore silver to its proper position of a circulating medium and gold will drop, and the usurers of the world who have the unfortunate people by the throat, will find their true level.

"For instance," continued he eagerly, "there are the national debts of the world. The interest upon these debts to-day, owing to the appreciation of gold, or, what is the same thing, the fall in prices, requires just twice as much human labour to pay them as used to suffice for that purpose. For example, you hold £1,000 in Consols."

"Alas!" said Madame Olga deprecatingly, "I only wish I did."

"But we will suppose you do," said he, waiving aside the objection. "For the taxpayer to pay you £30 interest on your £1,000 it is necessary for him to produce just twice as much wheat as would have sufficed for him to discharge his obligations a quarter of a century ago. That is to say, the burden upon the individual has just doubled, and the plutocrat, the creditor-class, profits, while the debtor suffers. That is the secret of the adversities which are coming upon this and other countries."

"But is it not a good thing for the people that food should be cheap?" asked Madame Olga.

"What is the good of having things cheap if you have no money to pay for them? And it is not worth while producing things if you get no money for them in the market. Take, for instance, wheat at 18s. a quarter; why, it costs nearly twice as much to produce it in the American farm. This kind of thing cannot last. The effect of it is simply this—to throw the monetary ascendency of the world into the hands of Asiatics. The question of the white money against the yellow money is really a question of the white man against the yellow man. Owing to the absurd devotion of the White man to the yellow money, the Yellow man with his white money is carrying all before him. That is the secret of Ping Yang Yaloo's immense fortune. Anything that brought silver back to its right relation to gold would send Ping Yang Yaloo higher than a kite. They are beginning to see this in America; but here every one is blind — excepting a very few independent statesmen. They are all bound hand and foot by old traditions and the authority of half a dozen men in the City who were reared upon text-books which were beginning to be antiquated when you and I were born."

"Then you hate gold?" said the Russian. "Now, my only complaint with it is that I have never been able to get enough of it. That is my currency grievance. It circulates too quickly—it always circulates away from me. At every turn you see people who need it more than you, and you give it away or lend it, which is really the same thing. If you could get a circulating medium which would stick to one's fingers and stay in one's purse, instead of gliding away imperceptibly, there would be something in it. But your currency question, I don't understand that."

"Ah," said Silvertongue, with a sigh, "it is as plain as A B C. I cannot understand how any one can fail to see it. But the difficulty is being solved, believe me, and that not by Governments, but by Nature. Prices have fallen because there is too little gold; prices will go up when there is more gold brought to the Mint. Gold mines richer than the fabled mines of Potosi are being opened out every day. Look at Coolgardie!"

"Where is Coolgardie?"

"Coolgardie is the gold-field which was opened up some few years ago in Western Australia, where there is more gold than water, and where out of a single shaft they have taken four hundred tons of quartz that has yielded an average of £300 sterling for every ton. Look at the Transvaal. Twelve years ago it yielded next to nothing; to-day it is yielding more gold than either the United States or Australia. Madagascar is coming——"

"Yes," interrupted Madame Olga, "and Siberia. Since Captain Wiggins opened up the passage to the Yenesei and enabled us to take crushing machinery, you will find that Siberia will be one of the greatest gold-producing countries in the world."

"No doubt," said Silvertongue. "From north and south and east and west, gold comes pouring in; but all these will do less than a little machine which I shall be delighted to show you at work on Lady Muriel's grounds."

"Really!" said Madame Olga; "what is this wonderful machine?"

"Ah! you laugh," said Silvertongue; "but it is the latest and most perfect method of extracting gold from the hardest ore that the world has ever seen."

She shook her head. "I hear that of some new machine every six months."

"No doubt," said Silvertongue. "But this is the machine."

"They all say that."

"Yes, but come and see it for yourself. The difficulty which has prevented the world from having as much gold as it needed was the impossibility of profitably extracting gold from refractory ores. It has been impossible to get anything like all the gold from the ore. All our stamping and crushing machinery has hitherto failed to extract more than a mere fraction of the gold which has been brought to bank. Now we shall be able to get 90 per cent. of the gold from the quartz which is brought up from the mine."

"No," said Madame. "I have heard this thing too often. I do not believe in your machine."

"Well," said Silvertongue despairingly, "if I make up a party to the gold mines in the Gorm Glen, will you join it?"

"With pleasure," said Madame Olga, "and all the more readily for I am sure of receiving the blessing promised in the beatitudes—'Blessed are they who expect nothing, for they will not be disappointed.'"

After dinner Mr. Silvertongue escorted a small party down a long and romantic ravine to the place where the much-talked-of gold mines of Lady Muriel were situated. The machine was at work. It was not very important looking, but as Silvertongue said, we must not forget that the invention of a pair of parallel bars revolutionised the transport of the world, and therefore his machine was not to be despised because it seemed insignificant.

"Ah," said Wilkes, who was one of the party, "this is the Comford Mill, is it not?"

"Yes," said Silvertongue, "you have seen it, then?"

"Yes, I have seen it at work. It is a wonderful mill. But it was very imperfect when I saw it last."

"It has been remodelled, and is now almost perfection," said Silvertongue enthusiastically. "This mill weighs little more than four tons, and crushes over ten tons of quartz in twenty-four hours. It reduces the quartz to so fine a dust that you would be able to pass it through a cambric handkerchief. It is an arrangement of steel balls which grind the quartz into a powder as fine as flour. There is the machine for opening up Siberia," said he, turning to Madame Olga. "You send that machine up the Yenesei by Captain Wiggins. It can be taken to any part of the country, and will turn out gold with the regularity of a clock."

"I suppose," said Wilkes, "the real advantage of this machine is that it pays to extract gold from ore which all other existing machinery would not do?"

"That is it exactly," said Silvertongue. "The Comford Mill is destined to put millions of money into the pockets of investors, who at the present moment are clinging to shares in gold-mines which have been abandoned because they would not pay for working. In another five years gold will be as much a glut in the market as silver. All prices will be turned topsy-turvy, and the ascendency of the Yellow man with the white money will be at an end. I am a white man," said Silvertongue pleasantly, "and I have a preference for men of my own colour."

While the others were gossiping round the mill, a messenger came up with a telegram for Mr. Wilkes. It was from his agent, informing him that Belsover Castle in Derbyshire, the ancient seat of his wife's family, was for sale, that Glogoul and Faulmann were in negotiation, and that it was necessary for him to return at once. He sighed, and handed the telegram to Silvertongue.

"Another turn of the screw!" remarked Silvertongue, after reading it. "What are you going to do?"

"Buy it," said Wilkes laconically, "and keep these scoundrels out, even if I have to sell the Hall."

"Lady Ænid?" queried Silvertongue.

"Is absolutely at one with me in this. The time is coming when all the solvent members of our noble families will have to make common cause against the plutocrat. They have got Chatsworth and Hardwicke, but they shall never have Belsover if I can help it."

When they returned to Westlands they found Lady Muriel in deep conversation with Sir Artegal. They also had had a telegram. Haddon Hall was in the market. Glogoul and Faulmann had made a bid which was so high that Sir Artegal feared it would be impossible for any one to outbid them.

Silvertongue drew Lady Muriel aside.

"Have you seen what the mill has been doing lately?" he asked.

"No," she replied.

"Believe me you have got a fortune in that gold-mine. If it keeps up at the present rate it will produce you gold at the rate of £100 a day. The profit on that gold-mine will help you to bear the cost of saving Haddon Hall. What do you think?"

"I think it is worth risking," she said. "I cannot bear to think of Haddon Hall, that flower of English history and romance, falling into the hands of a Mongolian. You had better tell Sir Artegal what you have told me. He knows more about the mine than I do."

The result of that conversation was that in five minutes telegrams were despatched from Westlands, the effect of which was that almost for the first time since they had commenced operations Messrs. Glogoul and Faulmann failed to secure the bargain on which they had set their minds.

And thus it came to pass that the ancient keep of Belsover passed once more into the hands of the descendants of its original possessors, while Haddon Hall became the property of Sir Artegal and Lady Muriel.

CHAPTER VI.

THE WILES OF LADY DOROTHY.

THAT night Glogoul and Faulmann were again in deep consultation. They had in the meantime received a cipher dispatch from Shanghai, which had caused them to open their eyes wider than ever. This dispatch, giving the latest order from Ping Yang Yaloo, intimated that it was necessary to control both Houses of Parliament, and to dictate the course of the Government upon the currency question; that, to do this, they were to spare no expense—even £10,000,000, as he stood to lose twice that amount if silver rose in value, or if the Lancashire competition could not be kept within bounds.

Faulmann rehearsed his conversation with Sir Peter Patterson, and asked Glogoul to accompany him the next day.

"No," said Glogoul; "like all guilty men, he is shy of every fresh face. It is only your honest men who are really trustful. Suspicion is the most obvious of all the signs of guilt."

"Well," said Faulmann, "but how much could we tell him?"

"Oh," said he, "we had better tell him the least that we could possibly get him for, as we shall have to spend a great deal of money ourselves."

"Quite so," said Glogoul.

"But have you thought out any plan of campaign?"

"Yes," said Glogoul. "I see my way pretty clearly just now. You say Ping Yang Yaloo must control both Houses of Parliament. Now the House of Commons is comparatively easy. Parties are pretty evenly balanced, and the number of venal members will increase with every election. With much less than a million we could buy up sufficient patriots, both Irish and English, not excluding Scotch and Welsh, who would vote to order; *i.e.*, we could cut the throat of the Ministry when we pleased. But that is not enough. Our Mandarin is after some other game—wants to control, not merely the House of Commons and the Government, but the House of Lords. How can that be done?"

"Blessed if I know," said Faulmann; "these fellows have no constituencies."

Glogoul contemplated him for a moment with a look of compassionate contempt. "No, they have no constituencies; but, what is much more serious for them, they have not got any cash, and as you said at the time when you and I first met, 'They are a race of Splendid Paupers,' living outside of their means with very few exceptions, and if a millionaire cannot keep up his own pack of paupers, use them as he pleases, and take them to market when necessary, then I'm a Dutchman, that's all."

"You are not a Dutchman," said Faulmann. "I wish you were, for then you would come to the point more directly. How in the name of fortune are we to control the peers?"

"Why, Faulmann," said Glogoul, "what have we been doing these last two years? Are we not engaged in the wrecking, or rather, in the salvage of the estates of the British aristocracy? Do you know we have had wonderful luck, although we started with quite a small capital? But just imagine what we could do if we had £10,000,000 at our back."

Faulmann's eyes sparkled.

"Glogoul, how was it you were not born a son of Israel? I see it all now."

Without another word they separated and went to bed. The next morning Faulmann presented himself before Sir Peter.

They were apparently alone, but Lady Dorothy was snugly ensconced in the interior of an old clock-case, from which she could see the visitor, and hear everything that was said.

"Now," said Faulmann, "I need not say that I hope you have not breathed a word of the conversation that passed between us yesterday to any living soul."

"Not a word has passed my lips," said Sir Peter, with emphasis. "On my honour, I have never breathed it to a human being."

"How well he does lie!" thought Lady Dorothy, in the clock-case. "But long practice, I suppose, has made him perfect."

"Have you any fresh news?" said Sir Peter.

"Yes," said Mr. Faulmann; "very serious cablegram arrived yesterday, after I left you."

Sir Peter's countenance fell.

Faulmann noticed this with a surprised chuckle, but went on—"The enterprise upon which my friend the Mandarin was engaged is even more arduous than I anticipated yesterday. He wants not only to control the House of Commons and the Government, but also the House of Lords."

"Pshaw!" said Sir Peter; "that is only his ignorance. You cannot expect a Chinaman to know that the House of Lords counts for nothing nowadays."

Faulmann smiled a little, and said, "The man who thinks that Ping Yang Yaloo does not know anything, usually wakes up some fine day to find himself mistaken.

THE WILES OF LADY DOROTHY.

If he wants to control the House of Lords, he has a reason for it; but that is not the matter upon which we wish to consult you. We have other plans in that direction for which co-operation is not necessary. What we look to you for is the control of the House of Commons."

"Well," said Sir Peter, "I have thought it over very carefully, but everything will depend upon the amount of money that can be placed at my disposal. For instance, I could purchase sufficient to place the Government in a minority upon any division that was not absolutely vital for —oh, quite a trifle—say, £25,000, but that is not what he wishes."

"By no means; that is no use at all, and £25,000 is a mere bagatelle—is not worth while talking about. What we wish to do is to have a permanent silver brigade in the House of Commons, which will defeat any Government that yields even a hair-breadth to the demand, no matter by whom it is backed, for a move in the direction of remonetising silver."

"Humph!" said Sir Peter. "I am afraid that will be difficult. You cannot buy the Irish in that fashion. You can buy a few by retail, but wholesale—no!"

"Besides," said Faulmann, "it will not be wise to rely upon the Irish alone. The Irish could be turned out of the House, and then where should we be?"

"You are quite right," said Sir Peter. "But how much do you think your Mandarin would be disposed to spend on the next general election, which we expect to take place next year?"

"It depends," said Faulmann cautiously. "If he could buy a working majority of the whole House, he would not shrink from half a million, or even more; but that is out of the question."

"Quite," said Sir Peter. "It is no use to discuss absurdities. What is necessary to be done is to keep the Liberals in office, but to keep the factions in power."

"Precisely," said Mr. Faulmann. "For instance, Mr. Balfour is coquetting dangerously with bimetallism, whereas the Liberals, so far as we can see, have no ideas at all on that question."

"But, at the same time, they must not be defeated," said Sir Peter; "and that means that, if possible, we should support a new group that would draw some support from the Conservatives, but above all injure and weaken the Liberals."

"Yes," said Mr. Faulmann. "But how can that be done?"

"Nothing can be done without money," said Sir Peter eagerly. "Have you ever heard of the Toilers' Industrial League?"

"Well," said Mr. Faulmann, "I know the Independent Labour Party."

"Yes, but that went up the spout long ago," said Sir Peter. "The Toilers' Industrial League, however, is the result of the seed which was sown by Keir Hardie and his colleagues."

"It has fallen into the hands of rogues," said Mr. Faulmann.

"Well," said Sir Peter, "we will put it mildly. Their personal ambitions seem predominant over other considerations, inducing them to forget the laws of arithmetic, to say nothing of the principle of the Ten Commandments."

"Well," said Mr. Faulmann, "we do not need to be too squeamish, you know, about instruments. They will do as well as any others."

"I think they will do better than others," said Sir Peter. "And I think if they were judiciously worked we could start candidates in some fifty or sixty constituencies, which would efficiently spoil all hope of a strong Liberal majority. Perhaps a dozen might get elected. We would pay their election expenses, and give those who are elected an allowance, which would, of course, be stopped the moment they voted on the wrong side."

"Well," said he, "that would be very well to begin with, but we ought to have a group of at least twenty-five, and that is a very small contribution to the necessary number."

"Oh, as for the others," said Sir Peter, "you can always find a dozen men out of seven hundred who can be got at. There are the guinea-pigs to begin with. They would much rather earn their £500 in a gentlemanly way by supporting a good Monometallist policy bound up in England's greatness than by giving their names to every swindle on the Stock Exchange. Then there are the Labour members. They are not more dishonest than any other members, but they are poorer, and where poverty is, there money has its power. Then you have the crofters, the Welsh members, and a contingency of the Irish. Ah, you need not be afraid! Give me money enough, and I will secure your group of twenty-five, who will hold the balance of power in their hands. But you have not yet told me how much you will be disposed to allow me?"

"Would a quarter of a million do?" said Faulmann tentatively.

Sir Peter's eyes glistened. "I think it might ——."

Inside the clock-case there was a perceptible movement. Faulmann started. "We are alone?" said he.

"Certainly," said Sir Peter.

"I heard a noise in that direction," pointing to the corner where the clock-case was.

"I suppose it was a mouse."

But Sir Peter took care to stand between the clock-case and his visitor.

"I think we understand each other," said Faulmann.

"Perfectly," said Sir Peter. "But you have not yet shown me your credentials."

"Ah, yes!" said Faulmann. "Here is a cablegram franked for Shanghai. Here is the message written out in accord with the cipher code. 'Can I trust Faulmann on your account for quarter of million?' Now, you send that cablegram, and before night you will have an affirmative reply. Will that satisfy you?"

"Certainly," said Sir Peter, as he accompanied Mr. Faulmann to the door.

When he returned to his room, he found his wife sitting at his desk. "Oh, you fool; you fool!" she cried.

"Well," said he, in an aggrieved tone, "what is the matter?"

"Why," said she, "I was so indignant that I very nearly forgot myself, and betrayed everything. Why did you not ask for half a million, when you were at it? You could have got it quite as easily as a quarter of a million. But it is just the way with you. You have no enterprise, no courage. I do not know what would become of you if it were not for me."

"Well, you would have made a pretty mess of it had you come out of the clock-case. As it was, you nearly spoiled everything."

"Fiddlesticks! I only made the faintest little sound in order to tell you to ask for more money. You are so dull, you cannot take a hint."

After which ebullition of natural indignation the worthy pair settled down to discuss their further plans. As the result, Lady Dorothy despatched a telegram to "Algernon Bradford, Toilers' Industrial League, Whitechapel. Lunch at 2.—DOROTHY."

Algernon Bradford was the honorary secretary of the Toilers' Industrial League, and the chief pet of Lady Dorothy. He was not much of a toiler, having been originally a member of the classes rather than of the masses.

His father had been a paymaster in the Royal Navy, and he had hoped to have seen his boy work his way in that profession; but money running short after he had begun his education, the boy had to be withdrawn from school, and apprenticed as a shop-lad in a drapery store. When eighteen or nineteen he had made the acquaintance of an actor; had fallen over head and heels in love with a ballet girl, and was convinced that his destiny in life was the stage. He had a somewhat pleasant appearance, a good head of hair, but there was a certain air of irresolution about him which rather detracted from his general appearance. He left his shop and joined a travelling company, which soon rubbed all the gilt off the gingerbread of the dramatic profession, but he remained sufficiently long on the boards to acquire some self-possession and a knowledge of one or two of the elementary laws governing the art of public speaking. He did not always stick his hands in his pockets when he stood before an audience, and he did not wrap up his voice in cotton-wool when he wanted the people to hear what he had to say. When the travelling company broke up he came back to town, and found himself more or less out at elbows. Posing on the strength of his dramatic experience, he took an active part in Saturday-night theatricals at certain East-end clubs, and when there, made the acquaintance of some of the tap-room politicians, who, finding that he had a good presence and a much better delivery than any one of their order, thought it well to push him forward a bit. He began to speak on Sundays in Victoria Park, and occasionally to put in a word of his own in discussions. His vanity and ambition, which had driven him to the stage, now impelled him to the wider theatre of politics. He took part in organising processions or an occasional great demonstration at Hyde Park, and at an election for the London County Council he was so active and so zealous that he was marked by the whips of the party as a likely man.

But Master Algernon's ambition soared far above that of being a mere political heeler. He aspired to be a politician on his own account, and hence, when the Independent Labour Party proclaimed that it was the sacred duty of Labour to revolt against both of the established parties, he eagerly threw in his lot with the I.L.P., and made ferocious speeches against the *bourgeoisie*, generally delivering capitalists and all their aiders and abettors to the infernal pit. As he had no ostensible means of living, the leaders of the I.L.P. looked rather askance at him, which led him, on more than one occasion, to express his doubts whether after all Keir Hardie was not as great a traitor as John Burns; and when the I.L.P. burst up in 1897 in an explosion of personal animosity between the leaders, Algernon was prompt to declare that he had seen it from the first, and that the principal thing to be done was to organise the Toilers' Industrial League, of which he himself would be secretary. As the League, at the moment of his appointment as secretary, consisted only of Algernon himself, no possible objection could be taken to this departure, and although afterwards the membership did not increase, the name of "Algernon Bradford, Secretary of the Toilers' Industrial League," figured at the foot of letters to the newspapers, and he was duly mentioned as being present at various meetings of a political and social nature, until it actually began to appear to others that the League had an existence.

At this stage, Lady Dorothy Patterson, ever on the look-out to gather any fish into her net, made some inquiries as to Algernon Bradford, and finding that he was a presentable young man, asked him to lunch, as she wished to take his opinion on the subject of the organisation of working women. Algernon was prodigiously flattered, but not a little embarrassed. He had not a suit of clothes which was not out at elbows; but the opportunity was too good to be lost, so he induced his room-mate to pawn his watch, and with the proceeds he hired a complete suit of clothes for the day only.

Very proud indeed was Algernon when he brushed his

"I SUPPOSE IT WAS A MOUSE."

hair and curled the ends of his moustache before starting on the eventful visit to Lady Dorothy.

She was alone, and apologised for the absence of Sir Peter, who had been called away upon a most important dramatic business. At that moment Sir Peter was lazily smoking a cigar in his back room, for it bored him to death to see all the cattle his wife persisted in cultivating.

The ups and downs in the young man's experience had not made him forget his manners, and Lady Dorothy was agreeably surprised to find that the Secretary of the Toilers' Industrial League was capable of talking intelligently, and behaving himself at table as if he had been accustomed to dine out. She made up to Algernon with even more than her usual effusion, and as for poor Algernon, well, he was only four-and-twenty, and Lady Dorothy represented to him all the unknown world of politics, culture, society and wealth, for which he had such longings, and from which he was so relentlessly shut out.

It was not surprising, therefore, that before the lunch was over he had become her devoted slave, while she felt she could count upon him for any services that she might need.

Sir Peter sneered; thought that her Algernon did not seem to him to amount to much, excepting as an additional charge upon what he called the Secret Service Fund, for Lady Dorothy soon found out the actual condition of Algernon's exchequer, and delicately furnished him with the actual money he needed to cut a presentable figure. Then she paid the expense of a hall, in which he summoned a meeting, and which she addressed, and from that moment the Toilers' Industrial League came to mean something more than its Honorary Secretary. Hence, it had already about a hundred members who subscribed a shilling a year, and boasted of branches in half a dozen towns; and Algernon indulged fond anticipations of the time when it would own a newspaper of its own.

It therefore need not be mentioned that Algernon tarried not when he received the telegram, but promptly appeared in his accustomed place at the table of his charmer. She began the subject delicately.

"Sir Peter," said she, "has every reason to believe that, in the next administration, he will be offered a high post, but of course it is out of the question to dream of serving under any one."

"Of course," said Algernon sheepishly. "Premiership, or nothing."

"Silly boy!" said she, looking at him, with a smile which would have been roguish if she had been twenty years younger; but even as it was it filled Bradford with delight.

"Well," said she, "you will be glad to know that the time is approaching when Sir Peter will be able to take his proper place before the country."

"Really," said Bradford. "Has that Will case then been——"

"Pshaw!" said Lady Dorothy, biting her lips, for she hated to be reminded of the one incident which had in a moment destroyed her husband's career, and blighted all the ambitions of a lifetime. "We never speak of that," said she reproachfully.

"I beg your pardon," said Bradford penitently; "what is it that you refer to?"

"It is this," said she, brightening up—"that he is going to support the Toilers' Industrial League as energetically as you and I have always wished he would. He hesitated for a long time, in order to see whether you were worthy of support, but your enthusiasm, your industry, your enterprise and your fidelity"—with a look from her blue eyes—"have so won him that he will support you—not publicly, of course; that would never do."

"Of course not!" said he.
"You know what I mean?"
Bradford's eyes sparkled. This was indeed good news.
"Yes," she said, "I thought you would be glad to hear it, but it will require very hard work on your part, my dear Algernon—Bradford, I mean."
"Oh, do not!" he said. "Please call me Algernon."
"Well, well," she said, accepting his hand, which he stretched out to her across the table, and giving it a delicate little squeeze. "Well, well, Algernon—be it so, if you like, but it will require very hard work."
"I will work," said her *protégé*, "I will work my fingers to the bone for Sir Peter."
"Or for Sir Peter's wife," thought the little woman, but she said nothing.
"Then," she continued, "how many candidates do you think the Toilers' Industrial League could put into the field?"

The question rather bothered Bradford. He had been counting up that day the members of the League who had sixpence in their pockets, which he thought of borrowing, but as he had come to the conclusion that there were only three who had it, he thought better of it.

So Algernon determined to put a bold face upon it, and said that they were prepared to start six candidates at a moment's notice.

"Six?" said she; "why, we want sixty!"
"Sixty!" gasped Algernon, "and we have only a hundred members of the League altogether!"

She appreciated the full his consternation, and went on quietly—"Yes, sixty candidates. Do you not think that they could be forthcoming?"

If she had asked for six hundred, Algernon, poor fool, would have made the same answer. Taking courage from despair, he said, "Certainly, certainly, Lady Dorothy; when do you want the list?"

"Well, not quite so fast," she said; "but I want to tell Sir Peter that, if he is able to guarantee the election expenses of a contest, and further, of a living wage—not more than a living wage—for the members who are elected, do you think you could get sixty?"

"Oh, easily," said he, with effusion—"easily!" and therein no doubt he spoke the truth.

"That will do," she said. "Sir Peter will be delighted. Of course, it must be a profound secret. Not one word as to where the money comes from, for Sir Peter always does good by stealth, and, in fact, I think the best plan would be for Sir Peter to have nothing to do with it at all but through me, and then it will be a personal obligation."

Algernon blushed to the roots of his hair, and kissing her hand with much greater effusion than if it had been the toe of St. Peter, he departed as if walking upon air.

Thus it was arranged that the Toilers' Industrial League was to cut a great figure in the coming General Election.

CHAPTER VII.
CHINAFYING CHATSWORTH.

HAVING left in the capable hands of Sir Peter Patterson the task of organising what may be described as the Gold Brigade in the House of Commons, Messrs. Glogoul and Faulmann were free to turn their attention to the duty of preparing Chatsworth for the residence of its future owner. Faulmann left this task chiefly to Glogoul, who had been in China and knew something of the tastes and life of the great Mandarin.

"The first thing to be done," said he when talking it over with Faulmann, "is to make Ping Yang Yaloo absolute lord and master of his own domain. We can have no trumpery vested interests standing in the way of his sovereign will and pleasure. I have a shrewd idea that we shall find the ground cumbered thick with all kinds of ancient privileges, traditional customs, and I know not what. It cost us a million to buy Chatsworth. I should not be surprised if it cost us another million before we had a free hand to deal with the estate as if it were our own property."

"Heaven forbid!" said Faulmann; "when the Duke sold, he sold everything he had to sell."

"Yes," said Glogoul, "but unless I am very much mistaken, there are no end of other interests in the Chatsworth estates which successive dukes have allowed to grow up, and it will cost us no end of trouble to get rid of them. There are rights of way, privileges of the public, etc., etc. However, I will go down and see just how things stand."

The result of Glogoul's visit to Chatsworth was, that he had considerably under-estimated rather than over-estimated the amount of money that would be needed to acquire the public rights existing on the Chatsworth estate and in its neighbourhood. In order to Chinafy the place it was necessary that the public should be excluded from the park, and as much of the neighbouring country added to the park as was possible. All access to the enclosed domain should be cut off. That was necessary for several reasons. Ping Yang loved seclusion, he hated Europeans, and was miserable unless he was absolute lord of every foot of ground on which he stood. He was extremely fond of the chase, which he followed more after the fashion of an Indian rajah than a Chinese Mandarin. He had a jungle specially preserved in Southern China, where he was wont to hunt tigers; and Glogoul well knew that, whatever else failed, the Mandarin would never consent to be without his tiger hunt in the centre of Derbyshire. "But," said Glogoul to himself, "the thing can be done. If English noblemen have reared pheasants like barn-door fowls for their annual sport, there is no reason why Ping Yang Yaloo should not rear tigers. In one respect it would be easier, for there is no likelihood of vagabonds poaching on our preserves. But before tiger-hunting can be followed in Derbyshire we must have our jungle, or at least our enclosed preserves, through which there will be no right of way excepting at peril of life."

Glogoul went over the estate with a local estate agent, merely telling him that the owner wished for privacy, and that he wanted to have as large a part of the county as possible for his exclusive use. The land agent stared, and said it was impossible.

Glogoul said, "All right; but let us at least overcome the impossible on the astral plane."

The agent shrugged his shoulders, but finding Glogoul peremptory he set to work. By evading Matlock, Buxton and some other large towns, and keeping as far as possible to the hills, which were only sparsely tenanted, and the valleys, which were occupied only by a few pit villages, they found that some very large tracts of country, one stretching from Chatsworth towards Ripley on the south, another including the Peak district to the north, a third coming close to the hill on which Belsover stands, and completely surrounding the ancient hall of Haddon, were available for their purpose. By this means they secured several hundreds of thousands of acres, from which it was conceivably possible the public might be excluded.

After spending a week over his plans the agent came to Glogoul in despair.

"I don't see how it can be done," he said. "Of course, you give all the tenants on your estates notice to quit—you may buy up the estates of other landlords and eject their tenants; but many hold leases which are not terminable for many years. There are a number of rights of way which cannot be extinguished. There are many roads, and the estate is crossed by one or two railways which cannot be interfered with."

"Nonsense!" said Glogoul. "Let me see your plans."

After studying them for some time he came to the conclusion that as a last resource it came to a matter of pounds, shillings and pence. The less important roads could be diverted, high walls could be built on either side of the railways and of the more important turnpikes.

"But," said the agent, aghast, "to build all these walls—and, as you say, you wish to have them from fifteen to sixteen feet high—would involve almost as much masonry as the Great Wall of China!"

"That is a mere detail," said Glogoul airily; for he already began to see how this gigantic building operation would facilitate certain other schemes. He had only twelve months' grace. At the end of that time Ping Yang Yaloo and all his retinue were to arrive at Chatsworth. Before that time the whole population must be cleared off the territory, and walls must be built round the whole estate, high enough to shut off Ping Yang Yaloo, his janissaries, and his tigers from the outside world.

The task was very much simplified owing to the depression which had prevailed for some years in Lancashire. This was the direct result of Ping Yang's successful competition. At least half the mines in Derbyshire were now idle. In the three districts which had been marked out as the tiger preserve, only two were still working. A portion had already migrated, and the distress had reduced the problem with which Glogoul had to deal to half its original dimensions. The district was poverty-stricken, and Glogoul calculated that it would not be difficult to buy up the leaseholders and clear out the remnant of the population. It was necessary, however, to "bear" the market for landed estate in that district. Faulmann suggested that there was nothing so likely to shake down the value of landed property as a sense of the insecurity of its foundations. "It is a mining county," said he, "and so many of the mines have been laid idle that it ought not to be impossible to do something of that sort."

"What do you mean?" asked Glogoul.

"Some time ago," said Faulmann, slowly, "when I was in Derbyshire, I saw an extraordinary phenomenon in the shape of the gradual subsidence of a whole tract of land. The pit props had given way, and the land was settling down, causing a kind of slow avalanche down the hillside into the valley below. Farms, houses, engine-rooms were all shaken. As long as the pit is working and the props are renewed, the natural consequences of mining are averted, but when the pit is idle the pit props decay, the ground falls in and depreciates the value of all the buildings on the surface. Could we not facilitate that process?"

"Humph!" said Glagoul; "I think that a little dynamite judiciously placed in the shallower workings might produce a useful psychological effect on the minds of property-owners on the surface. But it will have to be done very carefully."

In a few weeks the newspapers were full of an earthquake in Derbyshire which had occurred in the neighbourhood of the half-deserted town of Alfreton. It produced a panic which had led the population to seek refuge in the fields, dreading another shock. There was no doubt, the scientists said, that it was a shock of earthquake. The ground rose and heaved and then settled again. A distinct tremor was felt for several miles around the scene of the disturbance, which seemed to be in and about the neighbourhood of Alfreton. Newspaper reporters by the score visited the place, and whatever of sensation the earthquake had failed to produce was promptly manufactured by these diligent scribes, who, in the dearth of any genuine news, magnified the rumble of every passing cart into the approach of a coming shock.

In spite, however, of the diligence of the newspapers the panic was somewhat subsiding, and the inhabitants were returning to their shattered homes, when the country was startled by the report of a more disastrous earthquake close to the town of Ripley.

The old ironworks where, in former times, the great girders which span St. Pancras railway station had been constructed, had been idle for a couple of years. There were therefore no workmen employed at the time when the shock took place. The tall chimneys and the buildings were levelled with the ground. Up the hillside at Ripley the tremor had been distinctly felt, and all could see the great crack in the walls of the Town Hall. At the same time there was a renewal of the former shock at Alfreton, but it was not so violent as before.

About this time a renowned professor from the university of Tokio, in Japan, a country in which earthquakes are almost as familiar as thunder-storms, demonstrated completely to his own satisfaction, and to the bewilderment of the English public, that the county of Derbyshire had become the centre of a series of seismic shocks which, in all probability, would increase in intensity for a year or two, and then gradually die away; but in the course of that time the district would be rendered practically uninhabitable.

This article, which it is needless to say was handsomely paid for by Dr. Glogoul, produced a panic in the threatened region. Every one made haste to clear out at whatever sacrifice. The value of landed property fell by ten and twenty, and then, with leaps and bounds, by fifty per cent. It was impossible to let a house in the neighbourhood of Ripley and Alfreton. The roads were lined with inhabitants flying with their goods and chattels from the next shock, which they were assured would be more violent than those which had already taken place.

Many of the more hardy natives remained in their holdings, while some of a more sceptical turn of mind determined to wait for the further verification of the Japanese professor's predictions. The professor indicated that in accordance with the invariable law which had been discovered by the experts at the seismological observatory in Japan, the next shock would probably occur in a fortnight, some fifteen or twenty miles to the north. It would be followed directly by other shocks, which he thought would probably prove dangerous to the neighbourhood around Buxton.

Hardly a fortnight had elapsed before the newspapers reported that the prediction of the expert had been all but too truly realised. Immediately below the hill on which Peveril of the Peak had reared the castle of Belsover, there lie the remains of what was at one time known as the model colliery village, founded by a Newcastle coalowner, who used to boast that it contained neither publican, policeman, nor pauper—a boast which would have been better justified if as much care had been taken to supply good drinking water as there was to exclude the detested beer. With the decay of the Lancashire trade the mine had been laid idle, but a considerable number of the inhabitants continued to cultivate allotments, eking out a precarious living by the aid of odd jobs in the neighbourhood.

The third shock differed from its predecessors in occasioning a great loss of life. It occurred at midnight, and almost the whole population perished in the ruins of their houses. When Faulmann read the telegrams in the morning paper, he handed the paper to Glogoul, merely remarking, "That cost fifty lives. Was it necessary to kill so many?"

"Oh," said Glogoul, "what are fifty men?—a mere bagatelle; not one fifth of those who are constantly blown up in colliery explosions quite aimlessly, whereas now——"

"Of course," interrupted Faulmann, "it is quite different; the end justifies the means."

"Certainly," said Glogoul. "I think the time has come for us to play our next card."

So the great firm of Glogoul and Faulmann wrote a letter to the *Times* stating that his Excellency Ping Yang Yaloo, who had recently bought Chatsworth, had been filled with compassion on hearing of the fate of the unfortunate inhabitants of the district in which he was about to reside. He had, therefore, instructed them to state that from the depths of his commiseration, although his property might be the next to suffer, he wished to subscribe £10,000 towards the relief fund for the unfortunate victims, and in the meantime he would do what he could to give employment to those who had lost their means of subsistence by the catastrophes.

The newspapers were loud in their praises of the munificent Mandarin, and Messrs. Glogoul and Faulmann commenced the first section of the great wall which was to surround the estate. They had no lack of labour, and they got it cheap. Meanwhile, when the panic was at its height, Messrs. Glogoul and Faulmann, through secret agents, bought up almost all the property in the selected areas.

By this means within three months of the first earthquake at Alfreton, the whole of the land, with the exception of one plot, which stood almost in the centre of the estate, had passed into the possession of the firm. A few leaseholders here and there obstinately refused to part with their holdings; it was therefore necessary to re-enforce the argument of earthquake by one which would appeal more directly to the instinct of self-preservation.

While the northern wall was rapidly being pushed forward, there appeared another letter in the *Times* by the Japanese professor, whose warnings had been so signally verified by the event, calling attention to the fact that there was great danger of an outbreak of epidemic disease in the earthquake region, and recommending that the local sanitary authorities and resident landowners should take instant steps to examine their water supply and to look to their drains, otherwise the consequences might be most disastrous.

Now it happened that midway in the ground which Glogoul had selected for the Southern tiger preserve there stood a little village which centred round a Baptist chapel. This chapel was the only place of worship in the village. The pulpit had been occupied for many years by a pious and devout minister, who had promptly utilised the earthquakes as the occasion for a series of revival services which had led to the gathering of almost the entire population of the hamlet into the fold of his church. A religious exaltation took possession of him. He quoted the Psalms as to the protection of those who sheltered themselves under the everlasting arms, and regarded the immunity of his village from earthquake as a direct proof of Providential interposition. His flock, imbued with the same belief in the guardian care of Providence, refused to listen to any overtures of Glogoul and Faulmann, or of their agents. They were there, and there they meant to remain. It was therefore necessary to prove to them that their confidence in Providence was not proof against the resources of civilisation.

The village drew its water from a deep spring which bubbled up on the hillside, and which was conducted through a long pipe to the fountain in front of the chapel. When the professor's warning appeared in the *Times*, the medical officers of health for the county made a special examination of the sources of water supply, and reported that so far as they could see there was no sign that would justify a fear of an epidemic.

Two days afterwards the minister was suddenly taken ill. On a doctor being sent for he said that the symptoms were those of Asiatic cholera. In two days the minister was dead. The origin of the epidemic was shrouded in mystery to all excepting two men. The cholera germs which Glogoul had carefully preserved in ice since his return from China had been liberated at the hillside spring, and had done their work with the precision of trained assassins. The epidemic did not spread, but it was very virulent within a small area. By the time the last victim had been buried, the leases of all the land in the selected district were in the strong-box of Messrs. Glogoul and Faulmann.

The approach of winter brought with it the usual demonstration of the existence of widespread misery in the shape of the unemployed. Acting in accordance with the plan of campaign agreed upon with Sir Peter Patterson, Algernon Bradford was very active in organising demonstrations of the workless workers, poor wretches whose misery was sufficiently keen to make them follow any leader, no matter who he might be, if he gave them some hope, and it was a relief at least to make their grievances audible.

It was noticed by some curious observers that all the demonstrations of the unemployed which were organised by the Toilers' Industrial League were characterised by the same general features. Besides asking for work for the unemployed, they made a specific demand that the bloated aristocrats who had fattened for centuries on the blood and bones of the people should be compelled to disgorge their ill-gotten plunder. They further called for the organisation of a body of men, independent of party, who would be ready to follow any leader who would rally the forces of the suffering democracy against the aristocratic incubus. The Government at first took little notice of these demonstrations, but finding them growing in importance, sent out circulars to the Boards of Guardians suggesting that something should be done. This suggestion was greeted with howls of indignation by the Toilers' Industrial League. They were

A MYSTERY TO ALL BUT TWO MEN.

not paupers, and the unemployed refused to be dealt with by the guardians. There were several scrimmages, and in one or two places the bread-shops were looted, and everything seemed to indicate that matters would rapidly get worse.

At this juncture, deeming that the psychological moment had arrived, Messrs. Glogoul and Faulmann put themselves into communication with the Home Secretary and the President of the Local Government Board. They said that, in view of the extreme pressure of the distress, they were instructed by his Excellency Ping Yang Yaloo to provide work on the largest possible scale in the distressed district of Derbyshire. They had been at some difficulty to suggest the kind of work which should be undertaken, but in view of his Excellency's desire for privacy, and also of the importance of finding employment for the largest number of the unemployed at once, they hoped they would have the support of public sentiment in encircling the whole of his property with a lofty stone wall. One of his Excellency's reasons for this was that he was afraid the presence of his Chinese retainers would be an offence to the local residents, and so he desired to keep them to themselves. They submitted these proposals tentatively in the hope that they would not conflict with the wishes of Her Majesty's Government. At the same time, they intimated privately that they had received instructions to expend £500,000 on these relief works.

The delight of the Government can be imagined. They effusively thanked Messrs. Glogoul and Faulmann, and at all the meetings throughout the country which were organised by the Toilers' Industrial League, enthusiastic votes of thanks were passed to the great Chinese Mandarin, whose munificence they contrasted, with scathing invectives, with the beggarly efforts of the bloated aristocrats, most of whom were with great difficulty endeavouring to keep their own people employed throughout the hard winter.

In a very short time there were 20,000 men employed busily digging foundations, hauling stone, and making mortar to build the "Little Wall of China," as it was facetiously designated. Never in the history of England had such a wall been heard of. When it was pointed out that a high wall on either side of a turnpike road which had always run through open country was decidedly peculiar, to say the least, the questioner was always met with the answer that it made all the more work. The one man who ventured to oppose the construction of such walls was rudely set upon by the mob and beaten within half-an-inch of his life. What was all his sentimental talk about scenery compared with their need for bread?

So the work prospered. Messrs. Glogoul and Faulmann got their labour cheap, and the Little Wall of China was rapidly encircling the whole domain.

CHAPTER VIII.
A GIGANTIC CONSPIRACY.

THE success of the Comford Mill was no longer a matter of doubt. As fast as machines could be made, they were set to work, not only in Lady Muriel's mines in Inverness, but upon Lady Belsover's Welsh property, where gold existed in almost inexhaustible quantities, although the proportion of stone to gold was so great that hitherto it had not been worth the cost of extraction. The purchase of Haddon Hall and of Six Elms was completed, and the produce of the Scottish and Welsh Gold Mines came in very opportunely to enable them to carry out their plans for establishing themselves, the one on the right, and the other on the left of Chatsworth.

Lady Muriel somewhat demurred at the ordeal of having to live in a brand new house, which it was necessary to build close to the ancient and romantic Haddon, but it was unanimously agreed that it would be profanation to touch the hall as it now stands. That relic of the past must remain, bearing, with silent eloquence, its testimony to the love and the lives that have gone, illustrating the long and glorious chapter of English history and English romance.

Mr. Wilkes' task at Six Elms was very simple. The keep, unhurt by the storms of nearly a thousand years, was easily stripped of the profanations which its last occupant had accumulated within it. The ancient fountain in the gardens was soon repaired, the statues replaced in the ancient niches, but the huge ruin of the modern house, which had been so cruelly dismantled, demanded more extensive reconstruction.

"How indignant I always feel," said Lady Ænid, as she went over the roofless pile with her husband, "when I think of the reckless manner in which these stately buildings were abandoned to ruin. From a child I have always regarded this house as intimately associated with the close of the Renaissance of England. It was here the Marquis of Newcastle well-nigh ruined himself and the fortunes of his family by entertaining King Charles, with a regal hospitality of which nowadays, alas, we know little. On this spacious terrace, the masques were performed under the direction of Ben Jonson, in which the scions of the noblest houses in England took a leading part. On this raised dais the luckless monarch looked down on a festive scene, one of the last of those which remind me of the vanished Italian world. Between us and them there is a great gulf fixed."

"Yes," said her husband, "it is a great gulf indeed. Within a dozen years of the time when Ben Jonson was superintending merry masques on this terrace, Oliver Cromwell was levelling his artillery on the keep from yonder knoll, and when these great guns went off, they tolled the knell of that jocund time."

"But we shall bring it back," said Lady Ænid gaily—"the masques and music and all the bright revelry of the Elizabethan age."

Her husband sighed, and looked out over the valley, where a party of surveyors, under the orders of Glogoul and Faulmann, were marking off the limits of the Mandarin's domains.

"I fear, my love," said he, "that there will be sterner work to be done before England may be 'Merrie England' once more, but not just now."

"Come," said Lady Ænid, "I protest against this spirit of gloom. The Chinaman will come, and the Chinaman will go; but we of the old stock will remain for ever."

"I hope so," said he, "but it will be in the future as it has been in the past; not by isolation, nor by insistence on caste distinctions, but rather by the hearty union between the English democracy and its natural leaders."

When Glogoul found that Haddon Hall and Belsover Castle had been snatched out of his very grasp, he was indignant, but said nothing. He recognised the boldness of the challenge that was involved in the establishment of the two families on each flank of Ping Yang Yaloo at Chatsworth, but he had enough to do for the moment, and beyond determining to let them realise the unpleasantness of the neighbourhood in which they had so wantonly ventured, he did nothing.

When the earthquakes began in Derbyshire, Sir Artegal was, like every one, considerably alarmed. The fact, however, that Glogoul was acting as agent to Chatsworth suggested to Mr. Wilkes the idea that there was more of human than natural agency in these convulsions. He had no evidence by which to justify his suspicions, but he knew Glogoul, and knew him to be capable of anything.

During that winter, while they were slowly proceeding with the new Haddon House immediately behind, and out of sight of the romantic hall, they were much troubled with attempted strikes among their workmen. This was the more remarkable, because work was very scarce, and multitudes of unemployed men were tramping around, seeking employment at any terms. Sir Artegal and Mr. Wilkes both suspected that these things were brought about of set purpose, but there was no proof that the agitators who denounced them as bloodsuckers were acting in deference to orders, and as they always met their workmen with the utmost frankness, the interruptions of work were very brief.

What with the earthquakes and the outbreak of cholera, the agitation of the unemployed, and the difficulties with their own workpeople, the situation seemed serious enough to justify Sir Artegal in running up to town to talk the matter over with his friend the Prime Minister. He found the Premier much harassed with business. A general election it seemed impossible to stave off longer than another six months. The lack of employment at home was great. There was no cessation in the continually increasing pressure of Asiatic competition.

"Things are bad," said he, "and I am afraid they are going to be worse. I have just had a telegram from our Ambassador at Pekin, who hears that Ping Yang Yaloo is about to proclaim a still further reduction in the price of shirtings. If he does, that will mean the shutting up of the few remaining mills that are still running in Lancashire, and an addition of some 20,000 persons to the number of the unemployed. Fortunately, the promised expenditure of half a million in relief works in Derbyshire, will, to some extent, alleviate the distress; but it is a curious business—the same man to be throwing 20,000 operatives out of work in Lancashire, and employing 20,000 in building a perfectly useless wall around his domains in Derbyshire."

Sir Artegal did not disguise his alarm at the prospect, but found that the Prime Minister could give him little or no consolation. He hurried on his way from Downing Street, and was just in time to catch a great Jewish financier, who was usually supposed to hold in his hands the issues of peace and war.

"I want to tell you," said Sir Artegal, "two things. First, the machine is coining gold. In less than three months the production of gold will have doubled, and the depreciation of gold will begin. That is one fact. The second is that I have heard from a sure source that Ping Yang Yaloo is coming over here, not for any sentimental purpose, or any whimsical desire to change his residence, but in order to direct on the spot the operations that are necessary to enable him to command the markets of the world."

The Jew looked very grave. "Are you sure your information is correct?" said he at last.

"Absolutely certain. All this catering for popularity with the unemployed is but the first move in the great game. What the next will be I do not know, but I suspect."

"What do you suspect?" said the Jew.

"Well," said Sir Artegal, "no one knows better than you the present condition of most of our noble families. They are compelled to maintain their position in the counties, and keep up an appearance of affluence, when in reality they have hardly enough to buy themselves bread-and-cheese. They are keeping themselves afloat by increasing their incumbrances; and this process has gone on to such an extent that at the present moment, while more than half the land of England is supposed to belong to the peers, it is in reality, to all intents and purposes, the property of insurance companies and land mortgage companies; and, if the truth were told, a considerable number of our landlords may be foreclosed upon at any moment."

"Yes," said the other, "that is very, very true, but how does this bear upon the designs of Ping Yang Yaloo?"

"Well," said Sir Artegal, "I wish you would make inquiries as to whether there has been any attempt in any direction to obtain possession of the mortgages, bills, or any other obligations which are at present in the market, and which would enable their holders to exercise pressure upon the Peers."

"Certainly, I will let you know; but I cannot see what this has got to do with your Chinaman."

"Humph!" said Sir Artegal, "I may be mistaken, but I think I have seen signs that there is to be an attempt to corner the Peerage. If this Chinese Mandarin, who is given to audacious coups, were to find himself in such a position that he could foreclose on one-half the Peers of the realm, he would practically have the House of Lords at his mercy."

"True," said the other, "but, after all, that would not matter much. It is the House of Commons where the real power lies."

"Granted; and you may depend upon it that it is not left out of his calculations. I may be wrong, but it seems to me that the attack is being prosecuted simultaneously upon both Houses of Parliament. On the House of Lords, by the acquisition of all the obligations into which the Peers have entered; and on the House of Commons the move is rather in the direction of an attempt to disintegrate the Liberal Party, and to return to power a majority so small that it could hardly hold its own for a day. This is to be done by electing a group of Independents whom they think will become the balance-weight between the parties. Such, at least, is my reading of the situation."

The great financier paused for a moment, and then said, "I will make the inquiries you wish, and to-morrow I will let you know the result."

The next day Sir Artegal received a private letter from his friend in the City, confirming his worst fears. He reported that there had been going on for some time past a quiet buying up of all the securities, mortgages, bills and other liabilities held by the Peers. No one hitherto had been able to guess where and by whom this movement was directed; but the brokers were suspected of being hand and glove with Messrs. Glogoul and Faulmann, the well-known wreckers. Whoever they were, they had apparently ample funds at their disposal.

Sir Artegal locked the letter away in his desk, and then sauntered down to his club. On his way he met a newsboy, displaying a sensational placard and making the usual unintelligible cry which indicates that they have something of exceptional interest, without being able to articulate clearly enough to intimate what that subject is. He stopped the boy and bought the newspaper. Unfolding it, he found the chief place occupied by a manifesto by the Toilers' Industrial League:—

To the Workers of England (so it began),—How long are we to suffer and to pine in our millions, when a pampered few who have monopolised the land are battening in luxury upon all the delicacies of the earth? We do not seek for vengeance; we do not even plead for justice; we ask for bread—bread for our starving little ones; bread for our weeping wives; and work for the willing workers, who to-day, and every day, are seeking for work and finding none. Working Men of England, now is the hour to enforce your claim. The landlords of England cannot, for very shame, refuse to follow the noble example of the great philanthropic capitalist who has, at this moment, given employment to tens of thousands of our starving fellow-countrymen. What this heathen Chinee can do, our great nobles must be made to do. Up, then, and be doing! Assemble in your thousands before the mansions and the castles of the Peers. Associate with you all the ministers of the Church, all the preachers of the religion of humanity, of mercy, and place them at your head. Insist that the great nobles of England shall not fall behind the heathen Chinee in the services which he renders to his fellow-men.

Signed, on behalf of the executive committee of the Toilers' Industrial League.—Algernon Bradford.

Going on a little further, he met one of the best known, but most impulsive, Nonconformists in London.

"Have you seen the Manifesto?" said he eagerly.

"I have just been reading it, as you see," said Sir Artegal, holding up the paper.

"Isn't that great!" said he. "There is the opportunity—what an opportunity for the Christian Church! Once more, Labour has gone ahead of the Church."

"But what are you going to do?"

"Do!" said he. "We are going to have a Conference in the Memorial Hall at once, and we are going to rally the masses behind the Cross. It is impossible to resist such an appeal."

Sir Artegal remained silent. His companion looked at him in some surprise, and said—

"Does not this heathen barbarian of China put us to shame, with our boasted philanthropy and Christianity? I confess I should feel unable to lift my head and look a Chinaman in the face if I were not prepared to go at least as far as he has, poor benighted heathen, whom the Gospel has never touched. But I must away," said he. "The Conference meets in an hour, and I have to draft the resolutions."

So saying, he hurried away.

"A rare clever stroke that," said Sir Artegal to himself. "To think of invoking the Chinee to whip the Nonconformist Conscience into line. I wonder who thought of it."

A SCENE IN BOUVERIE STREET.

As a matter of fact, it was Lady Dorothy who had thought of that. After a sleepless night, in which she had tossed restlessly to and fro, she had risen at six o'clock, and had indited the Manifesto which was now flaming abroad in all the papers.

On the club steps Sir Artegal met the Duke of Pontiac. "Deucedly bad look-out this winter," said he, shrugging his shoulders. "Have you seen the new Manifesto?"

"Yes," said Sir Artegal. "What are you going to do?"

"Do!" said the Duke; "the fact of the matter is that I am just at the end of my tether. When the death duties were put on, I insured my life, in order to enable my heir to carry on the estate without being crippled. I am at my wit's end as to how to get the money to pay this year's premium. Now it seems that we have to be cornered by a howling mob, and enforced by all the fanatics of the Churches, insisting that we have to find work for the unemployed. By-the-bye," he added, "do you know anything about the firm of Glogoul and Faulmann?"

Sir Artegal smiled and said, "I think I do."

"Well, I received a confidential circular to-day telling me that they had reason to believe, from signs which they do not think could mislead, that there was going to be a revival in British agriculture at an early date, and that they were willing to negotiate loans for a short period at less than half the rate I have been able to get accommodation from Benzance Boss, the money-lender in Piccadilly."

"Take my advice," said Sir Artegal, "give that firm a wide berth. There is a snare in that offer."

"Really," said he, "and what must I do? 'Needs must when the devil drives;' and I would rather go to Glogoul and Faulmann than face Boss again." So saying, the Duke departed.

Sir Artegal had hardly seated himself in the library before he saw an old college friend, who was now leader writer on the staff of the *Daily Tribune*. With a few words of greeting it occurred to Sir Artegal that it might be well to give young Piper a hint. The *Daily Tribune* had for some years past nobly distinguished itself by the brilliance and intrepidity with which it had espoused the cause of the poor and the oppressed. It had often carried its advocacy far beyond the limits of prudence, being too much given to the belief that philanthropy could secure the success of a business enterprise. But when all allowances had been made, it had exercised for several years a healthy influence in English public opinion. It was alert, brimful of fight, and with a positive passion for flying at the highest game.

Piper was one of the young lions of its staff, and from old acquaintance Sir Artegal felt that he would be justified in giving him some inkling as to what was going to happen.

"I see the *Tribune*," said Sir Artegal somewhat drily, "has been going the way of all the papers, and falling down and worshipping at the shrine of Ping Yang Yaloo."

"Well," said Piper, "just think of it. Half a million of money to be spent in relief works. It is enough to put our aristocracy to shame. My chief is going to write a regular scorcher, and he told me to browse around, and pick up a few illustrations with which to drive his arguments in."

"Well," said Sir Artegal drily, "it would be very bad if I should spoil your scorcher. Will you oblige me by coming with me to the hall to see the latest telegrams?"

"Certainly," said Piper, wondering what on earth Sir Artegal was up to.

As they entered the hall, the tape machine ticked off a message, which, on being posted up, read as follows:—

SHANGHAI.—This morning, Shirting quoted ten per cent. lower than yesterday's rates.

"Do you know what that means?" said Sir Artegal, pointing to the quotation.

"No," said Piper.

"It means," said Sir Artegal quietly, "that Ping Yang Yaloo has played the card which has been feared for long, and the mills, employing 20,000 hands, will be closed to-morrow."

"You don't say so," said Piper.

"You may take that to your Chief from me as a fact. You may add also that I have reason to suspect a gigantic conspiracy on the part of this said philanthropic Mandarin, the ultimate object of which would be to leave both our commerce and our lands absolutely at the mercy of this Mongolian millionaire. Nothing that has ever been dreamed of in 'Corners' approaches the game which he is playing. You know I do not speak lightly," said Sir Artegal. "I never talk to newspaper men about affairs, but it seems to me the present situation justifies the departure from my usual rule."

That conversation was brief. But the evident earnestness of Sir Artegal produced its effect. The next morning, when every one turned to the *Daily Tribune*, expecting to find a scathing onslaught against aristocratic selfishness, with any amount of magniloquent reference to the union of religion and democracy, which was to bear such splendid results at the Memorial Hall—an onslaught which was to call in thunder-tones upon the pampered peers to provide work for a starving people—they found a leading article, full of dark, mysterious menace. The writer, taking "Fall of Shirtings" as his text, pointed out that, by the absolute monopoly of the cotton market, the great Chinese Mandarin was able to crush out the last remnants of the cotton industry in England, and that after this was done there was nothing to hinder him from raising his prices to any figure he pleased. "It is curious charity," the article concluded, "which provides millions in Derbyshire for building a Little Wall of China round Chatsworth, when at the same moment the same number of men are deprived of an opportunity of earning good wages by the arbitrary will of the Mongolian millionaire."

CHAPTER IX.

A SCENE IN BOUVERIE STREET.

WHEN Glogoul opened his *Daily Tribune* the next morning he could hardly believe his eyes. Up to this moment everything had been going swimmingly for the great game. He had taken a good deal of pains partly to bribe and partly to humour the other papers, in order to induce them to turn a blind eye on the possible dangers of his operations, but the *Daily Tribune* had been so eager in supporting anything and everything that tended to give immediate relief to the unemployed, that he was quite dumbfounded when that paper showed a disposition suddenly to double back on its track.

The moment Faulmann entered the sanctum a long consultation took place. The result was a cipher cablegram to Shanghai, the reply to which came back in a few hours, with the one monosyllable, "BUY!"

Dr. Glogoul threw the cablegram over to Faulmann, with the remark, "That's your business," and departed.

Faulmann had a lively remembrance of an adventure which a compatriot of his had experienced when Mr. Walledoff had sent him on a commission to buy any paper that might be worth having in the London market. That gentleman's method was marked by a primitive, not to say barbarian simplicity. It was not Faulmann's idea of conducting a delicate operation, to jump into a hansom and drive down to Bouverie Street, rush upstairs calling for the proprietor, and then to blurt out, almost before they had said "Good morning," that he wished to buy his paper.

At the same time Ping Yang Yaloo's business required haste, and it would not do to fool around the bush, so he sat for a moment and wondered. Then something occurred to him which seemed to give him pleasure, for he smiled, got up and walked backwards and forwards for a time, as if he were unravelling a clue. Then he smiled again, and sat down and rang for his bank-book. His balance was very high. They had only the previous week received a remittance of half-a-million from Shanghai, which had been placed for the moment in their drawing account; then, taking a blank cheque with him, he drove off, not to Bouverie Street, but to Waterloo Station, from which he took a ticket to Leatherhead.

Now, at Leatherhead there lived no newspaper proprietor nor newspaper editor, but a gentleman who was well known by Mr. Faulmann as the legal adviser to the proprietors of the *Daily Tribune.*

A short time before he had been lunching with this gentleman, who had in the course of a friendly gossip told him with what difficulty he had just extricated the *Tribune* from a worrying libel suit. It was one of those cases in which the editor had allowed his natural and justifiable indignation to outrun the producible evidence of the truth of the facts upon which he was commenting. It had cost the proprietor £5,000 in hard cash to get out of the lawsuit, which, if it had been pressed, would have resulted in his incarceration in Holloway Gaol. It was the memory of the freshness of this experience, and of the unpleasant exigencies of his position, which encouraged him to hope that he might be able to execute his commission.

He found his legal friend at home. He was surprised at receiving a visit from Faulmann at that time of day. The latter cautiously opened negotiations.

"I think," said he, "that your proprietor of the *Tribune* was somewhat badly hit over that lawsuit."

"Well, nothing like he might have been hit had it not been for me," said the lawyer cheerily.

"Just so," said he; "but even you may not be able to save him over this."

The lawyer pricked up his ears.

"What do you mean?" said he.

"Oh, nothing," said Faulmann; "but I thought it was more friendly to come and see you at once, than to let things go any further."

"What do you mean?"

"Have you seen the *Daily Tribune* this morning?"

"No, I have not looked at it yet; it is lying in the hall."

"Well," said Faulmann, "if you will just look at the first leader, I think you will understand why it is that I am here."

The lawyer read the article over very gravely twice.

"Well," said he, "what about this article? There is nothing in this article that is not perfectly fair and legitimate comment upon a question of public interest."

"Yes," said Faulmann, opening his eyes with affected simplicity, "I did not come to complain of that article; I only want to let you understand exactly why it is that I came here."

"Well," said the lawyer, looking somewhat mystified, "if you do not wish to complain of this article, why do you come here?"

"Because," said Faulmann quietly, "either the writer of that article believes that what he says is true, or he does not. Of course, you and I know that it is not true. It is all moonshine to talk about the mystery of the Mongolian millionaire, and it is a cruel, unjust libel to suggest that anything but the purest philanthropy has led him to incur such an expense to relieve your overcrowded market of England; but we need not discuss this article. I am looking to the future."

"Precisely," said the lawyer. "I am beginning to see your point."

"Of course you do. You always see a point quicker than any one else. You know what kind of a man your editor is. If he believes that there is this gigantic conspiracy, he is certain to use the *Tribune* day after day to the very uttermost limits to detect, unearth and denounce the conspiracy and all the conspirators."

"Yes," said the lawyer; "I guess that is pretty much what he will do. He is game enough to fight."

"Precisely," said Faulmann. "Now, as you know, he cannot go very far in that direction without coming across our firm, and I thought it kind and friendly just to come and tell you that, as we are peaceable men and dislike litigation, we never go to court if we can avoid it. But the first line that appears in the *Tribune* which is actionable—and he sails very near it to-day—will lead to proceedings, if possible, criminal proceedings, and we shall claim £100,000 damages. Of course, we have no wish to do any such thing, and would very much rather that we were let alone; but the best way to avoid trouble is to face it frankly before it comes. That is my business," added he, with a smile.

"But, stay!" said the lawyer. "I quite appreciate the danger. I quite see that it would be pretty difficult to defend a case against the munificent philanthropist whom you represent; but Ructions never cares for those things. Now, I should not be in the least surprised if he does not put his foot into it, and commit himself in the very next issue; in fact, I think it might be just as well if I came back to town with you. The position is much too delicate to permit of any fooling around."

"By all means," said Faulmann, pleased at the thought of having an uninterrupted gossip with the lawyer all the way to town.

After a glass of wine and a biscuit, Faulmann and his host went down to the station. Finding themselves in a carriage alone, they waxed confidential, and Faulmann intimated delicately—for he always did things delicately—that they had not yet decided upon their legal adviser, and as they had a very great deal of business in hand, he would receive it as a favour if Mr. Keeley could suggest a firm to whom they could safely entrust the gigantic interests of their principal.

Keeley's eyes twinkled. "My dear Faulmann," said he, "why not give that to me?"

"But," said Faulmann, "I never dreamed that you would be willing to take it."

"Take it!" said he, "why not? You know I have always been delighted to serve you."

"Well," said Faulmann, "that puts another face upon the matter. I had no idea that I could have your services, but I shall have to see my partner first, and in the meantime do I understand that you are at liberty to act on our behalf?"

"Certainly," said Mr. Keeley, delighted. "It would be good business for both of us," he said cheerfully.

Then Mr. Faulmann drew back, and for a whole five minutes he never spoke. At last, after making up his mind as if for a great deliberation, he approached Mr. Keeley and said, almost in a whisper—

"You are legal adviser to the *Daily Tribune,* are you not?"

"Yes," said he; "but the friendship between us would render it quite impossible for my clients to come to blows."

"I was not thinking of that," said Mr. Faulmann, and he was silent again.

A Scene in Bouverie Street.

Before he broke that silence the door opened and another passenger got into the carriage. All further conversation therefore was interrupted until they arrived at Waterloo.

"Now," said Mr. Keeley, "you will drive straight to Bouverie Street. Where shall I see you afterwards?"

"I shall be delighted if you will dine with me at my club," said he.

"All right," said Keeley. "At half-past seven to-night."

When Keeley reached Bouverie Street, he found affairs in a very lively condition in the office, and Mr. Ructions was closeted with the Rev. Tomkins Potts, who, full of righteous indignation, had come down to denounce the editorial in the *Tribune* as altogether unworthy of the situation.

"What was the use of having an organ of the British Democracy if, at the very critical moment, it was to go over to the enemy in that fashion?"

Mr. Ructions mildly intimated that, after all, even the editor of an organ had some right to have a judgment, and that he was responsible for his own editorials.

"What!" said Potts, indignantly storming up and down. "You dare to quote your judgment, your own and unaided judgment, against the clear leadings of Providence, shown by the union between associated labour and the whole church of God! Why, it is preposterous, sir!"

Mr. Ructions was a patient man, and accustomed to the outpourings of the righteous. He therefore only said, "I think we must agree to differ."

"We must not agree to differ," said Tomkins Potts, stamping his foot upon the floor of the office. "I am here, as a delegate from the executive committee appointed at the Memorial Hall yesterday, to insist that you shall——"

"Insist, Mr. Potts!" said Mr. Ructions, turning pale. "What right have you to insist as to how the *Tribune* shall be conducted?"

There was a menacing note in the editor's voice which showed his companion he had gone too far.

"I beg your pardon," said Mr. Potts. "We all know that you are quite sound. No one is sounder in all England; but even Jupiter sometimes nods, and able editors may sometimes make a slip. Come now, do not let us get to words about it. The fact is, that we have always relied upon the *Tribune* to be our banner-bearer in the fray, and we are truly at a loss to account for your extraordinary article of yesterday. Never was there such a chance for striking a deadly blow at the Peers. But all can be re-established, and what we want is a real scorcher of the old type—one that will raise blisters wherever it touches.

"Really, Ructions," continued he, extending his hand with a bland smile. "I feel this is a personal matter. I feel ashamed to call Ping Yang Yaloo a heathen. The old pagan philanthropist in Shanghai has put us to shame, and I felt humiliated to think that so magnificent, so truly Christian —as I may really call it—an initiative on his part had met with such a response in the organ which we have for so long been proud to follow."

Ructions shook his head, and said nothing.

Potts had no sooner disappeared than Keeley came in.

"Oh," said Ructions, with a sigh, "I am so glad to see you! The fact is, I have had a whole series of statements from various quarters which leads me to the very grave suspicion that we are on the verge of the worst conspiracy against the free government of this country, and against the prosperity of the people, that has ever been conceived."

Mr. Keeley looked with a quick piercing glance at Ructions.

"Ah!" he thought, "my good friend has got on to his hobby-horse, and it is running away with him. Now I must check this."

"What do you mean, Mr. Ructions?"

"I mean about this Ping Yang Yaloo."

"I thought so," said Keeley.

"Have you heard anything?"

"Yes," said Mr. Keeley, "that is why I am here. I have just had a visit from the representative of Ping Yang Yaloo to complain of the article in to-day's paper, and to give me formal notice that, if neither line appears in the same sense as that article, they will bring an action against the *Tribune*, claiming £100,000 damages."

Mr. Ructions sprang from his chair.

"There! That is the last link that I wanted, in order to prove the conspiracy. They know that we are on their trail, and now they have come to you to try to gag me. But they shall do nothing of the kind; no matter what you say."

"Sit down, Mr. Ructions," said Mr. Keeley shortly. "Sit down. I have something to say to you."

"What have you to say?" said Mr. Ructions.

"You remember," said Mr. Keeley quietly, "the trouble I got you out of about a month ago?"

"Yes," said Mr. Ructions; "I remember. It was very good of you. It only cost £5,000; it might have cost us £20,000."

"Precisely," said Mr. Keeley. "You know I have always been your friend. I like you personally, and I think you conduct the paper admirably. I shall be very sorry to see you come to grief. Mark my words, Mr. Ructions, you will inevitably upset the apple-cart if you have any more such articles."

"I am going to write one. I will go to the uttermost lengths."

"Stay!" said Mr. Keeley. "It is all very well for you to talk like that if the *Daily Tribune* is your own paper."

"No," said Mr. Ructions, "it is not my own property, but I have a free hand."

"Yes," said Mr. Keeley, "so long as you are on it, but no longer."

Mr. Ructions was striding backwards and forwards in the room. Stopping in front of Mr. Keeley, he said, "What do you mean?"

"Only this—by-the-bye, may I smoke?"

"Yes."

"Have a cigar?"

"No, I never smoke in the office."

"I think it would do you good, then. I think it would calm your nerves. Never get excited when you are discussing business. Now I am going to tell you something I never told you before. When I got my cheque from your proprietor for the £5,000, he took me aside and spoke to me seriously about you. He said that he liked you. very well, but he could not afford to pay away thousands of pounds like dirt in this fashion, and that he would really like me to consider whether or not he should give you notice."

"He said that?" exclaimed Ructions, starting from his chair. "He did? The scoundrel!"

"Come, come, Mr. Ructions, don't lose your temper. I told him that I thought it would be a thousand pities to terminate the relation between you; that he could not find any one to fill your place as well as you filled it; that libel suits were accidents to which every man was open; and soon I talked him out of it. But I could not induce him to abandon it entirely. His last words to me were—'Well, Keeley, I do nothing this time, but if ever Ructions gets into another libel suit, he goes; he goes that moment.'"

"I am glad you told me that," said Ructions calmly. "Because it makes my duty quite clear."

"It is?" said Mr. Keeley.

"To hand in my resignation at once."

"Come," said Keeley, "don't be a fool."

"No," said Ructions. "That is just what I do not want to be," and, seizing a memorandum, he began writing his resignation as editor of the *Daily Tribune*.

"Nonsense!" said Keeley, as he sat watching him, "what an idiot you are! What conceivable good will that do you, or your case, or any one else, writing in this headstrong fashion?"

"Well, but," said he, "what can I do? Here I am with the evidence in my possession of this conspiracy, assailed by people who do not know the facts, because I have gone so far, and yet I am not to be allowed to go any further."

"No," said Keeley. "You have just got to keep quiet, and do nothing."

"I'll be hanged if I will!" and he signed the resignation with a great flourish.

"Now," said Keeley, "I will see your proprietor and put the case before him, and come back here at ten. It is not a deadly matter. But do not go and throw yourself out of a situation, and generally put your proprietor to the great inconvenience of finding a new editor at the very shortest notice. Besides, my dear Ructions, I do not believe you have got any evidence to prove any such conspiracy, and I do not believe there is any conspiracy."

"But there is," said Ructions. "I do not mean to say that I have got legal evidence that I can produce in court, but I have got evidence that has convinced me."

"Just so; but evidence that cannot be produced in court is not evidence at all, from my point of view; and really you are not justified in going into this matter until I, as your legal adviser, can assure you that you are on safe ground."

Leaving the editor, the lawyer drove to the sanctum of the proprietor. He found that personage in a very ugly humour. He had been badgered all day by persons who had called upon him to expostulate about the article in the *Tribune*. The moment Keeley entered his room, he said, "I tell you what it is: I wish I had sacked this man. Instead of sacking him as I wanted to, you've let me into this!"

"Come, come," said Mr. Keeley, "he is a very good editor. Besides, there may be more in it than we know."

"More in it! I do not care what there is in it! He is a perfect fool—that man; not by being foolish, but by being too wise. He is always writing to-day about contingencies that only develop themselves on the day after to-morrow; whereas, if he would only be a day behind the fair, instead of being a day before, we might get some pickings. And upon my word," said the proprietor, as he sank into a chair, "upon my word, I am heartily sick of it. I wish Mr. Walledoff, or any other man, would buy the paper,

THE EDITOR SPRANG FROM HIS CHAIR.

lock, stock, and barrel. It would be a good riddance. I am sick and tired of the whole thing. People think it is all cakes and ale being a newspaper proprietor. If they had my place for a week they might know better."

"Come, come," said Keeley; "I have just left the office, where I have been trying to keep Ructions quiet. He is bent upon following up the line he has taken to-day."

"That he will not!" said Mr. Holmes viciously—"that he will not do!" and he began to write a letter to the editor.

"Well," said Mr. Keeley, "this looks as though things are coming to a crisis between you. What is the best way to get out of it?"

"I had better give him three months' notice," said Mr. Holmes, with a sigh, "or pay his salary for that time, and replace him with some one who will go straight, and not kick over the traces in this diabolical fashion. Upon my word, I have no patience for this! Why, even the *Daily News* is enthusiastic about the Memorial Hall meeting; and here is Ructions, of all men in the world, undertaking to throw cold water down the back of this ——"

But here Mr. Holmes stopped. He could not find enough eloquence with which to express his indignation.

Mr. Keeley was silent a bit, as if thinking. Then he said to him—

"Mr. Holmes, would you really like to sell the paper?"

"What?" said he. "Sell the paper? No; certainly not! Who put such an idea into your head?"

"Nobody," said Mr. Keeley; "I thought you said so just now."

"No," said Mr. Holmes. "Sell the paper, indeed! Why, look what a property it is!"

"Yes," said Keeley indifferently; "but properties can be bought."

"I would not sell it—no, not for £250,000!"

"That is a good deal of money," said Mr. Keeley, "especially as you only paid £25,000 for it ten years ago."

"Yes, but look what a position it has. Why, there is not a paper in London that has the pull we have to-day."

"That is rather Ructions' doing, isn't it?" said Keeley. "I would put another man in his place. There are as good fish in the sea as ever were got out."

"Well, he might make it awkward," said Keeley, drumming on the table. "Let us look at the question practically. If Ructions goes and finds some one else to back him to the tune of £250,000, would you be disposed to listen?"

"No, I would not. Not a penny less than £300,000. For £300,000—there! you can take it! For £300,000, and he may have the *Tribune*, or any one else, but not a penny less; not for Ructions, or for anybody."

CHAPTER X.

ROPING THEM IN.

Mr. Keeley, having obtained what he wanted, took up his hat and departed.

He met Mr. Faulmann at half-past seven. At 9.30 he had his cheque for £300,000 in his pocket, and was driving rapidly down to Bouverie Street.

He found Ructions looking even more pale and distraught than he was in the afternoon.

"Oh, Mr. Keeley, I am glad to see you! I am very much bothered. The very information on which I relied to prove the conspiracy has disappeared, and I have had a deputation from the Toilers' Industrial League, declaring that I have been guilty of the cruellest injustice to the most benevolent philanthropist of our time; and I would not like to feel," said he, "that I have been unjust to anybody." And the good fellow looked troubled.

"Never you mind," said Mr. Keeley. "I have seen Mr. Holmes, and I have seen the other people, too. I will tell you what we have fixed up. Believe me, there is no truth about this story of conspiracy. There is no conspiracy, and, what is more, Mr. Holmes is perfectly infatuated with admiration for Ping Yang Yaloo. The fact is, if it had not been for me, he would have written to you a letter which would have forbidden you to say another word against Ping Yang Yaloo." And Mr. Keeley rubbed his hands and laughed cheerfully.

"I do not care what he does. You see, I am awfully driven just now. My youngest child is lying between life and death at home, and I am shorthanded, as I have had to send Piper off down to Derbyshire to look into the matter on the spot, and I do not know really which way to turn."

"My dear fellow," said Keeley, who was a good-hearted man on the whole, and who knew too well what fate was hanging over Ructions' head. "Do not disturb yourself. Mark time. Leave the whole question open, and wait until events prove themselves. Do not publish another line of editorial about the whole subject until you see me again."

"All right," said Ructions, shaking his hand. "You have always been a good friend of mine. I think that is the best advice on the whole."

"I am quite sure it is," said Keeley. "Good-night, and get away home, and to bed."

Ten minutes later Mr. Keeley handed in Mr. Faulmann's cheque to Mr. Holmes, and received from him in return formal instructions to draw up a transfer of the *Daily Tribune*, and all the appurtenances thereof, to Messrs. Glogoul and Faulmann. The whole transaction, however, was to be kept a profound secret.

DAYLIGHT STILL FOUND HIM AT HIS VIGIL.

WHEN the Editor reached home he found his child much worse. His wife, harassed by long suffering, was threatened with imminent collapse. Wearily the editor turned to watch by the sick bed of his little one, who was tossing and moaning unconsciously. His wife had lain down to get a little sleep. He was alone, and there was no sound in the chamber except the ticking of the timepiece and the occasional moan of the little sufferer. Ructions had been under a severe strain for some time, and now he felt that everything was breaking beneath him. It was doubtful whether the child would be able to live through another day, his wife was distraught and wearied with long watching, and he was perplexed when confronting the inexplicable problems of life, and half wondered whether it would not be better for the child to be taken away from this evil world and be at peace. That did not, however, prevent him from gently smoothing the pillow of the little one, and giving it the draught which had to be administered every half-hour. Daylight still found him at his vigil beside the bedside of the child, who seemed, thank God, to be sleeping a little more quietly. The dim twilight which preceded sunrise gave place to the grey light of a winter morning, and still he was revolving many things, and wondering after all whether life was not a hideous mistake, and, that in endeavouring to make things a little better, he was only making confusion worse confounded.

He sat there, chewing the cud of many bitter thoughts, when the sharp rat-tat of the postman roused him from his reveries. It was the rude intrusion of the outer world, and he hastened to the door to receive his mail. There was only one letter, and that in the handwriting of Mr. Keeley. He opened it mechanically, not caring to speculate as to what its contents might be. It was very brief and very kind. It ran thus:—

My dear Ructions,—I was very distressed to see you looking so ill to-day. I have talked the matter over with Mr. Holmes, and we have agreed that you must have an instant rest and change of air. Please find cheque inclosed for £250, with which you will be able to take your wife and little one abroad as soon as it recovers, as I have no doubt it will. Mr. Piper will take your place in your absence.

At any other time Ructions would have been indignant at this sudden arrangement for his absence from the paper which he had conducted, and whose prosperity he had built up year after year. But on the whole he felt that it was the best that could have happened. He was fearfully run down, he knew, and he was in no fit condition to wage the life and death struggle which would be involved if that conspiracy really existed which he felt it might be his duty to unmask. Clearly the way opening before him was the best, and languidly dismissing the subject from his mind, he turned to his child's sick bed. To his great satisfaction he saw that the little one had opened its eyes and was looking at him quietly, and without any of the feverish fitfulness which it had previously exhibited. He felt its pulse, took its temperature, and a great thankfulness came into his heart. It seemed as if after all the little one was to be given back to them.

When he was still in the first glow of delight at the unexpected blessing of returning hope the door opened and his wife came in. She had slept soundly for six hours and felt that her strength had come back. She saw the change in the child at once, and she exclaimed with joy, "Oh, George!" and could say no more. They both bent over the couch in which their little one was lying, the whole being of both blending, as it were, in an exultation of gratitude too fervent to find expression in words.

That afternoon, when Mr. Ructions came down to the office, he found Mr. Piper already installed in his place. "Taken charge already, you see," said Piper pleasantly. "The fact is, we were all alarmed about you, and you must not put a pen to paper for another three months. Of course we shall be delighted to have your instructions," he continued deferentially, "but you have to go right away and leave us to steer the ship as best we can."

"How did you come back?" asked Ructions.

"Oh, Mr. Keeley telegraphed for me; said you were ill, and that I had to come back and take charge."

"Did you find anything?" asked Ructions.

"No," said Piper, "everything seems all straight there. It is surprising the number of men they have at work from the Peak to Ripley. The men are as thick as bees all along the line of the Little Wall of China. I can't say I like it very much," he added, "but after all there is work being done, and being paid for too. He is putting on whoever will do a day's work, and they are made to work and no mistake."

"Well, well," said Ructions, "keep your weather-eye open in that quarter while I am away, and wire me at once if things come to a crisis."

"All right," replied Piper, whereupon Ructions sat down and wrote cordial letters to Mr. Keeley and Mr. Holmes, and left the sanctum which had been the scene of his early triumphs, never to return to it more. Of that, however, he knew nothing, and with a light heart he set off home to find that his child was progressing favourably, and that the doctor held out every hope that in a few days they would be able to remove her to the south coast, from whence after a short stay they were to proceed to the South of France, there to forget in the land of flowers the cares and the worries of the last six months.

The same morning Faulmann told Glogoul how he had fared in his negotiations for the purchase of the *Tribune.*

"That is right," said Glogoul; "we must not appear in it at all; be warned by the ghastly mess that Walledoff made when he bought the *Latter Day Gazette.* There must be no ostensible change in the ownership, the editorship, or the policy of the paper. Keeley will see that nothing appears which is calculated to damage us, and it will not be difficult to work the oracle so as to convince the enthusiasts who get the paper that they are really carrying out their own programme. Meantime you had better see Sir Peter again and ascertain how things are going."

When Faulmann reached Kensington he found Sir Peter indisposed. "My wife," he said, "will tell you everything. Talk to her as if you were talking to me."

Faulmann, who naturally distrusted women, was inclined at first to depart in a huff, but on second thoughts he decided to see Lady Dorothy, and he had not been five minutes in the room before he saw that he had decided wisely. She spoke as if she had an absolute right of ownership in Sir Peter, and assumed throughout with a certain calm confidence that whatever she decided should be done, would be carried out. She expressed a violent antipathy to the aristocracy, and exulted in the success of the agitation which her dear Mr. Bradford was conducting.

"Yes," said Mr. Faulmann, "that is all very well; but now I am here I would like to suggest to you whether something could not be done to reduce the glut of the labour market."

"I wish there could," she replied. "But what do you suggest?"

"Well," said Faulmann, "when there is not enough work to go round, what do we do in order to secure a fair distribution of wages? We run short time, do we not?"

"Yes," she said hesitatingly.

"Now," said Faulmann, "do you not think that the time has come for a vigorous agitation for a six hours' day and whole holidays on Saturdays, especially in the textile trades?"

"It sounds well," said Lady Dorothy; "and no overtime, of course?"

"Of course no overtime," said Faulmann. "Overtime would spoil everything."

"But," she asked, "what about wages?"

"Oh," said Faulmann airily, "we must always stand for the living wage!"

"But how would you define the living wage?" asked Lady Dorothy.

"The living wage," said Faulmann pompously, "is the irreducible minimum of wage upon which a working man can keep himself and family in decent comfort; but practically," he added, with a smile, "the living wage is the actual wage as an irreducible minimum with as much as can be added to it by judicious agitation."

"I see," said Lady Dorothy, "a five-days' week, a six-hours' day, and a living wage never to fall below the present rate. That would no doubt catch on."

"I have no doubt of it," said Faulmann. "I hope Sir Peter will introduce a Bill to that effect next session."

"Oh," said Lady Dorothy, "certainly! There will be no difficulty about that."

"I am glad to hear it," said Faulmann, half sarcastically; and then, seeing that he had put things in train, he rose to go.

Sir Peter, whose indisposition did not seem to have been very severe, was playing billiards with a friend.

"When you have finished your game," said Lady Dorothy, looking in, "I should like to have a few words with you."

Half an hour afterwards he came up to her little office. "My dear," she said, "pray take a seat. Everything is going beautifully. You are to make a speech at an early date, in which you must express your opinion that the time has come for a new departure, and that, in view of the increasing lack of employment, it is necessary to put the textile industry of the country, as a beginning, upon the footing of six hours a day and five days a week."

Sir Peter stared at her for a moment, and then repeated, "Six hours a day and five days a week; and what about wages then?"

"Oh," said she glibly, "the living wage is to be insisted

upon! There are to be no reductions; that, of course, is a *sine quâ non*."

"But," objected Sir Peter, "there is practically no cotton industry left in the country."

"So much the easier," she replied, "to lay down sound principles—there will be no vested interests to stand in the way."

"Yes," said Sir Peter, "but is it not locking the door after the steed is stolen?"

"Never you mind that," said Lady Dorothy authoritatively; "you must have something to give body and substance to your labour programme. I am just going to telegraph for Bradford. You will get the Bill drafted, dear, won't you?"

He shrugged his shoulders with a kind of despairing acquiescence and returned to his billiards, saying to himself, "It is too mad for anything; but we must play the game, I suppose. At any rate," he added languidly, "she no longer bores me with her caresses."

And with good reason. Sir Peter had long since ceased even to disguise his distaste for such demonstrations; but there was another who in the ardour of his youthful devotion would have rejoiced to kiss even the hem of her garment. As it was, he was by no means confined to such Lenten fare, and Lady Dorothy experienced in the ardour of his affection something of the afterglow of the days of her somewhat skittish youth.

"Well, Algernon dear," she said, as he entered and covered her hand with kisses, "how goes the campaign?"

"Bravely, Lady Dorothy," said he; "nothing could go better. I have found an invaluable assistant who is going to stand for Blankshire."

"Really!" said Lady Dorothy. "Where young Wilkes was defeated?"

"Yes; it is the man who defeated him."

"You don't mean Lord Bulstrode?"

"Oh, dear me, no: I mean a Mr. Brassy. A wonderful man; knows every inch of the ground, and a marvellous organiser. He says that he knows of at least twelve good men and true who are ready to start for any part of England if their expenses are paid, and who will advocate any programme your ladyship pleases. They have such implicit confidence in your judgment, you see, my queen," he added, looking up into her face with an almost ecstatic devotion.

"Oh, you silly boy!" she said, passing her hand smoothly over his face. "What nonsense, to talk like that to an old woman like me."

The young man started as if some one had stung him. "Don't say that," he said bitterly, as if he were going to cry.

"Don't say what?" asked Lady Dorothy.

"Don't call yourself old," he said impetuously. "What are a few years by an almanack? To me you are radiant in immortal youth."

"Now, really, Algernon," said Lady Dorothy, "if you talk such nonsense I shall have to send you away, and we have so much business to transact." Then cutting short all further protestations she unfolded to him the new programme. He agreed that it was superb; but how was it to be launched?

"Oh, Sir Peter will do that!" said Lady Dorothy, "and you will see that the *Tribune* will take it up eagerly, and after a time all the Liberal papers will come into line."

"Sir Peter!" said Algernon, with an absent look. The young man was thinking in his vanity of the day when the promulgation of the new programme would be relegated, not to the husband who was on the retired list, but to the lover with whom it was arranged.

Lady Dorothy smiled to herself as she divined the train of thought passing through his mind.

"Never mind, dear," she said consolingly; "the whole success of the programme will depend upon you." Whereupon she tenderly pressed his hand, and he, grasping hers in both of his, raised it to his lips, pressed it passionately, and then departed.

No sooner had he gone than Lady Dorothy touched her bell. Her secretary appeared. "Isabel," she said, "you know where the Rev. Dawson Johnson lives?"

"Yes!" replied her factotum.

"Put on your hat and tell him I want to see him on important business at once."

In five minutes the Rev. Dawson Johnson was closeted with her ladyship. Lady Dorothy was one of those philosophers to whom all religions are equally false, and one of those politicians to whom they are all equally useful. She always put in an appearance at the Oratory on great occasions, made a point of consulting the Cardinal on all cases of conscience, regularly took communion at the parish church, but at the same time always attended any important gathering among the Nonconformists. The Rev. Dawson Johnson was one of her *protégés*. It was he who certified to her husband's admiring constituents the liberality with which she contributed to his collections whenever she attended his place of worship, and the good man honestly believed that Lady Dorothy in her heart of hearts was a Nonconformist.

"And what new work of mercy is it that you are contemplating now?" he asked, entering the room as if he were approaching a shrine, and remaining standing until she begged him to be seated.

"Sir Peter is not well, Mr. Johnson," she said. "He is suffering from insomnia, and the other night after he had been tossing restlessly for hours, he said to me, 'Dorothy, love, I cannot bear to think of those poor people down at the Derbyshire relief works without any spiritual consolation. You know there are twenty thousand of them, many of them with their families, and I am afraid that there is sore need for the faithful ministering of the Word.'"

"I have no doubt of it," said Mr. Johnson. "But what can we do? The charge of the souls of our own congregations lies too heavily upon us to allow the regular ministry to follow these sheep into the wilderness."

"Of course," said Lady Dorothy, "you don't dream for one moment that Sir Peter could think of depriving your congregation of your ministry. No, he said to me, 'If you could see Mr. Dawson Johnson and talk it over with him he might be able to arrange for some gospel services. If he would look after the spiritual side I should be glad to attend to the material.' To make a long story short, Mr. Dawson Johnson," she added, "Sir Peter has given me a cheque for a thousand pounds, which he desires me to place at your disposal for this purpose. There is, however, one condition, and that is that you must not allow any one to know to whom you owe this grant. Let not thy right hand know what thy left hand doeth! But I must apologise for quoting scripture to one who knows it so much better than myself."

"Oh, Lady Dorothy," said he, as his fingers closed over the cheque, "this is too much, too much! There are indeed some men of whom the world is not worthy."

Mr. Dawson Johnson hurried home, and immediately told his wife, and she, in the strictest confidence, communicated it to three of her intimate friends who happened to call that afternoon. By the evening there was not a person in Mr. Dawson Johnson's congregation who did not know the story of Sir Peter's bounty.

As for Sir Peter himself, when his wife told him what she had done, he merely looked at her with admiration, and remarked, "How you do rope them in!"

CHAPTER XI.

JIMJAMS AND CHOLERA.

THANKS to the agitation carried on by the Toilers' Industrial League, several of the nobles incurred considerable expenditure in providing work for the unemployed in their immediate vicinity. The Toilers' League insisted that every one who was employed on relief works should be paid full union wages, a rule which they allowed only to be relaxed at the great relief works in Derbyshire, where the men worked for their rations, with an extra allowance if they were accompanied by their wives and families.

In order to meet expenditure thus forced upon them by popular agitation, they had recourse to the money-lenders, would consent to a 25 per cent. reduction as ransom, this money to be applied in providing relief-works for the unemployed. The scheme was more popular than the Six Hours' Bill, which, however, had been enthusiastically adopted by the *Tribune*, and was in a fair way of becoming one of the leading planks of the Radical platform.

As for the brewers, they were for a time at their wits' end. But light at last dawned in the shape of a communication from Shanghai. The great man's private secretary wrote to Glogoul: "Rejoice, my friend, rejoice! Jimjams is the word; it is jimjams that will do the trick. After many experiments, we have succeeded in extracting from a weed which grows luxuriantly on our estates in Southern China, an essence which unites all the qualities of all the sedatives, stimulants and narcotics at present known to mankind. The

"YES, JIMJAMS IS A SUCCESS."

and in nine cases out of ten these money-lenders were either Messrs. Glogoul and Faulmann or their secret allies. Glogoul was in high spirits, for every week added to the number of tentacles which he was slowly but surely fastening round the estates of the nobility. With the exception of a few ennobled brewers and the owners of town property, he had almost every peer in the realm on his books. He grudged even these exceptions. Brewers and ground landlords must be got at somehow.

After a consultation with Faulmann, it was decided that the campaign against the ground-rents must be taken up with vigour. The Land Nationalisation League received, through Lady Dorothy, a cheque for £5,000, to be employed in an agitation, the central features of which were derived from the Plan of Campaign. No more ground-rents were to be paid excepting to trustees of the Toilers' Industrial League. They were to remain banked until the landlords

essence is made up in pellets about the size of buckshot: One of these pellets dissolved in a pint of water will make any one feel jolly, and half a dozen will make the hardest-headed toper gloriously drunk. Before communicating this information to you, we have tried it upon men of all nationalities at the Sailors' Home at Shanghai. It affects them all the same. When once men have begun to drink jimjams, they will drink nothing else. It is medicinal, aromatic, delightful to the taste, and can be produced for a mere nothing. We have got the secret, and I am convinced that there are millions in it. We are sending you over a first consignment by this mail."

Glogoul awaited with feverish impatience the arrival of the parcel. The moment it came Faulmann and he dissolved a pellet in a tumbler of water and tasted it. It was pleasant to the palate, and almost immediately it was swallowed the partners were conscious of a benevolent feeling towards each other and towards the world at large to which they had been strangers for some time past. Glogoul detected this, and said, "Let us increase the dose." They did so, and by the time Faulmann had taken four glasses he was lying helpless on the floor. Glogoul, who had a steadier head, dragged his partner to a couch and left him there, while he sat down in an easy-chair to analyse his feelings.

"Yes, jimjams," he said to himself, "is a success. The dreamy sensation it produces is not unlike opium. The effect, however, is much more rapid; and although I have only taken four pellets, I am beginning to feel something of the hallucinations of hashish. I wonder what the after-effects will be?" He determined, however, not to experimentalise any more that day.

In about three hours Faulmann slept off the stupor occasioned by the drug, and immediately asked for some more.

"No," said Glogoul, "jimjams is all very well for other people, but you and I have to keep our heads cool."

In vain Faulmann begged and implored to be allowed to have just one more pellet. Glogoul was obdurate. "Never again!" said he; "we have too much at stake. But I think I know of something that will cure your craving." He went to his cabinet and produced from a secret drawer a pill which he handed to Faulmann, who swallowed it eagerly. In a few minutes the room began to swim round him.

"You scoundrel," he shouted, "you have poisoned me!"

"No, I have not," replied Glogoul calmly; "lie still and you will soon be all right."

Faulmann remembered no more. When he awoke he was alone. His head was aching, but all craving for jimjams had left him. Next morning Glogoul and he discussed what should be done.

"Its effects," said Glogoul, "are too immediate for us to put it into general circulation. It must be sold as a patent medicine, and the ingredients kept a profound secret. But my own opinion is," he added, "that once the jimjams mania is set up the patient will go on taking it until it kills him. It will, at any rate, relieve the pressure of the labour market."

The next mail, however, brought him another letter from the great man's secretary. "We have," he wrote, "at last found the best way of using jimjams. It is not to supply the pellets to the public, they are too strong; and we have found, by experiment, that if a man once begins taking them he usually dies in three months. If, however, it is dissolved judiciously in distilled water it produces a mild and pleasing beverage. This is so weak that even a confirmed drunkard will last for one or two years."

It was after the receipt of this letter that a company, of which the well-known temperance reformer, Joseph Brassy of Rigby, was managing director, was established for the manufacture of the great new temperance drink, "Jimjams."

For once it seemed as if the temperance people had invented a popular beverage. The consumption of beer fell off day by day. There was a perfect rage for the new drink. The beer lords began to look anxiously to the dwindling value of their stock. In vain they tried to rally the market. Prices continued to fall. Then they set to work to combat this new and formidable rival. Stories began to be current as to the effect of the jimjams mania on persons of nervous temperament. The brewers produced an appalling array of statistics to show that the habit of drinking jimjams was destructive of what might be called the moral tissue of man. Its victim became lethargic, and soon exhibited all the traces of morphiamania. In many cases sudden death had resulted from the stoppage of the heart's action. These cases were attributed by the brewers to the deleterious effects of drinking jimjams. Prohibitory legislation was talked of, but the jimjamites laughed it to scorn. Sir Peter made an eloquent speech denouncing the plutocratic brewers who were trying to deprive mankind of the one innocent drink which would drive intemperance from the land.

Meanwhile a perfect labyrinth of walls had been constructed round the Derbyshire estates of Ping Yang Yaloo. It had been the original intention of the firm to run a wall as a kind of ring fence round the whole estate from the Peak in the north to Ripley in the south. But after a careful examination of the rights of way, the roads and the railroads, they decided to make three separate parks. One enclosed the Peak, another had Chatsworth as its centre, while the third was of an irregular shape stretching from Six Elms on the north towards Ripley and Alfreton. When the outer walls were finished the great hordes of labourers were employed in building extensive lairs, which were all lined with hot water pipes. The exact use of these buildings none of the workmen knew.

The President of the Local Government Board sent for Glogoul and Faulmann one day, and inquired what they intended to do with the labourers when the relief works were finished. They replied that they could not undertake to provide permanently for all this labour; but if the President had any suggestion to make, they would submit it to Ping Yang Yaloo, who might possibly authorise a further expenditure. The President thanked them cordially.

Articles appeared in all the papers praising the generosity of the Chinese millionaire, and a further sum of £100,000 was granted for the planting of Chatsworth with Chinese shrubs and plants. But, as Glogoul said to Faulmann, "This is only a palliative; nothing short of a good epidemic will solve the problem."

It must be admitted that everything seemed ripe for such a solution of the difficulty. The labour camps were filthy. Owing to the provident kindness of Glogoul and Faulmann, canteens were established in each centre, from which practically free drink was supplied to the workmen in the latter part of their engagement. Jimjams was supplied free as water, and those who took jimjams very seldom took anything else. The debilitated frame of the habitual jimjams drinker, the lacklustre eye and the bloodless face, all denoted a population incapable of offering any resistance to any serious epidemic which might break out.

Glogoul wrote to the medical authorities, calling attention to the dangerously insanitary condition of the camps, and offered to contribute £10,000 for the establishment of field-hospitals, where the sick could be treated. To one of these field-hospitals Ethel Merribel was appointed as head-nurse. She entered upon her task with considerable forebodings, but she was not prepared for the sudden apparition at her hospital of Dr. Glogoul.

"Miss Merribel," he exclaimed gallantly, "I am delighted to see you!"

"But, Dr. Glogoul, I am surprised to see you here."

"Why," said Glogoul, "did you not know that all these hospitals are practically of our providing?"

"No," said Ethel, "I did not. I was at the Derby Hospital, and they asked me if I would take charge of this place."

"I am extremely sorry to see you here all the same," replied Glogoul gravely, "for I am afraid there will be a very bad epidemic."

"Then it is the very place where I ought to be," she answered, smiling.

"The work is hard, my dear Miss Merribel," said Glogoul. "I advise you to exchange while yet there is time." There was something so serious in his look that she was alarmed.

"What do you mean?" she exclaimed.

"It seems to me that it will be strange if we escape an outbreak of cholera," he replied.

"If so," said Ethel, "it is not for me to desert my post," and all expostulations were in vain.

Dr. Glogoul, although capable of almost anything in the cause of science, or of what he considered to be business, shrank from letting loose the cholera until he could get Ethel Merribel out of the way. Finding that she was obstinate, he changed his plan, and as a result the cholera broke out, not in the Ripley district, as he had at first intended, but in the neighbourhood of the Peak, and spread southwards. The mortality was awful. The disease slew with the virulence of the Black Death. The deaths in the camp which it first struck reached as high as fifty per cent., and the remaining fifty per cent. fled, carrying with them the contagion far and near. By the end of the month the disease had travelled as far as Ripley, leaving death and desolation in its wake. Glogoul made a last despairing attempt to induce Miss Merribel to leave the district.

"No," she replied; "here I am and here I will remain. I am not going to desert these poor creatures in the hour of their trial."

"I warned you," he said, "while yet there was time. Why did you persist in choosing death?"

"It was my duty," said Ethel simply.

Glogoul blushed as the pale girl uttered these four words. Some sense of the divine in life glimmered before his hardened soul. He bowed and left the hospital.

Two days after cholera struck Ethel Merribel, and she lay prostrate, helpless, among the dying and the dead. She felt that her last hour had come, and with that certainty came a strange sense of ability to see the cause of things, of the invisible agencies which were working such havoc all around. As in the old hospital at Garlam she had seen the spectral forms of Bladud and Faulmann walking with death in their touch through the ward, she now saw One moving among the huddled crowd of cholera-stricken wretches, silent as the angel of death, ruthless and remorseless as a fiend from hell. Where his shadow fell, men writhed in torture; where he laid his hand, they stiffened and died. It was in vain they endeavoured to flee from that dreadful presence. And ever as he moved there went before him two fiends which did his bidding. One was the spirit of ENVY and HATRED, which set class against class and divided the masses from the classes, without whom they were but as dumb driven beasts, while an insatiable hunger was stamped upon the features of the other attendant spirit, and he grasped ever with the hand of AVARICE for more and yet more of the world's wealth.

As she looked, the walls of the hospital seemed to dissolve, and in place of the few wretched sufferers who were groaning and dying around her, she seemed to see the destroying Three go out throughout the length and the breadth of the land. They spared neither rich nor poor, high or low, fair or foul, and ever as the central figure pressed on, his attendant spirits made haste to make his way smooth and easy.

As she watched, the death dews gathered on her brow, and with parched lips she moaned, "How long, O Lord, how long?" Then it seemed to her as if a voice replied out of the firmament, "Until all who love unite in the service of all who suffer!"

As these words sounded in her ears she was conscious of a brightness more dazzling than the eye of man could look upon and live, and in that light the figure of the foul destroyer vanished as a dream, and she saw it no more.

But when the attendant came to her couch, Ethel Merribel was dead.

CHAPTER XII.

THE YELLOW MAN IN POSSESSION.

THE outbreak of cholera effectively disposed of the difficulty which confronted Messrs. Glogoul and Faulmann as to how to disperse the crowds which they had gathered together in Derbyshire. In other directions everything went well for the firm. They had added two famous north-country castles to the list of their desirable residences to let or sell which they circulated every month among the plutocracy of four continents.

They had also steadily and silently tightened their hold upon the peers, until they were in a position to foreclose on half the estates in England at three months' notice. In the House of Commons Sir Peter had not done amiss. He had introduced his "Six Hours a Day and Five Days a Week Bill" for the textile industries. That Bill was now the shibboleth of the Toilers' Industrial League. The campaign against ground-rents was being pushed on with relentless vigour, and Sir Peter had carried three-quarters of the Radical Party with him in a demand that a greatly increased proportion of local taxation should be thrown upon the landlords.

It was in vain that Mr. Hopton, now a member of Parliament, John Burns and Mr. Burt, together with the older Trade Unionists, demonstrated that the Six Hours a Day Bill was midsummer madness, when our one formidable rival was working his men sixteen hours a day for seven days a week. But a species of madness seemed to have seized the working classes. They were still under the influence of watchwords which might have had some meaning twenty years before, but which it seemed as if they had only begun to understand.

Similar phenomena are frequently to be observed in political history. It must have been from this that Baron Munchausen conceived the happy idea of frozen eloquence, which could be dissolved at a considerable period after the words had fallen from the speaker's lips. There is always a certain amount of frozen or latent suggestion in the public mind, which is thawed out some ten or twenty years after date. In the present instance, the latent suggestion of the wealth of the landed aristocracy, which was accurate enough when land represented the chief realised wealth of the community, was thawed out and became part of the circulating medium long after the circumstances had changed, and the landlords, instead of being the millionaires of the community, were little better than its paupers. In vain were facts and figures rained down upon Sir Peter and his supporters. The fixed idea of the mob was that the landowner was a Crœsus, and that the shortest cut to prosperity was to tax him out of existence by throwing upon his shoulders the whole of the expenses of administration and relief.

It is not surprising, therefore, under these circumstances, that a panic began to rage among the doomed class. They could see no way of relief; whichever way they turned they were confronted with the menace of ever-increasing burdens. Some of them sat still, as the mouse sits cowering under the eye of the snake, waiting helplessly for the moment when it will be engulfed down the scaly demon's jaws; others sold out for whatever they could get. Their estates always fell into the hands of Messrs. Glogoul and Faulmann. But a minority, headed by Sir Artegal and Lady Muriel, Mr. Wilkes and Lady Ænid, the Jew financier and a few of the more far-seeing of the clergy and Nonconformist ministers, set to work to redress the broken fortunes of the old order. The material basis upon which they relied was the continually increasing output of the gold which flowed from the Comford mill; their spiritual reliance was upon the innate honesty and sober commonsense of the English people, which would in time, they were certain, rid itself of the frenzy bred by the poison of those who set class against class, and who persuaded the masses that they should regard the classes, not as their natural leaders, but as their hereditary foes.

This minority of the elect found a powerful re-enforcement in Mr. Ructions. He had not been two months away from the country before he found that it would be impossible for him to direct the course of the paper in accordance with his own convictions and at the same time command the support of the proprietor. He had no idea, nor had any one in the office the slightest notion, that the paper had been sold to Ping Yang Yaloo's agents. Mr. Piper, who edited it, was in blissful unconsciousness that he was doing their bidding when he was advocating the Six Hours' Bill. As little did he dream that he was the conscious instrument of the Chinese conspiracy when he insisted upon increasing the burdens on land and taxing the ground landlords to the bone. Mr. Piper was an impressionable young man, and Mr. Keeley was genial and plausible. In a short time Mr. Ructions saw that the paper which he had conducted for so many years with such sweat of soul had passed beyond his control. Regretfully, but without hesitation, he resigned his post. Mr. Keeley wrote to him expressing extreme regret, and enclosing a cheque for £1,000, assuring him that his services on the *Tribune* would never be forgotten.

The *Tribune*, thanks to the prestige which it owed to its first editor, and to the great services which it had rendered to the cause of freedom, proved to be the most useful weapon in the hands of the conspirators. Ructions groaned in spirit as he saw the men, concealed behind his mask, stealthily striking at the very heart of English freedom. But for the moment he was helpless. It was not for long, however. Returning to London, he sought an interview with Sir Artegal, and after long consultation it was decided to start a London daily with localised weeklies in connection with it in all the large centres of population in the land. "England for the English" was the motto of this new organ, and Messrs. Glogoul and Faulmann saw with dismay the entry upon the field of an adversary so indomitable, wielding a pen so trenchant. By way of a counterstroke they bought up a series of evening papers in the country, doing it, not as Mr. Carnegie did a few years before, with a frankness which was quite foolishly aboveboard, but secretly, so that no one knew that the hand which controlled the editor was changed. Neither did the journals appear to be in communication with each other, but none the less every paper danced to the piping of Lady Dorothy, to whom Messrs. Glogoul and Faulmann had handed over the task of manipulating the press. She employed wherever possible, as editors, the impecunious scions of noble houses who had titles and brains, but neither principle nor cash.

So time wore on until autumn, when the great Mandarin was to take up his abode at Chatsworth. Everything for some time had been ready for his coming. Chatsworth had been refurnished throughout in Chinese fashion. Most of the pictures had been sold at Christie's, and such of the curios as it was possible to dispose of had been scattered to the four winds. The rest were done up in packing cases and stowed away in the cellars. The great conservatory on which the Duke some years before had spent £5,000 for repairs, merely for the amusement of the people who came from far and near to see the greatest greenhouse in the world, had been converted into a stable for his Excellency's elephants. One whole wing of the palace at Chatsworth was set apart for his harem, a convenient term which covered not merely his array of concubines, but many of those ministers to Oriental vice whose presence scandalised ancient Rome in the days of Heliogabalus. The village of Edensor had been laid out as a barracks for the Chinese bodyguard who were to arrive under the disguise of the livery of the Mandarin. In each of the three great parks into which his estate had been divided there were lairs for tigers, carefully warmed and provided with every convenience. Wild animals of all descriptions were allowed to roam over the desolation which had been established in the heart of Derbyshire. Deer of all kinds abounded, while here and there wallowing places were provided for the wild buffalo which had been brought from Africa.

It is not to be supposed that changes so extensive as these could have been carried out without exciting the bitter resentment of the multitude of the dispossessed. They were, however, silenced for the most part by the intimidation of the spokesmen of the Toilers' Industrial League, all of whom were unconsciously in the pay of the conspiracy. The *Tribune* and its weekly satellites demonstrated conclusively that whatever the hardship might be to individuals, Derbyshire had profited immensely by the building of this tiger preserve in the Midlands. No doubt there were fewer people on the soil, but those who were allowed to live within the Little Wall of China were better off than the miserable toilers whom they had superseded. The expenditure of capital also, it was proved, was much greater in keeping one tiger than in rearing a thousand sheep, to say nothing of the importance of varying the monotonous round of sport by the introduction of the manly and exciting pursuit of tiger-hunting.

But these sophistries no more sufficed to silence the murmur of discontent than similar arguments in our time help to reconcile the Scottish crofter to their supercession by the red deer. The spectacle of a great country laid desolate in order to provide sport for the alien from farther Asia, the dismantled homes, the ruined farmsteads, the fields once bright with corn now overgrown with all manner of noisome weeds, acted as a perpetual irritant to the smouldering discontent of the people.

The Rev. Ebenezer Brown, who had been Mr. Wilkes' right hand man at Rigby when he stood for Blankshire, had accepted a call to Chesterfield three years ago, and was a witness of the desolation which Glogoul and Faulmann had worked in the land. It got upon his nerves, and he preached sermons which read like latter day variants upon the invectives of the Hebrew seers. The scenes of horror which had followed the dispersion of the labour camps by cholera almost drove him mad. He would wander at night along the hilltops past the ruins of Six Elms, where the workmen in the daytime were busy re-building the seventeenth century palace, and pour out his soul in passionate entreaties to the Lord to smite with a fierce destruction the enemies of the people.

Some time before the day on which Ping Yang Yaloo was expected to arrive at Manchester in his steam yacht, an immense multitude gathered at the station of Rowsley to watch for the arrival of the mysterious millionaire. For several weeks previous to this his retinue had been arriving in driblets. A whole flotilla of steamers had been required to transport the belongings of the millionaire. The peculiarity of the costumes, the curious weapons, and the extraordinary nature of the merchandise offered unceasing topics for the conversation of the multitude. The first instalment of the harem had arrived some days before in closely curtained carriages. So great was the press of people to see the Chinese ladies that it was necessary to bring down a regiment of cavalry from Sheffield. Under the protection of their sabres the disembarkation of the Chinese menagerie continued. No such menagerie had ever before amazed the rustics of Derbyshire. The huge elephants, which made their way with ponderous tread to their appointed place, excited eager curiosity; but the interest was centred upon the great iron cages in which tigers and tigresses were conveyed to their quarters in the various preserves. From time to time there was a shout of anger or of fierce discontent from the crowd, but it was only momentary, and served but to punctuate the long rolling cheers which greeted each fresh arrival.

On the day on which Ping Yang was expected to arrive, Glogoul and Faulmann went down to Manchester to receive him. On their way thither Faulmann seemed to be smitten with an unaccustomed fit of remorse. Glogoul endeavoured in vain to cheer him.

"Don't be a fool, Faulmann," said he. "What is the matter with you?"

"I had a horrid dream last night," he replied. "It seemed to me that those wretches whose homes we have demolished, and whom we have destroyed with that accursed cholera of yours, stood around me. I felt as if I deserved to be damned."

"And so you do," said Glogoul heartily, "if you give way to feelings like these. We have only done what others have done before us who have died in the odour of sanctity, and whose praises are sung in all the churches."

Faulmann went on without heeding him. "The dynamite was bad, the cholera was worse, but, after all the miseries which that accursed jimjams has wrought, the rest of our crimes dwindle into insignificance."

"Well," said Glogoul, "let it be 'crimes,' if you will have it so. It is not our country, is it? And as for jimjams, what have we done more than the English have done to the Chinese? Jimjams is no worse than opium, any way; and after giving opium the free run of China for fifty years, you cannot possibly say that we

LADY DOROTHY DROPPED A CURTSEY AND OFFERED HER BOUQUET.

have balanced the account by giving jimjams a year's run in England."

"But," said Faulmann, "it has only begun."

"No doubt," said Glogoul, "but the opium habit is just as inveterate as that of jimjams. It has had a start of half a century, and jimjams is not going to make that up in a hurry. You should," said Glogoul, with a sinister smile, "regard yourself, like Lady Dorothy, as the Avenging Angel of Retributive Providence."

Faulmann did not reply, but looked out from the carriage window over the broad landscape through which the train was passing. It was only here and there, however, that he got a glimpse of the scenery, for the line was bordered on either side by the high wall which had been built to prevent the escape of the tigers.

"You may talk as you like, Glogoul," he said, "but when I look over the countryside and see for miles and miles not a chimney smoking or the glimmer of a single light from a peasant's cottage at night, I confess I feel bad."

"The more fool you," said Glogoul; "now, if you were a true humanitarian——"

"Like you, I suppose," said Faulmann savagely.

"Yes, like me," said Glogoul calmly. "I am the only true humanitarian, for my humanitarianism is based on science and intelligently directed to its logical end. The only service which you can render to this humanity of which you talk so much is to put an end to it. After all these whom we have put out of pain in the last twelve months, my conscience, if you like to call it such, only reproves me of one thing, and that is we have killed too few. How can you look out upon this pesthole of a world and not feel that the man who could devise a sleeping draught which the whole human race could take and never rise again, would be the supreme benefactor of the universe? We cannot attain to that yet, but we are approximating."

Faulmann did not reply; and the two were silent until they had reached their destination. Conspicuous on the gangway they saw Lady Dorothy Patterson, arrayed in a white satin costume more suitable to a girl of fifteen than to a matron of fifty. She stood holding a bouquet of hothouse flowers which she had herself selected—for she prided herself upon her taste—in order to present to His Excellency the moment his feet touched British soil. There was also the Mayor of Manchester with a special address of welcome, and Mr. Algernon Bradford dancing attendance on Lady Dorothy.

Within half an hour after their arrival the Mandarin's yacht drew up at the wharf, which was gaily decorated to receive him. Cannons fired salvoes of welcome, and immense crowds on either side of the canal all the way from Liverpool had almost deafened Ping Yang Yaloo with one incessant roar of cheering. His impassive countenance, however, showed no sign either of delight or of disgust or of weariness as he stepped upon the soft velvety carpet which was laid upon the gangway.

He had no sooner planted both his feet upon the wharf than Lady Dorothy pressed up to him with a smile which was meant to be irresistibly winning, dropped a curtsey, and gracefully offered him her bouquet. The millionaire looked at her with an imperturbable, stony look in his black eyes. He neither put out his hand nor manifested the slightest consciousness of her existence. Lady Dorothy blushed, and a horrible moment intervened. Before she had regained her self-possession, Ping Yang Yaloo had passed her, disdaining to take her flowers, and was abreast of the Mayor of Manchester. That functionary, with his gold chain and official air, succeeded in attracting for a moment the attention of His Excellency. No sooner, however, had Ping Yang Yaloo heard the first words of the address than he motioned to his secretary and moved on. No one attempted to detain him until he reached the saloon carriage, which he entered, leaving his secretary to wrestle with the intricacies of municipal etiquette. Ping Yang Yaloo was followed by the *élite* of his bodyguard, men armed to the teeth. These took up their quarters in the carriages in front and behind the car in which Ping Yang Yaloo was ensconced. The rest of the party filed into the various carriages, and the train started for Chatsworth.

It was a bright and beautiful day. The sun was shining as if to belie the Mandarin's impressions of an English climate. The excitement of the crowd was immense when the signals announced the approach of the Mandarin's train.

"WOE! WOE!"

It required all the tact and resolution of the soldiers to keep the crowd within bounds. Amid the enthusiastic cheering of the people, the train steamed slowly up to the platform of Rowsley Station. At the station carriages were waiting to convey the Mandarin, his guards, and his retinue to Chatsworth. As soon as the rest of his party had started, Ping Yang Yaloo took his seat on the luxurious crimson cushions of his carriage. His bodyguard, fierce-looking Tartars from the north of China, with pigtails, mounted and dressed exactly alike, so that no man in the crowd could tell one from another, formed an escort round the Mandarin's car.

Lady Dorothy, who had come up in the same train as his Excellency, was still carrying the slighted bouquet. Catching the eye of the Mandarin as she thought, she threw the flowers into the carriage.

They fell on the seat opposite. The great man stooped slowly, took up the bouquet-holder between his finger and thumb, gingerly, as if fearing it contained dynamite, and dropped it into the road at the moment the carriage drove off.

Mortified but undismayed, Lady Dorothy determined to retrieve her fortunes in the palace at Chatsworth, but on inquiring for a carriage, she was informed by the master of ceremonies that his Excellency's orders were precise: no white woman was to be allowed to enter Chatsworth gates.

Furious at this slight, Lady Dorothy departed, consoling herself as best she could with the devoted attentions of Algernon Bradford.

Just as the Mandarin's carriage was about to enter the gates of his park, a pale, slight figure broke through the cordon that kept the way, and stood with an outstretched hand in the centre of the road, right in the way of the approaching carriage. There was a wild cry from the crowd, but, above it, he was heard to shout in a voice which was rather a shriek than an articulate sound, "Woe! woe!"

The cry was heard distinctly by Ping Yang Yaloo, notwithstanding the jingling of the spurs and the clatter of the sabres of his escort. The postillions, seeing the minister standing in the middle of the road, slightly drew rein.

It was noted by some in the crowd that at that moment the eyes of all the escort were centred upon the impassive features of his Excellency. He did not speak, but raised his hand and made a slight signal, which, whatever it might mean, seemed to be perfectly understood.

In an instant one of the twenty members of the bodyguard rode forward at a gallop with a drawn sabre in his hand.

Every one present held his breath in amazement, not knowing what was about to happen.

In another moment the head of the Rev. Ebenezer Brown

rolled in the carriage-way, while his body, spouting blood, staggered for one moment and then fell.

That was all that could be seen; for the next moment the postillions whipped up their horses, the escort put spurs to their steeds, and the whole cavalcade, with the carriage in the centre, swept over the prostrate body of the minister, and on through the park gates.

Neither the policemen on duty nor any of the people present were able to identify, then or afterwards, the horseman whose razor-like sabre had given the "foreign devils" a taste of Chinese skill in decapitation. From that hour no English foot, save that of the Mandarin's secretary, was allowed to cross the threshold of Chatsworth Park.

On galloped the horsemen, while the state carriage swung and creaked on its springs, down by the riverside, where the rabbits were playing merrily in the autumn sunshine, past the artificial lake, and on until they clattered up to the great entrance.

The horses' hoofs struck fire from the stones. The carriage was all streaked and splashed with human blood.

Ping Yang Yaloo did not deign a look or a word to his obsequious retainers, who opened out to right and left, bowing low, as he stepped from his carriage into the entrance hall of his future home.

The great folding-doors were flung wide open, and a wild, barbaric tumult of horns was heard from within.

Slowly, with impassive features, His Excellency mounted the steps leading to the hall. The great folding-doors closed after him; Ping Yang Yaloo was established in the palace of Chatsworth.

Thus the old order changes, giving place to the new; and on the ruins of our old aristocracy, ruined by the fall in prices and the competition of Asia, there was reared the corner-stone of a new plutocracy, with all the vices of the old *régime*, and none of its virtues.

* * * * *

It is the custom in Christmas stories to wind up the affairs of the *dramatis personæ* as if the end of the story were the judgment day of the world. Things do not happen so in real life, and those who wish to know the result of the contest which was waged between His Excellency Ping Yang Yaloo on the one side, supported by the Toilers' Industrial League and Sir Peter and Lady Dorothy Patterson; and on the other by Sir Artegal and Lady Muriel, supported by all that was best and noblest in the dwindling remnant of the aristocracy and among the masses of the people, will have to wait until the destinies have spun a little more of the web of human life. For the great battle against the New Plutocracy, aided by a corrupt and self-seeking Demagogy, is a fight which is not yet finished, nor, indeed, has it hardly as much as begun. The prophetic vision fails us at present to carry further the story of this last rally of the Splendid Paupers.

LONDON: PRINTED BY WILLIAM CLOWES AND SONS, LIMITED, STAMFORD STREET AND CHARING CROSS.

ESTABLISHED OVER HALF A CENTURY.
The Mutual Life Insurance Company
OF NEW YORK.
RICHARD A. McCURDY, President.

A GOOD RECORD
THE BEST GUARANTEE FOR THE FUTURE.

Assets December 31st, 1893, exceed	£38,000,000
Paid to Policy-holders in 1893, over	£4,000,000
Returned to Policy-holders since 1843, over	£75,592,000
Received from Policy-holders since 1843, over	£101,000,000

"The importance of these figures cannot be gainsaid. The record here given, although brief, is unquestionably a very creditable one."—*Finance Chronicle, June 1st, 1894.*

"Truly a remarkable statement of this remarkable company."—*Banker's Magazine, Oct. 1894.*

"FIVE PER CENT." DEBENTURE POLICY.

The safe keeping and repayment of the principal is supported by a Guarantee unsurpassed by that of any other financial institution in the world.

SUMMARY.

The following Statement shows the amounts payable under the above contract should death occur before the end of twenty years.

Example: Debenture, £1,000; Annual Deposit, from £26 5s. 0d.

Death during	A Payable to Beneficiary immediately on Proof of Death.	B Annuity for 6 years following each of Insured, with Principal at end of 20 years or at Death of Beneficiary, if prior.		C If Beneficiary gives 20 Years Company will have paid	D Total Amount Paid for same.
		Annuity.	Principal.		
First Year	£50	£50	£1,000	£2,000	£6
Fifth Year	250	50	1,000	2,200	31
Tenth Year	500	50	1,000	2,500	263
Fifteenth Year	750	50	1,000	2,750	394
Twentieth Year	1,000	50	1,000	3,000	525

☞ Although this is a Life Contract, the Debenture and Profits may be surrendered for cash, or otherwise dealt with, if the Insured be living at the end of 20 years.

"Wherein is the potency of the charm which the Mutual of New York appears to have for assurers? The reason is, we think, to be found in the fact that this leviathan of the insurance world is, above all else, an up-to-date office."—*Money, June 6th, 1894.*

A SECURE PROTECTION FOR THE UNPROTECTED.

Executors, Trustees, and all interested in the Preservation of Property affected by

⇒* THE NEW DEATH DUTIES, *⇐

should at once apply for any particulars to any of the Branch Offices, or to—

D. C. HALDEMAN, General Manager for the United Kingdom, 17 and 18, CORNHILL, LONDON, E.C.

www.ingramcontent.com/pod-product-compliance
Lightning Source LLC
Chambersburg PA
CBHW032241080426
42735CB00008B/957